PREFACE

I was onstage at South Shields' Latir couldn't take it any longer. It was or that dotted the country in the 1960 identical: people dressed in suits, chicken in a basket and drinking w.. fringed lampshades and flock wallpaper; cabaret anu a compère in a bow tie. It felt like a relic from another period. Outside, it was winter 1967, and rock music was shifting and altering at such a breakneck pace that it made my head spin just thinking about it: The Beatles' Magical Mystery Tour and The Mothers of Invention, The Who Sell Out and Axis: Bold As Love, Dr John and John Wesley Harding. Inside the Latino, the only indication that the Swinging Sixties had occurred was my wearing a kaftan and some bells on a chain around my neck. They didn't work for me. I appeared to be a finalist in a search for Britain's least believable flower child.

Long John Baldry came up with the kaftan and the bells. Bluesology, his supporting band, had me on the organ. John had noticed all the other r'n'b bands going psychedelic: one week you'd go see Zoot Money's Big Roll Band playing James Brown songs, the next you'd find them calling themselves Dantalian's Chariot, wearing white robes onstage, and singing about how World War Three would kill all the flowers. He'd determined we should, at least sartorially, follow suit. As a result, we all received kaftans. Cheaper ones were manufactured for the backup musicians, while John's were custom-crafted at Take Six on Carnaby Street. Or, at least, he assumed they were custom-made until we played a show and he noticed someone in the audience wearing the same kaftan as him. 'Where did you acquire that shirt?' he said loudly in the middle of a song. 'This is my shirt!' This seemed to contradict the kaftan's connections with peace, love, and universal brotherhood.

Long John Baldry was one of my favorite actors. He was amusing, deeply weird, shamelessly homosexual, and a fantastic musician, possibly the best 12-string guitarist the UK has ever produced. He'd been a key figure in the early 1960s British blues explosion, performing with Alexis Korner, Cyril Davies, and The Rolling Stones. He knew everything there was to know about the blues. Being around him was an education in and of itself: he introduced me to so much music I'd never heard before.

But he was also an exceedingly nice and generous man. He had a talent for finding something special in artists before anybody else did, then nurturing them and taking the time to build their confidence. He'd done it earlier with Rod Stewart, who'd been one of the singers in John's previous band, Steampacket: Rod, John, Julie Driscoll, and Brian Auger. They were fantastic till they parted up. According to the account I heard, Rod and Julie had a dispute one night after a play in St-Tropez, and Julie splashed red wine over Rod's white suit--you can guess how well that went down--and that was the end of Steampacket. So Bluesology took over as John's supporting band, touring the country in hip soul clubs and blues cellars.

It was a lot of fun, even if John had some strange musical ideas. We played the most unusual sets. We'd start out doing hard-driving blues like 'Times Getting Tougher Than Tough,' 'Hoochie Coochie Man,' and so on. The audience would be in our hands, but then John would insist on playing 'The Threshing Machine,' a sort of smutty West Country novelty tune, the kind of thing rugby men sing when they're inebriated, like 'Twas On The Good Ship Venus' or 'Eskimo Nell'. Even John would sing it with an ooh-arr accent. After that, he'd ask us to sing something from the Great American Songbook, such as 'It Was A Very Good Year' or 'Ev'ry Time We Say Goodbye,' so he could impersonate Della Reese, the American jazz singer. I'm not sure where he got the idea that people wanted to hear him play 'The Threshing Machine' or impersonate Della Reese, but bless him, he stayed adamant that they did, despite some very persuasive evidence to the contrary. You'd look out in the front row, people who'd come

Rocket Man Revealed:
The Book Autobiography of Elton John

"That was just the mindset of the times: that happiness was somehow less important than keeping up appearances"

- Elton John -

By William Dominic Reynolds

TABLE OF CONTENTS

EPILOGUE

to hear blues icon Long John Baldry, and see a line of mods, all chewing gum and staring at us in terror, thinking, "What the fuck is this guy doing?" Even though I was asking myself the same thing, it was hilarious.

Then disaster struck: Long John Baldry had a massive hit single. This would normally have been cause for celebration, but 'Let The Heartaches Begin' was a dreadful album, a sugary, middle-of-the-road Housewives' Choice ballad. It was a million miles away from the music John should have been making, but it stayed at the top for weeks, never leaving the airwaves. I'd like to claim I had no idea what he was thinking, but I knew exactly what he was thinking, and I couldn't blame him. He'd been working for years and this was the first time he'd earned any money. When the blues cellars quit hiring us, we moved on to the supper clubs, which paid better. We'd frequently play two games in a row. They didn't care about John's important role in the British blues explosion or his mastery of the 12-string guitar. They simply wanted to watch someone who appeared on television. I get the impression that they weren't much interested in music. Some clubs would just close the curtains on you if you went over your allowed time. On the plus side, supper club audiences liked 'The Threshing Machine' more than mods did.

Another huge issue with 'Let The Heartaches Begin' was that Bluesology couldn't perform it live. I don't mean we refused to participate. I mean, we couldn't even play it. The song featured an orchestra and a female choir, and it sounded similar to Mantovani. We were an eight-piece horn-powered rhythm and blues ensemble. We had no way of reproducing the sound. So John came up with the idea of recording the backup music. When the big time arrived, he'd drag a massive Revox tape machine onto the stage, push play, and sing along. The rest of us would have to do nothing but stand there. We were dressed in kaftans and bells. People were eating chicken and chips. It was agonizing.

In reality, the only thing enjoyable about John's live rendition of 'Let The Heartaches Begin' was that women started shouting every time he performed it. They'd abandon their chicken and chips and sprint to the front of the stage, apparently overcome by desire. Then they'd start clutching at John's microphone cord, attempting to pull him towards them. I'm sure this occurred to Tom Jones every night and he handled it well, but Long John Baldry wasn't Tom Jones. Rather than basking in the praise, he'd become enraged. He'd stop singing and yell at them, 'IF YOU BREAK MY MICROPHONE, YOU'LL PAY ME FIFTY POUNDS!' This terrible warning went unheeded one night. I noticed John elevate his arm as they continued to pull on the cord. Then there was a loud thud that rattled the speakers. With a sickening feeling, I realized it was the sound of a lust-filled fan being slapped over the head with a microphone. In retrospect, it's a wonder he wasn't arrested or sued for assault. So, for the rest of us, the main source of entertainment throughout 'Let The Heartaches Begin' was wondering if tonight would be the night John clobbered another of his screaming followers.

It was the tune that was playing when I had my epiphany in South Shields. I'd wanted to be a musician since I was a child. Those fantasies had taken numerous forms: I was Little Richard, Jerry Lee Lewis, and Ray Charles at various periods. But, whatever shape they took, none of them involved Long John Baldry standing onstage in a supper club outside of Newcastle, not playing a Vox Continental organ and alternately crooning to the accompaniment of a tape recorder and angrily threatening members of the audience with a fifty-pound fine. Nonetheless, here I was. I had to do something else, as much as I liked John.

The problem was that I didn't have a lot of other possibilities. I had no idea what I wanted to achieve or even what I was capable of doing. I knew I could sing and play the piano, but I was clearly not a pop star. For one thing, I didn't look like a pop star, as my inability to pull off a kaftan demonstrated.

For another, I was known as Reg Dwight. That's not the name of a pop star. 'Tonight on Top of the Pops, Reg Dwight's new single!' It was obviously not going to happen. Bluesology's other members have names that you might envision being announced on Top of the Pops. Stuart Brown is an actor. Gavin, Peter. Dean, Elton. Dean, Elton! Even the saxophonist sounded more like a pop star than I did, and he had no desire to be one: he was a real jazz fan, wasting time with Bluesology until he could start honking away in some free improvised quintet.

I could have changed my name, but what was the point? After all, not only did I believe I wasn't pop star material, but I'd been informed I wasn't. I'd auditioned for Liberty Records a few months prior. LIBERTY RECORDS WANTS TALENT, they advertised in the New Musical Express. But it was not my talent, as it turned out. I'd gone to see Ray Williams, played for him, and even recorded a couple of tunes in a small studio. Ray saw potential in me, but no one else at the label did: thanks but no thanks. So there you have it.

In fact, I only had one other choice. I'd told Ray that I could write songs, or at least half-write songs, when I auditioned for Liberty. I could compose music and write melodies, but not lyrics. "We might be such a happy pair, and I promise to do my bit," I'd tried in Bluesology, and the effects could still lead me to wake up in the middle of the night in a cold sweat. Ray had handed me an envelope almost as an afterthought, or as a consolation reward after rejecting me. Someone who responded to the same advertisement sent in some lyrics. Ray didn't seem to have read any of them before passing them on to me.

The person who penned them was from Owmby-by-Spital in Lincolnshire, which isn't exactly the world's rock and roll capital. He was supposedly employed on a poultry farm, transporting dead birds in a wheelbarrow. His lyrics, on the other hand, were quite good. Esoteric, Tolkien-influenced, similar to Procol Harum's "A Whiter Shade Of Pale." Most importantly, none of them made me want to rip my own head off with embarrassment, indicating that they were far superior to anything I'd come up with.

Furthermore, I discovered that I could write music to them quickly. Something about them struck a chord with me. And something about him appeared to click with me as well. He came to London, we had coffee, and we hit it off right away. Bernie Taupin turned out to be anything but a country bumpkin. For a seventeen-year-old, he was extraordinarily sophisticated: long-haired, quite gorgeous, well-read, and a major Bob Dylan lover. So we started composing songs together, or rather not creating songs together. He'd give me the lyrics from Lincolnshire, and I'd write the music at home, in my mother and stepfather's Northwood Hills flat. That way, we'd come up with dozens of songs. We hadn't actually gotten any other artists to buy the bloody things yet, and if we committed to it full-time, we'd go bankrupt. But, other than money, what did we have to lose? Twice a night, a wheelbarrow full of dead hens and 'Let The Heartaches Begin'.

I informed John and Bluesology that I would be leaving following a December show in Scotland. It was OK, no hard feelings: as I previously stated, John was an extremely generous man. On the way home, I decided to alter my name after all. For some reason, I recall thinking I needed to come up with something different immediately. I assume it was all meant to represent a clean break and a new beginning: no more Bluesology, no more Reg Dwight. I opted for pinching other people's names because I was in a rush. Elton comes from Elton Dean, and John comes from Long John Baldry. John Elton. Bernie Taupin and Elton John. Elton John and Bernie Taupin are songwriters. It sounded fantastic to me. Unusual. Striking. On the bus back from Heathrow, I told my now-ex-bandmates about my decision. They all burst out laughing and wished me good luck.

CHAPTER 1

Elvis Presley was introduced to me by my mother. Every Friday after work, she would pick up her pay, then swing by Siever's, an electrical store that also sold records, and purchase a new 78. Waiting at home to see what Mom would bring back was my favorite part of the week. She appreciated big band music (Billy May and His Orchestra, Ted Heath) and American vocalists (Johnnie Ray, Frankie Laine, Nat King Cole, Guy Mitchell singing "she wears red feathers and a huly-huly skirt"). But she brought something else home with her one Friday. She said she'd never heard anything like it, but it was so good she had to buy it. I knew the words Elvis Presley as soon as she pronounced them. I'd been perusing through magazines in the local barber shop while waiting for my hair to be trimmed the previous weekend when I came across a photo of the strangest-looking man I'd ever seen. Everything about him stood out: his clothes, his hair, even the way he stood. He might as well have been bright green with antennas sticking out of his forehead compared to the people outside the barber shop window in the north-west London suburb of Pinner. I'd been so engrossed that I hadn't read the accompanying piece, and by the time I arrived home, I'd forgotten his name. But there was only one Elvis Presley.

As soon as Mum turned on the album, it was clear that Elvis Presley sounded like he came from another planet. In comparison to the music my parents usually listened to, 'Heartbreak Hotel' scarcely counted as music at all, an opinion my father would continue to expound on for years. I'd heard rock and roll before - 'Rock Around The Clock' had been a great hit earlier in 1956 - but 'Heartbreak Hotel' didn't sound like it. It was raw, sparse, sluggish, and eerie. Everything was soaked in this strange echo. You couldn't understand a word he was singing: I realized his baby had abandoned him, and then I completely lost the thread. What exactly was a 'dress clerk'? Who was this 'Bidder Sir Lonely' he kept referring to?

Whatever he was saying didn't matter because something almost physical happened when he was singing. You could really feel the weird energy he was emitting, as if it was contagious, as if it was coming straight from the radiogram speaker into your body. I already considered myself a music fanatic, and I even had a little collection of my own 78s, which I paid for with record tokens and postal orders I received for birthdays and Christmas. Winifred Atwell, a huge, jovial Trinidadian lady who performed onstage with two pianos - a baby grand for light classical and a broken old upright for ragtime and pub ballads - had been my hero up until that point. I adored her exuberance, the slightly campy way she'd say, 'And now, I'm going to my second piano'; the way she'd lean back and stare at the audience with a great grin on her face while she was playing, as if she was having the finest time in the world. I thought Winifred Atwell was fantastic, but I'd never had an experience like this when listening to her. Nothing like this had ever happened to me before. As 'Heartbreak Hotel' began to play, it felt as if everything had altered, as if nothing could ever be the same again. As it turned out, something had happened, but nothing was there.

And thank God for that, for the world needs to change. I grew up in 1950s Britain, and before Elvis and rock and roll, it was a fairly depressing world. I didn't mind living in Pinner - I've never been one of those rock stars who felt compelled to leave the suburbs, and I liked life there - but the country as a whole was in a horrible way. It was sly, scared, and judgmental. It was a world of individuals with unhappy expressions peering through their curtains, of females being taken away because they'd gotten into trouble. When I think of 1950s Britain, I remember sitting on the stairs of our house, listening to my mother's brother, Uncle Reg, try to talk her out of divorcing my father: 'You can't get divorced! What will people say?'At one point, I recall him saying, 'What will the neighbors say?Uncle Reg wasn't to blame. That was simply the mindset of the time: happiness was somehow less important than appearances.

My parents should never have married in the first place, in my opinion. Although I was born in 1947, I was basically a war baby. I was probably conceived while my father was on leave from the RAF; he had signed up in 1942, during the height of World War II, and had chosen to stay on after the war ended. And my parents were unquestionably a war couple. Their story appears to be romantic. They met the same year my father joined the army. He was seventeen years old and worked in a boat building yard in Rickmansworth that specialized in canal narrowboats. Mum was sixteen, her maiden name was Harris, and she delivered milk on a horse and cart for United Dairies, a profession that a woman would never have done before the war. My father was an enthusiastic amateur trumpet player, and when on vacation, he supposedly spotted my mother in the audience while sitting in with a band performing at a North Harrow hotel.

But the reality of Stanley and Sheila Dwight's marriage was far from romantic. They simply did not connect. They were both headstrong and short-tempered, two great traits that I was fortunate enough to inherit. I doubt they ever truly loved each other. People rushed into marriage during the war since the future was unknown, even at the time of my parents' wedding in January 1945, and you wanted to seize the moment, so that could have played a role. Perhaps they once loved one other, or at least thought they did during their brief time together. They didn't even seem to like each other anymore. The rows went on and on.

At the very least, they subsided while my father was away, which he was frequently. He was promoted to flight lieutenant and was frequently transferred abroad, to Iraq and Aden, so I grew up in a house full of ladies. We resided at 55 Pinner Hill Road with my maternal grandmother, Ivy, the same house where I was born. It was the type of council house that had popped up all throughout the country in the 1920s and 1930s: three bedrooms, semi-detached, red brick on the ground floor and white-painted render on the upper floor. The residence did contain another male occupant, though you wouldn't have known it. My grandfather had died of cancer when I was little, and Nan had remarried to a man named Horace Sewell, who'd lost a leg in World War One. Horace had a kind heart, but he wasn't one of life's big talkers. He seems to spend most of his time outside. When he wasn't working at the local nursery, Woodman's, he was in the garden, growing all of our vegetables and cutting flowers.

Maybe he was just trying to avoid my mother, in which case I couldn't blame him. Mum had a bad temper even when Dad wasn't present. When I go back to my youth, I remember Mum's moods: dreadful, gloomy, miserable silences that came on the home without warning, during which you walked on eggshells and carefully chose your words in case you set her off and were whacked as a result. When she was pleased, she could be warm, charming, and lively, but she always seemed to be looking for a reason not to be happy, for a fight, for the last word; Uncle Reg famously said she could start an argument in an empty room. For years, I blamed myself, thinking that maybe she never wanted to be a mother because she was only twenty-one when I was born, locked in a marriage that plainly wasn't working, forced to live with her mother because money was so tight. But her sister, my auntie Win, said she was always like that - that when they were kids, it was as if a dark cloud followed Sheila Harris about, that other kids were afraid of her, and that she appeared to enjoy it.

She had some very strange notions about parenting. It was a time when you kept your kids in line by stomping on them, when it was widely believed that there was nothing wrong with children that couldn't be fixed by stomping the living daylights out of them. This was a philosophy to which my mother was devoted, and it was terrifying and humiliating if it occurred in public: there's nothing like getting a hiding outside Pinner Sainsbury's in front of a visibly curious audience of bystanders to wreck your self-esteem. However, some of Mum's behavior would have been regarded as troubling even by today's standards. Years later, I discovered that she had toilet-trained me when I was two by striking me with a wire brush until I bled if I didn't use the potty. When my grandmother found out what was going on, she went insane, and they didn't talk for weeks. Nan had gone insane when she saw my mother's constipation treatment. She threw me on the kitchen draining board and stuffed carbolic soap in my arse. If she liked scaring people, she must have been pleased when I was afraid of her. I loved her - she was my mother - but I spent my youth on high alert, always trying to avoid doing anything that may irritate her: if she was happy, I was happy, if temporarily.

My grandmother never had such issues. She was the person I had the most faith in. It felt like she was the family's focal point, the only one who didn't go to work - my mother had progressed from running a milk cart during the war to working in a series of stores. Nan was one of those amazing old working-class matriarchs: no-nonsense, hardworking, caring, and humorous. I admired her. She was the best cook, had the greenest fingers, and enjoyed a drink and a card game. Nan had had an extremely difficult existence; her father had abandoned her mother while she was pregnant, so she was born in a workhouse. She never mentioned anything, but it seemed to have left her as someone who could handle anything, even when I came wailing down the stairs with my foreskin caught in my pants zip and requested her to get it out. She just sighed and went about her business, as if pulling a small boy's penis from a zip was something she did every day.

Her place smelled of roast meals and open fires. Auntie Win or Uncle Reg, or my cousins John and Cathryn, or the rent guy, or the man from Watford Steam Laundry, or the man who delivered the coal, were always at the door. And music was continually playing. Two-Way Family Favourites, Housewives' Choice, Music While You Work, and The Billy Cotton Band Show were almost always on the radio. If it wasn't, records were playing on the radiogram, typically jazz but occasionally classical.

I could spend hours just looking at those records and learning about the various labels. Blue Deccas, red Parlophones, bright yellow MGMs, HMVs, and RCAs, both of which had that picture of the dog looking at the phonograph on them for reasons I never understood. They appeared to be magical items; the idea that you could poke them with a needle and sound miraculously emerged astounded me. After a while, the only things I wanted for Christmas were music and books. I recall being disappointed when I came downstairs and saw a large box wrapped neatly. Oh no, they've captured Meccano.

We also had a piano that belonged to my grandmother. Auntie Win used to enjoy it, and I ultimately did as well. There were many family myths about my enormous aptitude on the instrument, the most common of which was that when I was three, Win seated me on her lap and I promptly picked out the music of 'The Skaters' Waltz' by ear. I'm not sure if that's accurate, but I was definitely playing piano at an early age, around the time I started at my first school, Reddiford. I'd play songs like 'All Things Bright and Beautiful' that I'd heard at church. I was simply born with a good ear, in the same way that some individuals are born with photographic memories. If I heard something once, I could go to the piano and play it almost perfectly. I began lessons at the age of seven with a lady named Mrs Jones. My parents began bringing me out to play 'My Old Man Said Follow The Van' and 'Roll Out The Barrel' at family gatherings and weddings not long after that. For all the albums in the house and on the radio, I believe my family's favorite type of music was an old-fashioned sing-song.

When my father was on leave, the piano came in handy. He was a typical 1950s British guy in that he seemed to see any manifestation of emotion other than rage as proof of a fatal flaw in character. So he wasn't tactile, and he never confessed his feelings for you. But he liked music, and if he heard me playing the piano, he'd say "well done," and maybe put his arm around my shoulder, giving me a sense of pride and approbation. I was briefly in his good graces. And staying in his good graces was crucial to me. I was just slightly less scared of him than I was of my mother because he wasn't there as much. When I was six, my mother decided to move us away from Pinner and all her family and to Wiltshire, where my father had been assigned to RAF Lyneham, near Swindon. I don't recall anything about it. I remember having fun playing in the countryside, but I also remember feeling disoriented and puzzled by the shift, and falling behind in school as a result. We weren't there long - Mum must have realized she'd made a mistake immediately - and when we returned to Pinner, Dad seemed more like a visitor than someone who lived with us.

But everything changed when he came to visit. All of a sudden, there were new rules for everything. I'd get in trouble if I kicked my football off the grass and into the flower bed, but I'd also get in trouble if I ate celery in The Wrong Way. If you're curious, the Right Way to Eat Celery was supposedly not to produce too loud a crunching sound when biting into it. He once beat me because I was allegedly taking off my school blazer wrongly; however, I appear to have forgotten The Right Way to Take Off a School Blazer, as important as this knowledge undoubtedly was. Auntie Win was so shocked by the spectacle that she ran off in tears to inform my grandmother what had happened. Nan, presumably exhausted by the arguments over potty training and constipation, told her not to get involved.

What was the situation? I'm at a loss for words. I have no notion what my father's problem was, nor do I know what my mother's was. Maybe it had something to do with him being in the army, where everything had regulations. Perhaps he felt a little jealous, as if he was being excluded from the family because he was gone so much: all these restrictions were his way of asserting himself as the head of the household. Maybe that's how he was raised, even if his parents - my grandfather Edwin and grandma Ellen - didn't appear particularly tough. Or perhaps both of my parents just found raising a child tough since they had never done so before. I'm not sure. I do know that my father had a very short fuse and didn't seem to understand how to utilize words. There was no cool answer, no 'now come on, sit down'. He'd just blow up. The Dwight Family's Temperament. It was the scourge of my existence as a child, and it remained the bane of my existence once it was discovered to be hereditary. Either I was naturally inclined to losing my rag, or I learnt by example unconsciously. Whatever it was, it was a disaster for myself and everyone around me for the most of my adult life.

Muffin the Mule on TV and Saturday morning children's matinees at the Embassy in North Harrow; the Goons on the radio and bread and dripping for tea on a Sunday night if it hadn't been for Mum and Dad. I was completely content while I was not at home. When I was eleven, I transferred to Pinner County Grammar School, where I was noticeably unremarkable. I was neither bullied nor a bully. I wasn't a snob, but I wasn't a crybaby either; I left that to my friend John Gates, who was one of those kids who seemed to spend their entire childhood in detention or outside the headmaster's office, with no difference in the range of punishments inflicted on him. I was a little overweight, but I was fine at sports and was never in danger of becoming a famous athlete. Other than rugby, I played football and tennis. They put me in the scrum because of my size, and my major function was to get kicked in the balls by the opposition team's prop. No, thank you.

Keith Francis was my best buddy, although he was part of a large group of friends, both guys and girls, who I still see now. I host class reunions at my home on occasion. I was nervous the first time since it had been fifty years, I was renowned, I lived in a big mansion, what would they think of me? They, on the other hand, couldn't care less. It could have been 1959 when they came. Nobody appeared to have altered all that much. John Gates still had a glint in his eye, indicating that he might be a bit of a handful.

For years, I led a life where nothing much happened. A school trip to Annecy, where we stayed with our French pen pals and gasped at the sight of Citroen 2CVs, which were unlike any automobile I'd ever seen on a British road, with seats that looked like deckchairs, was the pinnacle of excitement. Or the Easter holiday when, for reasons unknown, Barry Walden, Keith, and I decided to cycle from Pinner to Bournemouth, an idea I began to doubt when I realized their bikes had gears and mine didn't: there was a lot of frantic pedaling up hills on my part, trying to keep up. When I started talking about records, the only threat any of us faced was that one of my pals might become bored to death. Collecting them was insufficient for me. I made a note of it in a book every time I bought one. I jotted down the A and B side names, as well as the writer, publisher, and producer information on the label. I then memorized everything, becoming a walking musical encyclopedia. An innocent question about why the needle skipped when you tried to play 'Little Darlin" by The Diamonds would lead to me informing everyone within earshot that it was because 'Little Darlin" by The Diamonds was on Mercury Records, who were distributed by Pye in the UK, and Pye were the only label that released 78s made from new-fangled vinyl, rather than old-fashioned shellac, and needles made from shellac responded differently to vinyl.

But I'm not moaning about life being boring; I prefer it that way. Things were so taxing at home that a mundane life beyond the front door sounded strangely appealing, especially when my parents decided to try full-time living together again. It was shortly after I began working at Pinner County. My father had been assigned to RAF Medmenham in Buckinghamshire, and we all relocated to 111 Potter Street in Northwood, just 10 minutes from Pinner. We stayed for three years, long enough to prove beyond a shadow of a doubt that the marriage was failing. It was dreadful: incessant fighting, sporadically interrupted by frigid silences. You couldn't unwind for a second. If you spend your life waiting for your mother's next outburst of rage or your father's announcement of another rule broken, you'll end up not knowing what to do: the uncertainty of what's going to happen next fills you with anxiety. So I was really insecure, terrified of my own shadow. Furthermore, I believed I was partially accountable for the status of my parents' marriage because many of their disagreements were about me. My father would scold me, my mother would step in, and there would be a great debate about how I was raised. It didn't make me feel good about myself, and it led to a lack of confidence in my appearance that lasted well into adulthood. I couldn't handle looking at myself in the mirror for years. I despised what I saw: I was too overweight, too short, my face looked odd, and my hair would never do what I wanted it to, especially not fall out prematurely. Another long-term effect was a fear of confrontation. That continued for decades. I persisted in terrible business and awful personal relationships because I didn't want to upset anyone.

When things became too much for me, I would always flee upstairs and shut the door, just as I used to do when my parents argued. I'd head to my bedroom, where I kept everything nice and orderly. I didn't simply collect records; I also collected comic books, books, and periodicals. I was quite particular about everything. If I wasn't scribbling down the contents of a new single in my notebook, I was copying all the singles charts from Melody Maker, the New Musical Express, Record Mirror, and Disc, then collecting the results and averaging them into a personal chart of charts. I've always been obsessed with statistics. Even now, I receive the charts on a daily basis, including the radio chart places in America, as well as the box office charts for films and Broadway shows. Most artists aren't interested in doing so. When I chat to them, I know more about their single than they do, which is absurd. The official explanation is that I need to know what's going on because I now operate a firm that produces films and manages artists. The truth is that I'd do it if I worked in a bank. I'm simply a nerd.

A psychologist would probably argue that I was attempting to create order in a chaotic environment as a child, with my father coming and going and all the reprimands and rows. I had no influence over it, nor over my mother's moods, but I did have power over the items in my room. Objects could not injure me. I found them soothing. I spoke to them and acted as if they had feelings. I'd be upset if something was shattered, like if I'd killed something. During one particularly heated argument, my mother hurled a record at my father, shattering it into who knows how many pieces. 'The Robin's Return' by Dolores Ventura, an Australian ragtime pianist, was the song. 'How can you do that?' I wondered. How could you possibly break such a lovely thing?'

When rock 'n' roll arrived, my record collection exploded. Other exciting changes were afoot, things that suggested life was moving on, out of the gray post-war world, even in suburban north-west London: the arrival of a TV and a washing machine in our home, and the arrival in Pinner High Street of a coffee bar, which seemed unimaginably exotic - until a restaurant serving Chinese food opened in nearby Harrow. But they happened slowly and gradually, over a few years. That was not the case with rock 'n' roll. It seemed to appear out of nowhere, so quickly that it was difficult to comprehend how drastically it had transformed everything. One minute, pop music meant Guy Mitchell and 'Where Will The Dimple Be?' the next.', as well as Max Bygraves singing about toothbrushes. It was polite and schmaltzy, intended for parents who didn't want to hear anything too exciting or upsetting because they'd had enough of that living through a war. Then there were Jerry Lee Lewis and Little Richard, these guys who sang incoherently, as if they were foaming at the mouth, and who your parents despised. Even my mother, an Elvis fan, left when Little Richard appeared. 'Tutti Frutti' was merely a horrible noise to her.

Rock & roll was like a never-ending sequence of explosions that were so dense and quick that it was difficult to understand what was going on. Suddenly, it seemed like there was one unbelievable record after another. 'Hound Dog,' 'Blue Suede Shoes,' 'Whole Lotta Shakin' Goin' On,' 'Long Tall Sally,' 'That'll Be The Day,' 'Roll Over Beethoven,' and 'Reet Petite' are some of the songs on this album. To stay up, I had to obtain a Saturday job. Fortunately, Mr. Megson of Victoria Wine was searching for someone to help him out in the rear of the store, stacking empty beer bottles in crates. I had a vague concept of saving some money, but I should have understood that idea was doomed from the start: Victoria Wine was next door to another record shop. Mr Megson might have cut out the middleman by depositing the ten bob he paid me directly into their till. It was an early manifestation of what would become a lifelong shopping attitude: I'm just not very good at keeping money in my pocket if there's anything I want to buy.

Sixty years later, it's difficult to describe how revolutionary and shocking rock and roll looked. Not only the music, but the entire culture it represented, including the clothes, films, and attitude. It felt like the first item that we truly owned, something geared solely at us, something that made us feel distinct from our parents, something that made us believe we could achieve something. It's also difficult to describe how much the elder generation loathed it. Take every case of moral panic produced by pop music since - punk and gangster rap, mods and rockers, and heavy metal - and double it by two: that's how much indignation rock & roll caused. People absolutely despised it. No one despised it more than my father. 'Look at the way they dress, the way they act, swiveling their hips, flashing their dicks,' he said. You are not to become involved.' If I did, I would become what was known as a wide lad. A wide boy is an old British word for a type of petty criminal - a confidence trickster, someone who performs a little wheeler-dealing or conducts the occasional scam. He was adamant that rock and roll would result in my absolute degradation, presumably because he was already aware that I might go off the tracks due to my inability to eat celery properly. The mere mention of Elvis or Little Richard would set him off on an angry rant in which my inevitable transformation into a wide boy figured prominently: one minute I'd be happily listening to 'Good Golly Miss Molly,' the next I'd be fencing stolen nylons or duping people into playing Find-the-Lady on the mean streets of Pinner.

There didn't seem to be much danger of that happening to me - there are Benedictine monks who are crazier than I was as a teenager - but my father was not taking any chances. By the time I began at Pinner County Grammar School in 1958, you could see a shift in how people dressed, but I was explicitly barred from wearing anything that made me appear to be associated with rock and roll. Keith Francis was making a break for it in a pair of winkle-picker shoes with pointed toes that seemed to arrive in class several minutes before he did. I was still clothed in the manner of a little imitation of my father. My shoes were the same length as my feet, which was terrible. My prescription glasses were the closest I came to sartorial rebellion, or rather, how much I wore my prescription glasses. They were solely meant to be used for viewing the chalkboard. I wore them all the time, certain that they made me look like Buddy Holly, and they absolutely ruined my eyesight in the process. I had to wear them all the time after that.

When it came to sexual experimentation, my declining eyesight had unanticipated implications. I can't recall the specific circumstances under which my father discovered me masturbating. I believe I was attempting to dispose of the evidence rather than engaging in the act itself, but I remember not being as humiliated as I should have been, owing to my lack of knowledge. When it came to sex, I was a late bloomer. I wasn't very interested in it until I was well into my thirties, though I made an extremely strong attempt to catch up after that. But at school, I'd overhear my pals discussing it, and it'd leave me perplexed: 'Yeah, I brought her to the movies, got a little of it.' How? Why? What was the significance of that?

So I believe what I was doing was more about enjoying a pleasant experience than expressing my increasing sexuality in a frenetic manner. In any case, when my father caught me, he used the tired line about how if I kept doing that, I'd go blind. Obviously, boys all around the country were given the same warning, understood it was nonsense, and ignored it. It, on the other hand, preyed on my psyche. What if that was correct? I'd already harmed my eyesight in my mistaken quest to seem like Buddy Holly; perhaps this would put an end to it. I concluded it was better not to risk it. When many musicians will say Buddy Holly had a huge influence on their lives, I'm probably the only one who can say he unwittingly stopped me wanking, unless Holly managed to walk in on The Big Bopper doing it when they were on tour or something.

But it was too late for my father to persuade me not to get involved in rock and roll, despite all the regulations about clothing and warnings about my sure-fire spiral into criminality. I was already up to my neck in it. At the movies, I saw Loving You and The Girl Can't Help It. I began attending live performances. Every week, a large group of students traveled up to the Harrow Granada: me, Keith, Kaye Midlane, Barry Walden, and Janet Richie were the most ardent, regular members, along with a guy named Michael Johnson, who seemed to be as concerned with music as I was. He appeared to know things about me that I didn't. A few years later, he showed up at school with a copy of 'Love Me Do' by The Beatles, whomever they were, proclaiming that they were the biggest thing since Elvis. I felt that was a bit much until he played it to me, and then I realized he could have a point: another musical infatuation was born.

A Granada ticket cost two and sixpence, or five bob if you wanted the good seats. Because they crammed the performances with singers and musicians, either felt like good value. A night would have ten musicians, each doing two songs until the main act, who would perform four or five. Everyone appeared to play there at some point. Johnny And

The Hurricanes, Little Richard, Gene Vincent, Jerry Lee Lewis, Eddie Cochran. If someone declined to appear at the Harrow Granada, you could take the tube up to London, where I saw Cliff Richard And The Drifters at the Palladium before they changed their name to The Shadows. Other, smaller venues in the suburbs began to host bands: the South Harrow British Legion and the Kenton Conservative Club. As long as you had the money, you could easily watch two or three shows per week. The weird thing is, I don't recall ever seeing a bad show or being dissatisfied, despite the fact that some of the shows must have been dreadful. The noise must have been terrifying. I'm very sure the South Harrow British Legion didn't have a PA system capable of truly communicating the violent, feral power of rock and roll in 1960.

When my father was not present, I would play Little Richard and Jerry Lee Lewis songs on the piano. They were my true role models. It wasn't only their playing style, which was fantastic: they played with such aggression, as if they were smashing the piano. It was the way they stood up while playing, kicking the stool and jumping on the piano. They made playing the piano look just as visually thrilling, seductive, and wild as playing the guitar or singing. I'd never considered any of those possibilities before.

I was sufficiently enthused to do a few shows at local youth clubs with a band called The Corvettes. It was nothing serious; the other members were all still in school - they attended Northwood, the local secondary contemporary - and it only lasted a few months: we were paid in Coca-Cola for most of the performances we did. But then I had an epiphany about what I wanted to do with my life, and it had nothing to do with my father's ambitions for me, which revolved around either joining the RAF or working in a bank. I'd never say it out loud, but I secretly decided he could stuff both of those schemes up his arse. After all, rock and roll might have transformed me in the rebellious way Dad feared.

Or maybe we never had anything in common other than football. My father's happy childhood memories are all tied to football: he hailed from a football-crazy family. Roy Dwight and John Ashen, two of his nephews, played professionally for Fulham in south-west London. He used to take me to Craven Cottage to watch them from the touchline when Jimmy Hill was their inside right and Bedford Jezzard was their top scorer. Even off the field, Roy and John struck me as extraordinarily glamorous figures, and I was always slightly taken aback when I met them. After his career ended, John became a very intelligent businessman with a penchant for American vehicles; he'd come to see us in Pinner with his wife, Bet, and park an unbelievable-looking Cadillac or Chevrolet outside the home. And Roy, a right-winger who moved to Nottingham Forest, was a superb player. He appeared in the 1959 FA Cup Final for them. I watched it on TV at home, armed with a stash of chocolate eggs I'd hoarded from Easter in preparation of this historic occasion. I didn't so much eat the chocolate as put it in my mouth in a fit of frenzy. I couldn't believe what I saw on the television. Roy scored the first goal after ten minutes. He was already on the verge of being called up to the England squad. He'd almost certainly sealed his fate by now: my cousin, a real relative of mine, was going to play for England. It appeared as absurd as John's car choice. They were bringing him away on a stretcher fifteen minutes later. He'd shattered his leg in a tackle, which sealed his fate. His football career all but ended. He tried, but he was no longer the same player. He eventually ended up working as a PE teacher at a boys' school in south London.

Watford were my father's team, and they were far less flashy and intimidating. When he first took me to see them play, I was six years old. They were slogging it out at the bottom of the football league's Third Division South, which was as low as you could go without being kicked out totally. In fact, not long before I began attending Watford games, they had performed so poorly that they were kicked out of the football league; they were permitted to return after appealing for reelection. Their home ground on Vicarage Road appeared to reveal everything about the team. It just had two ancient, rickety, and little covered stands. It also functioned as a greyhound racing track. If I'd been smart, I'd have taken one look at it, evaluated Watford's previous form, and backed a club that could genuinely play football. I could have saved myself twenty years of nearly unending pain. But football doesn't operate that way, or it shouldn't. It's in your blood: Watford was my father's team, so Watford was my team.

And, besides, I didn't care about the dirt, the team's hopelessness, or the bitter cold. I fell in love with everything right away. The thrill of seeing live sport for the first time, the thrill of taking the train to Watford and walking through town to the ground, the newspaper sellers who came around at half-time and told you the scores from other games, the ritual of always standing in the same spot on the terraces, an area near the Shrodells Stand called The Bend. It was like taking a drug and becoming addicted to it right away. When I wasn't constructing my chart of charts in my bedroom, I was cutting football league ladders out of my comic books, pasting them to my wall, and making sure the scores on them were absolutely up to date. It's an addiction I've never broken because I've never wanted to, and it was inherited from my father.

My piano teacher had recommended me for the Royal Academy of Music in central London when I was eleven years old. I passed the exam, and for the following five years, Saturdays were spent studying classical music in the morning and watching Watford in the afternoon. The latter was preferable to the former. The Royal Academy of Music seemed to smell of anxiety at the time. Everything about it was intimidating: the massive, towering Edwardian structure on Marylebone Road, its illustrious history of producing composers and conductors, and the fact that anything other than classical music was strictly prohibited. It's completely different now; whenever I go there, it's a wonderfully happy place; the students are encouraged to do pop, jazz, or their own writing in addition to their classical instruction. But, back then, simply discussing rock and roll at the Royal Academy would have been heresy, akin to showing up to church and telling the priest that you truly want to worship Satan.

The Royal Academy could be entertaining at times. I had a wonderful teacher named Helen Piena, and I loved singing in the choir and playing Mozart, Bach, Beethoven, and Chopin, all of the melodic things. At times, it seemed like a chore. I was a slacker in school. Some weeks, if I hadn't done my homework, I didn't bother showing up at all. I'd call from home, pretending to be ill, and then take the train up to Baker Street, hoping my mother wouldn't notice. Then I'd take the tube home. I'd spend three and a half hours going round and round the Circle Line, reading The Pan Book of Horror Stories instead of practicing Bartók. I knew I didn't want to be a classical musician from the start. For starters, I wasn't good enough. I don't have the necessary hands. My fingers are too short for a pianist. If you look at a snapshot of a concert pianist, you'll notice that they all have tarantula-like hands. And, for another, it wasn't what I was looking for in music: everything regulated, playing the right notes at the right moment with the right feeling, no space for creativity.

In some ways, it's ironic that I was appointed a Doctor and an Honorary Member of the Royal Academy years later - I was never going to win an award for best student when I was there. In another sense, it isn't ironic at all. I would never, ever suggest that the Royal Academy was a waste of my time. I'm very proud of myself for going there. I've done benefit concerts to collect funds for a new pipe organ for them; I've toured with the Royal Academy Symphony Orchestra in Britain and America; and every year, I pay for eight scholarships there. The space was packed with individuals I'd end up working with years later as Elton John: producer Chris Thomas, arranger Paul Buckmaster, harpist Skaila Kanga, and percussionist Ray Cooper. And what I learnt there influenced my music: it taught me about teamwork, chord patterns, and songwriting. It inspired me to write with more than three or four chords. When you listen to the Elton John album, and almost every album I've made afterwards, you can hear the impact of classical music and the Royal Academy somewhere.

My parents finally split while I was enrolled at the Royal Academy. To be fair to them, they had attempted to make their marriage work despite the fact that it was evident they couldn't bear each other; I suppose because they wanted to provide stability for me. It was absolutely inappropriate, but they made an effort. Then, in 1960, my father was sent to Harrogate, Yorkshire, where Mum met someone else. That's all there was to it.

My mother and I moved in with her new boyfriend, Fred, a painter and decorator. It was a very difficult financial period. Fred, too, was divorced; he had an ex-wife and four children, so money was tight. We lived in a dreadful Croxley Green flat with peeling wallpaper and wet. Fred put forth a lot of effort. On top of decorating, he did window cleaning and odd jobs: anything to ensure we had food on the table. It was difficult for both him and my mother. Uncle Reg was correct - there was a stigma attached to divorce in those days.

But I was overjoyed that they'd divorced. My mother and father's everyday conflict was no longer present. Mum had gotten what she wanted - ridding herself of my father - and it seemed to change her. She was content, and her contentment filtered down to me. There were less mood swings and less criticism. And I had a thing for Fred. He was generous, warm-hearted, and easygoing. He saved his money and bought me a drop-handlebar bike. When I started speaking his name backwards and nicknamed him Derf, a nickname that stuck, he thought it was hilarious. There were no longer constraints on what I could wear. Years before he and Mum married, I began referring to Derf as my stepfather.

Most importantly, Derf enjoyed rock and roll. He and my mother were extremely supportive of my musical endeavors.

I suppose there was an added incentive for my mother because she knew that encouraging me would irritate my father, but she seemed to be my biggest fan for a while. And Derf landed me my first paying job as a pianist at the Northwood Hills Hotel, which wasn't really a hotel at all, but rather a tavern. Derf was drinking a pint there when he found out from the owner that their regular pianist had departed, and he suggested they give me a shot. I'd play whatever I could think of. Songs by Jim Reeves, Johnnie Ray, Elvis Presley, and 'Whole Lotta Shakin' Goin' On'. They were huge fans of Al Jolson. But not as much as they adored old British pub tunes that everyone could sing along to: 'Down At The Old Bull And Bush,' 'Any Old Iron,' 'My Old Man,' the same songs my family used to sing after a few drinks. I made a lot of money. My pay was only a pound a night, three evenings a week, but Derf would accompany me and carry a pint pot collecting tips. Sometimes I'd end up with £15 a week, which was a lot of money for a fifteen-year-old child in the early 1960s. I saved up and bought an electric piano - a Hohner Pianette - as well as a microphone to make myself heard above the din of the tavern.

The bar pianist's work had another purpose in addition to earning me money. It made me a pretty bold performer, because the Northwood Hills Hotel was by no means Britain's most opulent venue. I played at the public bar, not the more fancy saloon next door, and there was almost always a brawl once enough booze had been consumed. I don't mean a verbal brawl; I mean a true brawl, with glasses flying and tables being shoved over. At first, I'd keep playing in the misguided belief that music might make things better. If a burst of 'Bye Bye Blackbird' didn't accomplish the intended enchantment, I'd have to seek assistance from a bunch of travelers who frequented the tavern. I'd grown acquainted with one of their kids, and she'd even invited me to their caravan for dinner, and they'd make sure I was okay when the pub started up. And if they weren't on that night, I'd have to turn to my final recourse. This entailed climbing out the window next to the piano and returning later after things had cooled down. It was terrifying, but at the very least it prepared me mentally for playing live. I know artists who have been absolutely wrecked by the experience of performing a horrible gig in front of an unappreciative crowd. I've played awful shows in front of unappreciative crowds before, but they never had a lasting influence on me. If I don't have to quit performing and jump out a window in fear of my life, it's still a step forward from where I started.

My father met a woman named Edna in Yorkshire. They married, relocated to Essex, and established a paper shop. He must have been happier because they had four more sons who all adored dad, but he didn't seem any different to me. It was as if he didn't know how else to act around me. He was still aloof and rigid, still lamenting the awful effect of rock and roll, still gripped by the fear that I would turn into a broad boy and bring shame to the Dwight family name. Taking the Green Line bus to Essex to see him was the consistent low point of any week. I stopped traveling to Watford with him because I was old enough to stand alone on The Bend.

Dad must have gone insane when he found out I was planning to leave school before finishing my A-levels to work in the music industry. He didn't think it was a good career for a boy with only a high school diploma. To make matters worse, it was his own nephew who got me the job: my cousin Roy, he of the FA Cup goal, who had maintained close relations with my mother following the divorce. Footballers looked to have connections with the music industry, and he was acquaintances with Tony Hiller, the general manager of the Mills Music publishing company in Denmark Street, Britain's Tin Pan Alley. I learned about a job opening in the packaging department through Roy; the compensation was only £4 per week, but it was a start. And I knew I had little chance of passing my A-levels in the first place. My education had begun to slip somewhere between the Royal Academy, practicing playing the piano like Jerry Lee Lewis, and often slipping out the window of the Northwood Hills Hotel.

I say he must have gone insane because I can't recall his reaction. I know he wrote to my mother demanding that she stop me, but you can imagine how she reacted: she was overjoyed. Everyone else seemed happy for me, including Mum and Derf, and even my school's principal, which seemed nearly magical. Mr Westgate-Smith was a tough, serious guy. I was afraid when I went to visit him to tell him about the job. But he was really lovely. He said he knew how much I loved music and the Royal Academy, and that he would let me go if I agreed to work hard and give the project everything I had. I was taken aback, but he meant it. He might have easily refused; I would have gone anyhow, but I would have left school with a cloud over my head. Instead, he was quite encouraging. Years later, when I'd achieved success, he'd write to tell me how pleased he was of what I'd accomplished.

In a strange way, my father's attitude aided me as well. He never changed his opinion regarding my profession. He never said thank you. His wife Edna just wrote to me and informed me that he was proud of me in his own way, but it wasn't in his makeup to express it. But the fact that he never said anything made me want to prove to him that I'd made the correct decision. It motivated me. I believed that the more successful I became, the more he would be shown wrong, whether he realized it or not. Even now, I wonder whether I'm attempting to show my father what I'm made of, despite the fact that he's been deceased since 1991.

CHAPTER 2

My first employment on Denmark Street came at the perfect time, as Denmark Street was in terminal decline. It had been the heart of the British music industry ten years before, where authors went to sell their songs to publishers, who would then sell them to musicians. Then came The Beatles and Bob Dylan and changed everything. They didn't need professional songwriters' help because it turns out they were professional songwriters themselves. More bands with songwriters began to arise, including The Kinks, The Who, and The Rolling Stones. That was clearly how things were going to be from now on. There was still just about enough work to keep Denmark Street running - not every new band could compose their own material, and there was still a legion of vocalists and easy-listening crooners who got their tunes the old-fashioned way - but the writing was on the wall.

Even my new position at Mills Music seemed like a relic from another era. It has absolutely nothing to do with pop. My responsibilities included packaging sheet music for brass bands and delivering them to the post office across the street from the Shaftesbury Theatre. I wasn't even in the main building: the packing department was on the other side. The fact that it couldn't have been less glamorous was highlighted when Chelsea's star midfielder Terry Venables and a few of his teammates showed up unexpectedly one afternoon. They were being hunted by the press at the time - there was a story about them going out drinking after a game against the manager's orders - and had chosen to hide out in my new employment. They were football pals, like my cousin Roy, and had plainly grasped that the packing department was the last place in London you would check if you were looking for someone famous.

But I had a great time. It was a stepping stone into the music industry. Even though Denmark Street was on its final legs, it still maintained a special place in my heart. There was some glitz there, albeit fading glitz. There were guitar stores as well as recording studios. Lunch would be served at either the Gioconda coffee shop or the Lancaster Grill on Charing Cross Road. There were no celebrities in there - they were restaurants for people who couldn't afford anything better - but there was a buzz about them: they were full of aspirants, would-be, would-never-bes, and individuals who wanted to be noticed. People seem to like me.

Back in Pinner, my mother, Derf, and I had moved out of the damp and peeling wallpaper leased flat in Croxley Green and into a new house a few miles away in Northwood Hills, not far from the tavern whose window I'd scrambled out of on a frequent basis. From the exterior, Frome Court appeared to be a typical detached suburban house, but on the interior, it was divided into two-bedroom flats. 3A was ours. It seemed like a home, as opposed to our old residence, which felt like a punishment for Mum and Derf's divorce: you've done something bad, so you have to live here. And I was playing the electric piano I'd bought with the earnings from my pub appearance in a new band formed by Stuart A Brown, another ex-member of The Corvettes. Bluesology was far more serious. Stuart was a tremendously good-looking person who was convinced he was going to be a celebrity. We had a saxophonist. We practiced a set of obscure blues tracks by Jimmy Witherspoon and J. B. Lenoir in a Northwood bar called the Gate. We even had a manager, a Soho jeweler named Arnold Tendler, who employed our drummer, Mick Inkpen. Arnold was a charming little man who wanted to go into the music business and had the unfortunate misfortune of selecting Bluesology as his big investment opportunity after Mick persuaded him to come watch a show. He sunk his money into us and stage outfits - matching polo neck jumpers, trousers, and shoes - and received nothing in return, unless you include us always moaning at him when things went wrong.

We began playing local gigs in London, and Arnold financed for us to make a demo at a studio in a prefabricated hut in

Rickmansworth. Arnold was able to get the demo to Fontana Records by some miracle. Even more astonishing, they released a single, 'Come Back Baby,' a song I'd written - or rather, the only song I'd written. It made no difference. It was aired a few times on the radio, most likely on the less savory pirate stations that would play anything if the record label gave them some money. We gathered around the screen because there was a rumor that it will be on Juke Box Jury one week. It was not included on the Juke Box Jury. Then we released another track, 'Mr Frantic,' which was also penned by me. There was no rumor that it will be on Juke Box Jury this time. It simply vanished.

We received a position with Roy Tempest, an agency who specialized in bringing black American musicians to Britain, near the end of 1965. He kept piranhas in his office, and his business practices were as keen as their teeth. If he couldn't get The Temptations or The Drifters to cross the Atlantic, he'd find a few obscure black singers in London, dress them up in suits, and book them on a nightclub tour under the guise of The Temptin' Temptations or The Fabulous Drifters. When someone objected, he pretended to be unaware, saying, 'Of course they're not The Temptations!' They're known as The Temptin' Temptations! 'A totally different band!' So, in a sense, Roy Tempest invented the tribute act.

Bluesology got off lightly in their dealings with him in certain ways. Major Lance, Patti LaBelle And The Blue Belles, Fontella Bass, and Lee Dorsey were among the acts for whom we were hired as a supporting band. And the job meant I could quit packaging brass band music for a paycheck and pursue a career as a professional musician. I didn't have much of a choice. There was no way I could work a day job and keep up with Tempest's gig schedule. Unfortunately, the pay was horrible. Bluesology was paid fifteen pounds each week, which we used to pay for van gas, food, and lodgings: if you played too far out from London to drive home after the gig, you would book into a B&B for five pounds per night. I'm sure the celebrities we were supporting weren't getting much more. The workload was taxing. Night after night, I drove up and down the highway. We went to the big regional clubs: Manchester's Oasis, Sheffield's Mojo, Hanley's Place, Newcastle's Club A Go Go, and Derby's Clouds. We went to hip London clubs like Sybilla's, The Scotch of St James, where The Beatles and Stones drank whiskey and Coke, and the Cromwellian, which had a wonderful bartender named Harry Heart, who was almost as renowned as the pop stars he served. Harry was a total jerk who spoke in Polari and kept a bizarre vase full of transparent liquid on the counter. When you offered to buy him a drink, the puzzle was solved: 'Gin and tonic, please, and have one for yourself, Harry.' He'd say something like, 'Ooh, thank you, love, bona, bona, just one for the pot, then.' And he'd pour a measure of gin into the vase and drink from it in between serving customers. The real puzzle was how a man who drank a huge vase full of neat gin every night remained upright as the evening progressed.

And we went to the most unusual clubs. There was a venue in Harlesden that was just someone's front room, and another in Spitalfields that featured a boxing ring instead of a stage for reasons I never quite understood. We played a lot of black clubs, which should have been daunting because we were a bunch of white kids from the suburbs trying to play black music to a black audience, but it never was. For one thing, the audience appeared to enjoy the music. For instance, if you've spent your adolescence trying to play 'Roll Out The Barrel' while the patrons of a Northwood Hills tavern beat the living shit out of each other, you're not easily scared.

in fact, the only time I felt uneasy was at Balloch, which is located just outside of Glasgow. When we got to the site, we discovered that the stage was around nine feet tall. This was quickly revealed to be a security precaution: it prevented the audience from attempting to climb onstage and kill the performers. With that avenue of pleasure closed to them, they resorted to attempting to kill each other. They formed a line on either side of the club as they arrived. The first note of our set clearly signaled the start of the evening's festivities.

Suddenly, pint glasses were flying and blows were being hurled. It wasn't so much a show as it was a minor riot accompanied by an r'n'b band. It resembled the State Opening of Parliament on Saturday night in the Northwood Hills.

We played two jobs practically every night, and even more if we tried to supplement our income by performing our own performances. Roy scheduled us to play an American services club in Lancaster Gate at 2 p.m. one Saturday. Then we hopped in the van and traveled to Birmingham, where we played two performances he had arranged for us: the Ritz and the Plaza. Then we got back in the van, traveled back to London, and performed at Count Suckle's Cue club in Paddington, which he had hired for us. The Cue was a cutting-edge black club that blended soul and ska, and it was one of the first venues in London to book not only American but also West Indian acts. To be honest, my greatest memory of it isn't its pioneering blend of American and Jamaican music, but rather the fact that it featured a food counter that offered delicious Cornish pasties. When it's six a.m. and they're starving to death, even the most devoted music fan has a somewhat different set of priorities.

Roy Tempest occasionally made disastrous bookings. He brought The Ink Spots here, evidently thinking that because they were a black American singing group, they had to be a soul band. They were, however, a vocal harmony group from a different age, pre-rock 'n' roll. They'd start singing 'Whispering Grass' or 'Back In Your Own BackYard,' and the crowds would fade - great tunes, but not what the youths in the soul clubs wanted to hear. It was heartbreaking - until we arrived at Manchester's Twisted Wheel. The audience there was filled with music fans who were well-versed in the history of black music. They showed up with their parents' 78s to be signed by The Ink Spots. They practically lifted them off the stage and carried them around the club on their shoulders at the end of the set. People talk about Swinging London in the mid-1960s, but those Twisted Wheel youngsters were way more informed, switched-on, and cool than everyone else in the country.

In reality, I didn't mind the money, the workload, or the rare unpleasant gig. For me, the entire experience was a dream come true. I was performing with musicians whose records I owned. Billy Stewart, a huge guy from Washington DC who was signed to Chess Records, was my favorite. He was a fantastic singer who had turned his weight problem into a gimmick. His songs continued mentioning it:'she stated I was her pride and pleasure, that she was in love with a fat lad'. He had a legendary temper - it was rumored that when a secretary at Chess took too long to buzz him in, he retaliated by drawing a rifle and shooting the door handle off - and, as we soon discovered, a legendary blader. If Billy requested that the van pull over on the highway to urinate, you have to cancel your plans for the remainder of the evening. You had been there for several hours. The roar coming from the bushes was incredible: it sounded like someone using a fire hose to fill a swimming pool.

It was unnerving to play with these folks, and not just because some of them were said to fire objects when they got angry. Their mere brilliance was terrifying. It was a fantastic education. It wasn't only the quality of their voices; they were also terrific entertainers. The way they danced, how they spoke in between songs, how they could influence an audience, and how they dressed. They had such panache and charm. They had some odd eccentricities - for some reason, Patti Labelle insisted on performing a version of 'Danny Boy' for the audience at every event - but you could learn so much about artistry by watching them onstage for an hour. I couldn't believe they were nothing more than cult figures over here. They'd had tremendous American singles, but in the UK, white pop stars had taken their songs, covered them, and been far more popular. Mr. Wayne Fontana And The Mindbenders appeared to be the main culprits, having re-recorded Major Lance's 'Um Um Um Um Um Um' and Patti LaBelle's 'A Groovy Kind Of Love' and massively outsold the originals. Billy Stewart's dud 'Sitting In The Park' was replaced by Georgie Fame's smash. This clearly irritated them, and appropriately so. In fact, I got a decent indication of how much it irritated them when a mod in the audience at Windsor's Ricky-Tick club yelled sarcastically, "We want Georgie Fame!" while Billy Stewart sang "Sitting In The Park." I've never seen a man his size move so quickly. He jumped offstage, into the audience, and pursued him. The child literally sprinted out of the club, as you would if a trigger-happy twenty-four-stone soul singer suddenly took a dislike to you.

Bluesology traveled to Hamburg in March 1966, lugging our instruments on the ferry and then on the train, to perform at the Top Ten Club on the Reeperbahn. It was renowned since it was one of the first venues where The Beatles performed before they became famous. They were residing in the attic of the club when they recorded their first single with Tony Sheridan. The setup had remained unchanged in the five years after. The band's quarters were still in the attic. Just down the street, there were still brothels with prostitutes in the windows, and at the club, you were still expected to perform five hours a night, alternating with another band: an hour on, an hour off, while the clientele flowed in and out. It was easy to envisage The Beatles living the same life, not least since the bed linens in the attic appeared to have not been changed since John and Paul had slept in them.
We performed as Bluesology, and we also supported Isabel Bond, a Scottish vocalist who had relocated from Glasgow to Germany. This sweet-looking dark-haired girl who turned out to be the most foul-mouthed woman I'd ever encountered was funny. She'd sing old standards but tweak the lyrics to make them dirty. She's the only artist I've ever heard who could incorporate the words 'give us a wank' into 'Let Me Call You Sweetheart'.

But I was so young. I seldom drank and was still uninterested in sex, owing to the fact that I'd reached the age of nineteen without having gained any true knowledge or comprehension of what sex was. Aside from my father's dubious claim that masturbation caused blindness, no one had told me anything about what you did or were meant to do. I had no concept of penetration or a blow job. As a result, I'm probably the only British musician from the 1960s who went to work on the Reeperbahn and returned with his virginity intact. I was in one of Europe's most known fleshpots, with every possible kink and inclination provided for, yet the racist thing I did was buy a pair of flared pants from a department store. I was just interested in playing and visiting German record stores. I was completely engrossed in music. I was quite ambitious.

And I knew in my heart that Bluesology wasn't going to make it. We didn't measure up. It was self-evident. We'd progressed from obscure blues to the same soul songs that almost every British r'n'b band played in the mid-sixties - 'In The Midnight Hour,' 'Hold On I'm Coming'. The Alan Bown Set or The Mike Cotton Sound could play them better than us. There were far superior vocalists than Stuart out there, and far superior organ players to me. When I was a pianist, I wanted to hammer the keys like Little Richard, and attempting to do so on an organ can ruin your entire day. I lacked the technical expertise required to play an organ properly. The worst instrument was the Hammond B-12, which was permanently mounted on the stage of Wardour Street's Flamingo club. It was a massive wooden item, similar to playing a chest of drawers. It was encrusted with switches and levers, as well as draw bars and pedals. All of them would be used by Stevie Winwood or Manfred Mann to make Hammond scream, sing, and soar. I, on the other hand, didn't dare to touch them because I had no idea what any of them were doing. Even the small Vox Continental that I typically used to play was a technical quagmire. One key had a propensity of becoming stuck. It happened in the middle of a set at The Scotch of St James. The next thing I knew, I was playing 'Land of a Thousand Dances' and my organ was generating a cacophony that sounded like the Luftwaffe had arrived over London to give the Blitz another try. The rest of the band cheerfully continued dancing in the alley with Long Tall Sally and twisted with Lucy doing the Watusi as I panicked madly. I was about to dial 911 when The Animals' lead singer, Eric Burdon, took the stage. Alan Price, the Animals' keyboard player, was clearly blessed with the intricate technical expertise I lacked - he thumped the instrument with his fist and the key was released.

'That happens to Alan all the time,' he said as he walked away.

So we weren't as good as the other bands doing the same thing as us, and the other bands weren't as good as the bands that wrote their own material. When Bluesology was scheduled to perform at Birmingham's Cedar Club, we arrived early to find a rehearsal in process. It was The Move, a local quintet who were plainly on the rise. They had a crazy stage show, a manager with the gift of gab, and a songwriting guitarist named Roy Wood. We crept in and observed them. They not only sounded incredible, but Roy Wood's songs sounded better than the cover versions they played. Only a clinically insane person would have claimed that about the few songs I'd composed for Bluesology. To be honest, I'd only written them because we had one of our extremely infrequent recording sessions coming up and wanted at least some of our own songs. You could tell I wasn't putting my heart and soul into them. But I recall getting a revelation while watching The Move. Isn't this the end? This is the way to go. This is exactly what I should be doing.

In fact, if Long John Baldry hadn't come into the scene, I might have left Bluesology sooner. We were at the right place at the right time to get the work with him. Bluesology happened to be performing in the south of France when Long John Baldry found himself without a supporting band for a show at St-Tropez's Papagayo club. His original plan was to form a band similar to Steampacket with himself, Stuart Brown, a kid named Alan Walker - who I believe got the job because Baldry fancied him - singing, and a girl named Marsha Hunt, who had just arrived in London from the US, taking the female vocalist's part. Bluesology were to be his backup band, at least once he'd significantly updated the line-up: a couple of musicians he didn't like received the ax and were replaced by others he thought were better suited. It wasn't exactly what I had in mind. That lineup was a significant step down for John, in my opinion. I was aware of Julie Driscoll and Rod's abilities. Rod had blown me away when I saw him play with John at the Kenton Conservative Club while the band was still called The Hoochie Coochie Men and I was still in school. And Brian Auger was a true musician's musician: he didn't seem like the type of organist who'd ever need The Animals' lead vocalist to walk onstage and provide a helpful thump in the middle of a show.

As a result, I had misgivings. The lineup that included Alan Walker and Marsha Hunt didn't survive long: Marsha looked stunning, this magnificent, tall black girl, but she wasn't a great singer. Even yet, I had to agree that having Long John Baldry around made things a lot more interesting. Indeed, if your life is becoming a little normal, a little monotonous, I highly advocate going on tour with a hugely crazy six-foot-seven gay blues singer with a drinking problem. Things will brighten up significantly.

I really enjoyed John's company. He'd drive up to Frome Court in his van, which had its own record player, and greet me by reaching out the window and screaming 'REGGIE!' at the top of his lungs. His life seemed full of incidents, many of which were related to his boozing, which I quickly realized was self-destructive: the major indication came when we performed at the Links Pavilion in Cromer and he got so pissed off after the gig that he slid down a neighboring cliff in his white suit. However, I had no idea he was gay. In retrospect, it seemed incredible. This was a man who named himself Ada, addressed other men as she' or 'her,' and constantly updated you on the state of his sex life: 'I've got this new partner called Ozzie - lovely, he spins around on my dick.' But, once again, I was so stupid that I honestly had no idea what being gay meant, let alone that the term might have applied to me. 'What?' I'd sit there pondering. He's spinning on your dick? How and why? 'What the hell are you talking about?'

It was all very entertaining, but it didn't change the fact that I didn't want to be an organist, a backup musician, or a member of Bluesology. Which is why I ended up at Liberty Records' new offices, just off Piccadilly, prefacing my audition for the label by pouring out my woes: the stasis of Bluesology's career, the horror of the cabaret circuit, the tape machine and its role in our legendary non-performance of 'Let The Heartaches Begin'.

Ray Williams, on the other side of the desk, nodded sympathetically. He was blond, gorgeous, well-dressed, and quite young. As it turned out, he was so young that he lacked the authority to provide anyone with a contract. The decision was made by his superiors. They might have signed me if I hadn't chosen 'He'll Have To Go' by Jim Reeves as my audition piece. My reasoning was that everyone else would sing 'My Girl' or a Motown song, so I'd try something unusual and stand out. And 'He'll Have To Go' is one of my favorites. I felt comfortable singing it because it used to knock people out in the Northwood Hills public bar. If I had paused for a moment, I might have realized that it was unlikely to elicit much enthusiasm among those attempting to launch a progressive rock label. The Bonzo Dog Doo-Dah Band, The Groundhogs, and The Idle Race, a psychedelic band lead by Jeff Lynne, who went on to join the Electric Light Orchestra, were all signed to Liberty. The last thing they needed was Pinner's Jim Reeves.

Perhaps singing 'He'll Have To Go' was exactly the appropriate thing to do. Ray might not have provided me with Bernie's lyrics if I hadn't passed the audition. And I'm not sure what would have occurred if he hadn't handed me Bernie's lyrics, though I've spent a lot of time thinking about it because it seems like such an unbelievable twist of fate. I should mention that Ray's office was in shambles. There were stacks of reel-to-reel cassettes and hundreds of envelopes everywhere: he'd been contacted not only by every budding musician and writer in the country, but also by every nutcase who'd seen Liberty's 'talent wanted' post. He seemed to pull the envelope out at random, just to give me something to take away so the meeting didn't feel like a waste of time - I'm not sure if he'd even opened it before handing it to me. And yet, that envelope contained my future: everything that has happened to me since has occurred as a result of what it contained. You try to figure it out without getting a headache.

Who can say? Without it, I may have found another writing partner, joined another band, or forged a career as a musician. But I know my life and career would have been extremely different, most likely significantly worse - it's difficult to imagine how it could have ended out any better - and I guess you wouldn't be reading this right now.

Because Liberty Records was uninterested in the first tracks Bernie and I composed together, Ray offered to sign us to a publishing firm he had established. There was no money in it unless we actually sold some tunes, but that didn't seem to matter at the time: Ray believed in me. He even tried to connect me with a couple of other lyricists, but it didn't work out like it did with Bernie. The others wanted us to collaborate, writing music and words at the same time, which I couldn't do. Before I could write a song, I needed to have the words written down in front of me. I needed that push, that inspiration. And there was just something magical that happened when I saw Bernie's lyrics that inspired me to compose music. It started the instant I opened the letter on the tube train home from Baker Street, and it hasn't stopped since.

The songs were pouring out of us. They were better than anything I'd written previously, which was saying a lot. Actually, just a few of them were better than anything I'd previously written. We composed two types of tunes. The first were songs we hoped to sell to Cilla Black or Engelbert

Humperdinck, for example: big weepy ballads and peppy bubblegum pop. They were terrible - I shuddered at the notion of the weepies sounding similar to the dreadful 'Let The Heartaches Begin' - but that was how you made money as a songwriting duo for hire. Your intended market was those big middle-of-the-road stars. Every time, we missed the mark. The largest person we managed to sell a song to was actor Edward Woodward, who moonlighted as an easy-listening crooner on occasion. His record was titled This Man Alone, which foreshadowed its audience.

Then there were the songs we wanted to write, inspired by The Beatles, The Moody Blues, Cat Stevens, and Leonard Cohen, the kind of stuff we were buying from Musicland, a record shop in Soho that Bernie and I frequented so much that the staff would ask me to help out behind the counter when one of them needed to get some lunch. We were nearing the end of the psychedelic era, so we created a lot of charming songs about dandelions and teddy bears. We were essentially putting on other people's styles and learning that none of them fit us, but that's how the process of establishing your own voice works, and it was a lot of fun. Everything was enjoyable. Bernie had relocated to London, and our friendship had blossomed. We got along so well that it felt like he was the brother I'd never had, which was exacerbated by the fact that we were, at least temporarily, sleeping in bunk beds in my Frome Court bedroom. We'd spend our days composing, with Bernie scribbling lyrics on a typewriter in the bedroom, bringing them to me at the upright piano in the living room, then running back to the bedroom as I began to arrange them to music. We couldn't be in the same room when we were composing, but when we weren't, we spent all of our time together, at record stores and at the movies. We'd go to shows or stay out at musicians' clubs at night, watching Harry Heart drink his vase full of gin and conversing with other young hopefuls. We met a hilarious little guy who had changed his name to Hans Christian Anderson to fit in with the flower-power craze of the moment. When he opened his mouth and a heavy Lancashire accent came out, the illusion of fairy tale otherworldliness generated by this moniker was partly deflated. He eventually reverted to his given name, Jon, and became the lead singer of Yes.

We recorded both types of songs in a tiny four-track studio in the New Oxford Street offices of Dick James Music, which administrated Ray's own publishing company: it later became famous because it was where The Troggs were covertly recorded shouting and cursing at each other for eleven minutes while trying to write a song - 'you're talking out the back of your fucking arses!' 'Fuckin' drummer - I shit him!' - a tape that became known as the Troggs Tape. Caleb Quaye, the in-house engineer, was a multi-instrumentalist with a smoldering joint between his fingers. Caleb was cool, and he made sure you knew it. He spent half his life laughing at things Bernie and I said, did, or wore that revealed our pathetic lack of cool. However, he, like Ray, seemed to believe in what we were doing. When he wasn't writhing on the floor in laughter or wiping tears of hopeless mirth from his eyes, he was giving our songs more time and attention than they deserved. We worked on them late into the night, breaking company regulations by enlisting the help of session musicians Caleb knew and testing out arrangements and production ideas after everyone else at DJM had gone home.

It was wonderful until we were apprehended by the office manager of the company. I'm not sure how he found out we were there - I imagine someone driving by saw a light on and assumed the property was being burgled. Caleb was worried about losing his job and, probably out of desperation, told Dick James what we'd been up to. Dick James volunteered to publish our tunes instead of firing Caleb and tossing us out. He was going to pay us a weekly retainer of £25: tenner for Bernie and fifteen pounds for me (plus an extra fiver because I had to play piano and sing on the demos). It meant I could leave Bluesology and focus only on songwriting, which was precisely what I desired. We left his office in a stupor, too stunned to be excited.

The only disadvantage of this new arrangement was that Dick believed our future rested in ballads and bubblegum pop. He worked with The Beatles, running their publishing company Northern Songs, but he was primarily a Tin Pan Alley publisher. DJM was an unusual setup. Half of the company was like Dick: middle-aged, from the old Jewish showbiz world rather than rock and roll. Caleb, Dick's son Stephen, or Tony King were among the younger and more fashionable members of the other half.

Tony King worked from a desk he rented on the second level for a new company named AIR. George Martin founded AIR, an association of independent record producers, after seeing how little EMI paid him for working on The Beatles' records, and Tony handled their publishing and promotion. It would be an understatement to say Tony stood out in the DJM offices. Tony would have been seen in the midst of a Martian invasion. He donned clothes from the coolest tailors in London, with orange velvet trousers and satin details. He wore love beads around his neck and one or more of his antique silk scarves floated behind him. His hair was highlighted blond. He was a die-hard music aficionado who has worked with The Rolling Stones and Roy Orbison. He was close to The Beatles. He, like Long John Baldry, was openly gay and didn't care who knew. 'Sorry I'm late, sweetie, the telephone got tangled up in my necklaces,' he wafted through the office. He was just hilarious. I was completely enthralled by him. More than that, I wished to emulate him. I aspired to be that fashionable, outrageous, and exotic.

His fashion style began to affect mine, with some startling effects. I developed a mustache. I got an Afghan coat, but it was on the cheap side. The sheepskin hadn't been thoroughly cured, and the resulting stench was so awful that my mother wouldn't let me in the flat if I wore it. I couldn't afford the stores Tony frequented, so I bought a length of curtain fabric with Noddy pictures on it and had a seamstress friend of my mother make me a shirt out of it. In the advertisements for my first song, 'I've Been Loving You,' I donned a faux fur coat and a mock-leopardskin trilby hat.

When the single was released in March 1968, the sight of me dressed in this spectacular attire failed to entice record consumers. It was a complete failure. I was unsurprised. I wasn't even let down. I didn't want to be a solo artist; all I wanted to do was write songs, and my record deal had happened by chance. Dick's son Stephen had been sending tapes of our songs to various labels in the hopes that one of their artists would record them. Someone at Philips had indicated they loved my voice, and before I knew it, I had a deal to release a few singles. I wasn't sure, but I agreed because I felt it may be a good way to get some publicity for the tunes Bernie and I were writing. We were getting better as songwriters. We were inspired by The Band's rootsy Americana and a new breed of US singer-songwriters like Leonard Cohen, whom we discovered in Musicland's imports area. Something about their impact rang true in our writing. We'd started making material that wasn't derivative of other people's work. I'd listened to a song we'd written called 'Skyline Pigeon' over and over and couldn't think of anyone else it sounded like - we'd finally made something our own.

But Dick James had chosen 'I've Been Loving You' as my debut single, presumably after a lengthy but ultimately profitable search for the most boring song in my collection. He managed to locate something absolutely unremarkable for which Bernie hadn't even written the words, and which we'd planned to sell to a middle-of-the-road crooner. Dick's old-school Tin Pan Alley roots were clearly visible. I knew that was the incorrect decision, but I didn't want to argue about it. He was the Denmark Street legend who'd worked with The Beatles, and he'd granted us a contract and a record deal when he should've thrown Bernie and me out on the street. The advertisements stated it was 'the finest performance on a "first" CD', that I was '1968's great new talent,' and concluded, 'YOU HAVE BEEN WARNED'. The British public reacted as if they'd been informed that every copy was polluted with raw sewage, and 1968's great new talent was forced to start over.

At this moment, there was one more unanticipated issue in my life. I'd proposed to a woman named Linda Woodrow. We first met in late 1967, during a Bluesology show at Sheffield's Mojo club. Linda knew the club's resident DJ, the Mighty Atom, who stood four feet eight inches tall. She was tall, blonde, and three years my senior. She was unemployed. I'm not sure where her money came from; I believed her family was wealthy, but she was a woman of her own means. She was extremely nice and seemed to be interested in what I was doing. A post-gig talk had escalated into a meeting that felt suspiciously like a date, which had escalated into another date, which had resulted in her going down to visit Frome Court. It was an unusual connection. There wasn't much physicality, and we never had sex, which Linda saw as evidence of old-fashioned chivalry and romanticism on my part, rather than a lack of interest or willingness: in 1968, it wasn't uncommon for couples not to sleep together before they married.

But, sexual or not, the relationship began to take on its own pace. Linda decided to relocate to London and look for a place to live. Linda could afford one, so we could share a place. Bernie could be our roommate.

I'd be lying if I claimed I didn't feel uneasy about everything, not least because Linda had begun to express reservations about the music I was making. She was a tremendous lover of an American crooner named Buddy Greco, and she made it clear that she thought I should model myself after him. My anxiety, though, was surprisingly easy to tune out. I liked the notion of leaving Frome Court. And I suppose I was doing what I believed I should be doing at twenty - finding someone to settle down with.

So we ended up at Furlong Road, Islington, in a flat with me, Bernie, Linda, and Caspar, her little Chihuahua. She got a job as a secretary, and the topic gradually shifted to getting married. The sound of alarm bells had become difficult to ignore by this point, because those closest to me kept sounding them. My mother was adamantly opposed to the concept, and the words of the song he later wrote about the experience, 'Someone Saved My Life Tonight,' give you a pretty clear picture of what Bernie thought. It's hardly a favorable assessment of Linda's many virtues: 'a controlling queen','sitting like a princess perched in her electric chair'. Bernie had no feelings for her. He was afraid she was going to ruin our music by bringing up Buddy Greco. He believed mom was overbearing, and he was enraged because she'd had him take down a Simon and Garfunkel poster he'd hung in his room for some reason.

I was able to ignore the warning signs thanks to a combination of stubbornness and my aversion to confrontation. We got engaged on my twenty-first birthday - I'm not sure who proposed to whom. A wedding date has been set. Preparations were being made. I began to panic. The obvious course of action was to be truthful. The apparent course of action, however, did not appeal - actually telling Linda how I felt was beyond me. Instead, I decided to stage a suicide attempt.

Bernie, who came to my aid, has never forgotten the specifics of my alleged effort to end it all by gassing myself. Someone who truly wishes to commit suicide will do so alone, in order to avoid detection; they will do it at night or in an area where they are alone. I, on the other hand, did it in the middle of the afternoon in a crowded flat: Bernie was in his room, Linda was napping. I'd not only placed a pillow in the bottom of the oven to rest my head on, but I'd also turned the gas to low and opened all the kitchen windows. When Bernie dragged me out of the oven, it was fairly dramatic, but there wasn't enough carbon monoxide in the room to kill a wasp. I expected awful shock, followed by Linda's quick revelation that my suicidal anguish was founded in dissatisfaction about our impending marriage. Instead, there was moderate amusement. Worse, Linda seemed to believe that if I was depressed, it was because 'I've Been Loving You' had failed to top the charts. Clearly, now would have been an excellent time to tell her the truth. Instead, I remained silent. The suicide attempt was forgotten, and the wedding was written down in the diary. We started looking for a flat in Mill Hill jointly.

Long John Baldry had to tell me what I already knew. We'd remained excellent friends after I left Bluesology, and I'd asked him to be my best man at my wedding. He appeared amused by the fact that I was getting married at all, but agreed. We agreed to meet in Soho's Bag O' Nails club to finalize the plans. Bernie came along for the ride.

From the moment John walked in, there was something odd about his demeanor. He seemed preoccupied. I had no notion what to do with it. I assumed there was something going on in his personal life. Ozzie might have refused to spin around on his dick, or whatever they did in private. It took a few glasses for him to tell me exactly what the problem was.
'Oh fucking hell,' he exclaimed. 'Why are you living with a fucking woman? Get out of bed and smell the roses. You're a gay man. You adore Bernie more than she adores you.'

There was an awkward pause. I knew he was correct, up to a point. Linda was not someone I loved enough to marry. I adored Bernie. Not sexually, but he was my best buddy in the entire world. I was significantly more concerned with our musical collaboration than with my fiancée. But what about gay? I wasn't sure about that, mostly because I wasn't sure what being homosexual entailed, though thanks to a few candid chats with Tony King, I was getting a better notion. Perhaps I was gay. Maybe that's why I admired Tony so much: I saw part of myself in him, not just his clothing and air of urbane sophistication.

There was a lot to think about. Rather than doing so, I argued back. John was being completely ridiculous. He was inebriated yet again and making a big deal out of nothing. I couldn't possibly back out of the wedding. Everything was in order. We'd requested a cake.

But John refused to listen. He continued to attack me. If I went through with it, I'd wreck both my life and Linda's. I was a complete moron and a coward. The conversation began to draw attention as it became more heated and passionate. People from adjacent tables got involved. Because it was the Bag O' Nails, the folks at adjacent tables were all pop stars, which added to the strange atmosphere. Cindy Birdsong of The Supremes joined in; I remembered her from the Bluesology days, when she was one of Patti LaBelle's Blue Belles. Then P. J. Proby became involved in the conversation. I'd love to tell you what the trouser-splitting, ponytail-wearing enfant terrible of mid-sixties pop had to say about my impending wedding, its potential cancellation, and, indeed, whether or not I was a homosexual, but by then I was incredibly pissed, and the exact details are a little hazy, though at some point I must have caved and admitted that John was right, at least about the marriage.

The rest of the night is a jumble of images in my mind. Walking up the road to the flat as daylight broke, arm in arm with Bernie for moral support, and stumbling against cars and knocking over dustbins. Linda threatened to kill herself during the squabble. A muddled chat over whether or not Linda was going to kill herself was held via the locked door of Bernie's room - he'd made himself very scarce shortly after our arrival. Another chat through Bernie's door, this time asking him if he wouldn't mind unlocking it so I could sleep on the floor.

There was another argument the next morning, and a desperate phone call to Frome Court. 'They're coming in the morning with a vehicle to take me home,' Bernie wrote in 'Someone Saved My Life Tonight'. That was some poetic license. There was no 'they' or 'truck,' just Derf in his little decorator's van. However, Bernie and I were taken home. We returned to the bunk beds at Frome Court. Bernie hung up his

Simon & Garfunkel poster. Linda was never seen by either of us again.

CHAPTER 3

In principle, Bernie and I were just returning to Frome Court temporarily until we found our own place. It gradually dawned on me that we would be staying for the foreseeable future. We wouldn't be able to get somewhere on our own since we couldn't afford it. We couldn't finance our own studio since British singers were staunchly resistant to singing our tunes. We'd occasionally hear that an artist's manager or producer was interested in something we'd written. You'd get your hopes up, then... nothing. The rejections began to pile up. Cliff, I'm afraid, says no. Sorry, Cilla does not believe it is suitable for her. Octopus does not desire 'When I Was Tealby Abbey'. Octopus? Octopus, who were they? I literally knew nothing about them except that they didn't like our songs. We were being rejected by people we'd never heard of.

There was nothing moving. Nothing was going on. It was difficult not to become depressed, though one advantage of living at Frome Court was that my mother was always around, ready with her patented manner of snapping me out of it. This included a straight-faced proposal that I give up my songwriting career and instead work in a neighborhood shop: 'Well, you've got a choice, you know. If you're interested, there's a job opening in the laundromat.' You're talking about the laundromat, right? Hmm. As appealing as a job managing the tumble dryers sounds, I guess I'll stick to songwriting for a while longer.

Instead of leaving, we attempted to make a bedroom with bunk beds look like a suitable place for two adult men to reside. I joined a Reader's Digest book club and slowly accumulated leather-bound versions of Moby Dick and David Copperfield. We acquired a stereo and two sets of headphones from the Littlewoods catalog since you could pay in installments. We purchased a Man Ray poster from Athena on Oxford Street, then went next door to India Craft to purchase some joss sticks. Bernie and I could convince ourselves that we were artists living a bohemian existence at the cutting edge of the counterculture while lying on the floor with our headphones on, our latest buy from Musicland on the turntable, and the air heavy with incense smoke. Or, at least, we could until my mother knocked on the bedroom door, wondering what that bleeding smell was and, by the way, what we wanted for dinner.

Tony King had utilized his connections at AIR Studios and Abbey Road to get me work as a session musician, so I had a little more money than Bernie. If you worked at Abbey Road, you were paid £3 an hour for a three-hour stint in cash. Even better, if the session lasted even a minute over the allocated time, the Musicians' Union rules stipulated that you were paid for a session and a half: roughly fifteen quid, which was the same as I earned in a week at DJM. The AIR Studios secretaries Shirley Burns and Carol Weston would be an added bonus. They were fantastic, always up for a chat and always willing to recommend my name if they heard of a job opening. Something about me seemed to trigger their maternal instinct, and they would quietly pass me their luncheon vouchers. So, on top of everything else, I got a free supper - I felt I'd died and gone to heaven.

But forget about the money: the session work was an incredible experience. Pickiness is not an option for a session musician. You accepted any work that came your way, no matter what it was. You had to work swiftly and accurately since your colleagues' session musicians were some of the top musicians in the country. The Mike Sammes Singers, who sang backup vocals for everyone, were frightening - they looked like middle-aged aunties and uncles who'd arrived at the studio straight from a golf club dinner dance. But if you had to sing with them, they suddenly instilled fear in you because they were so skilled at what they did.

You also had to be adaptive because you were expected to play a wide range of songs. One day you'd be singing backup vocals for Tom Jones, the next you'd be working on a comedy record with The Scaffold, arranging and playing piano with The Hollies, or attempting to come up with a rock version of Zorba the Greek's theme for The Bread and Beer Band, a Tony King project that never really took off. You were always meeting new people and making new connections: musicians, producers, arrangers, and record business personnel. Paul McCartney walked into the studio one day while I was recording with The Barron Knights. He sat in the control room for a time, listening. Then he proceeded to the piano, stated that he was performing this in a neighboring studio, and performed 'Hey Jude' for eight minutes. That certainly brought what The Barron Knights were doing - creating a novelty record about Des O'Connor competing in the Olympics - into sharp focus.

Sometimes a session was fantastic because the music you were playing was terrific, but other times it was fantastic because the music you were playing was so bad. For a company called Marble Arch, I did a lot of covers albums: quickly knocked-out renditions of current chart singles featured on compilations with titles like Top of the Pops, Hit Parade, and Chartbusters that were sold inexpensively in supermarkets. People talk about my involvement in them as a desperate low time in my career: the impoverished, undiscovered artist reduced to anonymously singing other people's songs to earn a crust. With the benefit of hindsight, you could look at it that way, but it didn't feel that way at the time, because the sessions for the covers albums were hysterically entertaining.

The producer Alan Caddy's directions were incredible - one utterly ridiculous request after another. 'Can you perform "Young, Gifted, and Black"?' That's not a song that makes much sense sung by a white guy from Pinner, but I'll give it a shot. 'We're going to do "Back Home" next, and we want you to sound like the England World Cup squad.' OK, there are only three vocalists here, and one of us is female, so it won't sound exactly like the original, but you're the boss. On one occasion, I was asked to sound like Robin Gibb of The Bee Gees, a wonderful vocalist with a distinct vocal style: an unsettling, tremulous, nasal tremolo. I couldn't accomplish it unless I literally grasped my throat and wobbled it around as I sang. I believed this was a genuine brainstorm, but it caused complete chaos among my other musicians. I stood there wailing, fingers clutched around my neck, desperately trying not to look across the studio at the two session singers, David Byron and Dana Gillespie, who were holding each other and laughing.

I went back and performed one after my solo career took off, which shows how much I enjoyed the sessions for the covers albums, this apparently awful artistic bottom in my professional existence. I can promise you that I am not making this up. 'Your Song' had been written, the Elton John album had been released, I'd been on Top of the Pops, and I was about to embark on my first tour in America when I went back into the studio and happily belted out shonky versions of 'In The Summertime' and 'Let's Work Together' for some terrible album sold in a supermarket for fourteen and sixpence. It was, as usual, hilarious.

The session work, however, was far from the most significant aspect of my friendship with Tony King. He had a terrific group of pals, almost like a gang, largely made up of gay males who worked in the music industry. They were record producers, BBC employees, promoters and pluggers, and a young, ambitious, confident, and witty Scottish man named John Reid. He was rapidly rising through the ranks of the music industry. He eventually became the UK label manager for Tamla Motown, dealing with The Supremes, The Temptations, and Smokey Robinson, a high position that Tony marked appropriately by always referring to John as Pamela Motown after that.

Tony's group wasn't particularly outlandish or controversial - they had dinner parties or went out to restaurants and pubs together rather than frequenting London's gay clubs - but I really enjoyed their company. They were intelligent, witty, and hilarious: I enjoyed their camp sense of humor. The more I thought about it, the more I realized there was something strange about how entirely at ease I felt around them. I'd never been a loner; I'd always had a lot of friends - at school, in Bluesology, on Denmark Street - but this was different; it felt more like a sense of belonging. I felt like one of the children in Mary Poppins, being thrust into this fantastic new world. Twelve months after John Baldry had drunkenly shouted to everyone within earshot at the Bag O' Nails that I was queer, I determined he was correct.

As if to emphasize the point, my libido chose to show up for the first time, like a frantic latecomer to a party that was supposed to have begun ten years ago. At twenty-one, I seemed to be going through a type of belated adolescence. There were a lot of quiet crushes on men all of a sudden. For one thing, it wasn't only John Reid's sense of humor and encyclopedic knowledge of American soul that drew me in. Of course, I never followed through on any of them. I couldn't have done it. I'd never intentionally struck up a conversation with someone before. I'd never gone to a homosexual bar before. I had no idea how you found someone to date. What should I have said? 'Would you like to go to the movies with me and maybe get your knob out later'? That's the main recollection I have of realizing my sexual orientation. I don't remember feeling anxious or tortured. I only remember wanting to have sex but having no idea how to do it and being frightened of getting it wrong. I didn't even tell Tony I was gay.

I had other things on my mind, after all. Bernie and I were summoned to a meeting at DJM with Steve Brown, who had recently taken over as studio manager from Caleb. He said he'd heard the tunes we'd been working on and believed we were wasting our time.

'You need to stop this nonsense. You're not particularly good at it. 'In fact,' he nodded, apparently warming to this depressing issue, 'you're hopeless. You'll never make a living as songwriters. You're not going to be able to do it.'

I sat there stunned. Oh, very nice. That's all there is to it. The Northwood Hills laundromat calls. Perhaps not; there was always session employment. What about Bernie, though? The poor sod would find himself back in Owmby-by-Spital, wheeling his wheelbarrow full of dead chickens around, the only evidence of his musical career one flop single he didn't actually write and a rejection message from Octopus, whomever they were. We hadn't even paid off the stereo's HP.

As my thoughts raced, I became aware that Steve Brown was still speaking elsewhere in the room. He was talking about 'Lady What's Tomorrow,' one of the songs we'd written but hadn't bothered to try to sell. It was influenced by Leonard Cohen, and Cilla Black was plainly not interested. Steve Brown, on the other hand, appears to be.
'You should write more songs like that,' he added. 'Do what you want to do, not what you think will sell. I'm going to talk to Dick about doing an album.'

Bernie and I sat at the pub afterwards, trying to understand what had just happened. On the one hand, I had no aspirations to be a solo artist. On the other hand, the chance to stop penning the weepies and bubblegum pop was too good to pass up. And we still thought that releasing Elton John CDs would be a fantastic way to showcase the type of tunes we liked. The more people heard our songs, the more possible it was that another, more famous musician would hear them and decide to record one.

There was one issue. The agreement with Philips was for singles only; they wanted a follow-up to 'I've Been Loving You,' not an album. So, following his direction to stop trying to be marketable and do what we enjoyed, Steve Brown recorded a new song that Bernie and I had written. 'Lady Samantha' was the name, and it seemed like a breakthrough.

At this point in my career, making a single that I could listen to without yelping involuntarily would have been a breakthrough, but 'Lady Samantha' was a very excellent tune. It sounded nothing like 'I've Been Loving You': it was heavier, hipper, and more confident. It was a 'turntable hit' when it was released in January 1969, which was a polite way of saying it was a song that got a lot of radio play but no one really bought.

Following its failure, we discovered that Philips was not interested in renewing our contract: for some odd reason, they appeared quite averse to supporting an album by an artist who had so far done nothing but cost them money. Dick James hinted at putting it out himself, establishing a true label, rather than merely licensing tracks to other record companies, but he seemed more interested in discussing the Eurovision Song Contest. Much to Dick's pleasure, one of the supposed forgotten attempts at middle-of-the-road songwriting has now been proposed as a prospective UK entry. Lulu was scheduled to perform six songs on her TV show, and the British audience would vote to determine the winner. To suggest Bernie reacted calmly to the news would be an understatement. He was shocked. Eurovision wasn't exactly the orgy of disgrace it is now, but it wasn't like Pink Floyd and Soft Machine were lining up to participate. Worse, despite the fact that his name was in the credits, he had had nothing to do with the song. I had written the lyrics myself. It was like hearing 'I've Been Loving You' all over again. We were abruptly back where we had begun.

Bernie's greatest worries were realized as we sat down to watch the Lulu concert in Frome Court. Our song, my song, was absolutely unremarkable and forgettable, which was more than you could say about the others. Every other songwriter seemed to have come up with a horrible notion that you couldn't forget if you tried. One sounded like something intoxicated Germans in a Bavarian beer hall would slap their knees to. Another had the abominable pairing of a huge band and a bouzouki. 'March' was the name of another. The month was not mentioned in the title. The song was literally about marching, with a military brass band arrangement to emphasize the point. Steve Brown was correct. We couldn't do anything like this, as evidenced by our song being last in the public vote. The German oompah tune was victorious. 'Boom Bang-A-Bang' was the name of the song.

We came to DJM the next day to find that the Daily Express had published a piece explaining that our song had lost because it was clearly the weakest of the bunch. Dick grudgingly admitted that it could be better if we stopped wasting everyone's time and instead recorded our own CD. If Philips did not release it, he would employ a publicity and promotions person and launch his own record label.

As a result, we were locked away in the small DJM studio, with Steve Brown producing and Clive Franks operating the tape machine. Clive was the man behind the recording of The Troggs Tape; years later, he ended up co-producing some of my albums, and he still works with me today, performing sound engineering for my live shows. We all threw everything we had at the new tunes. Psychedelic sound effects, harpsichords, Caleb's backwards guitar solos, flutes, bongos, stereo panning, improvisational jazz interludes, trick endings where the songs faded out then unexpectedly returned, Clive whistling. You could hear the kitchen sink being hauled into the studio if you listened closely. We could have been better off if we had learned that sometimes less is more, but when you're producing your debut album, you don't think like that. There's a whisper in the back of your mind telling you that you might never make another, so you might as well try everything while you can. But, God, that was such a thrilling journey. The album's title was Empty Sky. On June 6, 1969, it was released on Dick's new DJM label. When I first heard the title track, I thought it was the best thing I'd ever heard in my life.

Empty Sky wasn't a big hit (it only sold a few thousand copies), but I could feel things starting to move slowly. The reviews were mixed, but they were an improvement over being told by the Daily Express that you couldn't produce a song as good as 'Boom Bang-A-Bang'. We received a phone call shortly after the record's release informing us that Three Dog Night had covered 'Lady Samantha' for their new album. Night of the Three Dogs! They were from the United States! One of our tracks had been recorded by a genuine American rock band. A hip, popular American rock band, not a light performer with a Saturday-night variety show on BBC1, not a Eurovision Song Contest participant. Bernie and I had a song on an album that reached the top twenty in the United States.

And Empty Sky provided me with the material, which allowed me to perform live. The first few gigs were a little shaky. I was still nervous: the last time I was onstage, Long John Baldry had his tape recorder out and I was in a kaftan, suffering a complete collapse of the will to live. But the gigs improved as I became more at ease, and they really took off when I formed my own band. Nigel Olsson and Dee Murray were hanging around DJM when I met them. Nigel was in a band called Plastic Penny, who had a tremendous hit single in 1968 and, unbelievably, had purchased one of the tracks Bernie and I had been trying to sell the year before. It was indicative of our misfortune that they recorded it on an album released just as Plastic Penny's period in the spotlight ended and their career went downhill. Meanwhile, Dee had been a member of The Mirage, a psychedelic band that had released singles for years without getting anywhere. They were wonderful musicians with whom we instantly connected. Dee was a fantastic bassist. Nigel was a Keith Moon and Ginger Baker drummer, a showman with a kit that took up most of our rehearsal area with his name plastered across his dual bass drums. They were both capable of singing. We didn't require the services of a guitarist. The sound we generated as three was already massive and harsh. Plus, there's something about performing as a trio that allows you to be completely spontaneous. It didn't matter that we couldn't duplicate the intricate arrangements of the album: instead we could spread out and improvise, play solos, convert songs into medleys, suddenly launch into an old Elvis cover or a version of 'Give Peace A Chance'.

I began to consider how I appeared onstage more. I wanted to be a frontman, but I couldn't because I was stuck behind a keyboard. I couldn't strut around like Mick Jagger or smash my instrument up like Jimi Hendrix or Pete Townshend: bitter subsequent experience has taught me that if you get carried away and try to smash up a piano by pushing it offstage, you end up looking more like a furniture removal man having a bad day. So I remembered the piano players I'd admired as a kid, and how they'd managed to convey joy while stuck behind the old nine-foot plank, as I affectionately referred to it. I remembered Jerry Lee Lewis throwing his seat away and jumping on the keyboard, Little Richard standing up and leaning back while he played, and Winifred Atwell grinning to the audience. They all had an impact on my performances. When you have arms as short as mine, playing the piano standing up like Little Richard is bloody hard work, but I persisted. We didn't sound like anyone else, and we certainly didn't look like anyone else. Whatever else was going on in pop as the 1960s gave way to the 1970s, I was fairly positive there were no other piano-led power trios whose vocalist was attempting to combine the outrageousness and ferocity of early rock and roll with Winifred Atwell's bonhomie.

The shows became crazier and the music got better as we traveled around campuses and hippy places like the Roundhouse, especially when we started playing the latest batch of tunes Bernie and I had written. I admit that I'm not always the best judge of my own work - after all, I am the man who loudly declared that 'Don't Let The Sun Go Down On Me' was such a terrible song that I would never countenance releasing it, of which more later - but even I could tell that our new material was in a different league than anything we'd produced before. They were simple songs to compose - Bernie got the lyrics to 'Your Song' over breakfast one morning in Frome Court, handed them to me, and I wrote the music in fifteen minutes flat - because we'd already done the hard work. The way they sounded was the culmination of the hours we'd previously spent attempting to write together, the gigs I'd been playing with Nigel and Dee that had improved my confidence, the years I'd spent, much against my will, at the Royal Academy, and the evenings on the club circuit in Bluesology. 'Border Song' and 'Take Me To The Pilot' had the funk and soulfulness I'd picked up supporting Patti LaBelle and Major Lance, but they also had a classical influence from all those Saturday mornings forced to study Chopin and Bartók.

They were also the result of the Frome Court bedroom. Two artists were continually playing on the Littlewoods stereo while we were writing. Delaney and Bonnie were a rock/soul duet. I was immediately smitten by the way their keyboardist, Leon Russell, performed. It was as if he'd gotten into my thoughts and figured out just how I wanted to play the piano before I did. He'd managed to combine all of the music I adored - rock & roll, blues, gospel, and country - into a single, perfectly natural sound.

The Band was the other. We listened to their first two albums over and over. Their music, like Leon Russell's piano performance, felt like someone turning on a torch and showing us a new road to take, a way to do what we wanted to do. 'Chest Fever,' 'Tears Of Rage,' 'The Weight': these were the songs we wanted to write. Bernie was enthralled by the lyrics. 'Virgil Caine is the name, and I served on the Danville train, 'til Stoneman's troops arrived and tore the tracks up again,' he'd enjoyed gritty stories of old America since he was a youngster. They were white musicians who made soul music without covering 'In The Midnight Hour' or creating a poor imitation of what black artists performed. It was an epiphany.

Dick was blown away when we played him the demos of the new tunes. Despite the success of Empty Sky, he stated that he wants to release another album. Furthermore, he was going to give us £6,000 to make it happen. That was an incredible leap of faith. It was a lot of money to spend on an album back then, especially one by an artist who hadn't sold many records yet. There's no denying Dick believed in us, but I believe his hand was a touch forced. Bernie and I had made friends with Muff Winwood, Stevie's brother, who worked for Island Records and lived near Frome Court - I believe we ran into him on a train back to Pinner one day. We'd go over to his house a couple of nights a week with a bottle of Mateus Rosé and a box of chocolates for his refined wife Zena, play table football or Monopoly, and ask Muff for music business advice. He was ecstatic when he heard the new tracks and wanted to sign us to Island, a far bigger and cooler label than DJM. Dick may have been motivated to bring his chequebook out after hearing about a competition.

Whatever the cause, the money allowed us to leave DJM and move into a decent studio, Trident in Soho. Steve Brown suggested we hire an outside producer, Gus Dudgeon, who had produced David Bowie's number one single, 'Space Oddity,' which we all loved the sound of. We could afford strings and an arranger, Paul Buckmaster, who had also worked on 'Space Oddity'. Paul appeared dressed like D'Artagnan, with long center-parted hair, a goatee beard, and a large hat. He appeared quirky, which turned out to be a false initial impression. Paul wasn't the least bit eccentric. He was so out of the ordinary that it was possible he was insane. He would stand in front of the orchestra and make noises with his mouth to indicate what he wanted them to do: 'I don't know how to articulate what I want, but I want you to produce a sound like this.' They were spot on. He was an absolute genius.

But everything about the sessions was strangely amazing. Everything had been planned in advance by myself, Gus, Steve, and Paul - the songs, the tone, the arrangements - and it all just fell into place. I'd never played a harpsichord until we hired one for 'I Need You To Turn To'; it was a difficult instrument to master, but I did it. I was terrified of performing live with an orchestra, but I psyched myself up by convincing myself that this was it, that something was finally happening. All those bad clubs with Long John Baldry and his tape recorder, all the session work, Derf carrying his pint pot about for tips at the Northwood Hills Hotel, Bernie and me escaping from Furlong Road, and Linda's fantasies of turning me into Buddy Greco: it was all leading up to this. And it was effective. The entire record was completed in four days.

We knew we'd created something special, something that would propel us to the next level. We were correct. When it was released in April 1970, Elton John received rave reviews; John Peel aired it, and it slid to the bottom of the charts. We started getting offers to play around Europe, but every time we went, something strange happened. In Paris, we were booked as the opening act for Sérgio Mendes and Brasil '66. An crowd expecting an evening of bossa nova booed us off, expressing their satisfaction at having their musical horizons suddenly enlarged. When we arrived in Knokke, Belgium, we discovered we weren't performing at all: it was a televised song contest. We flew to Holland to appear on a TV show, but instead of having us play, they insisted on filming me in a park, miming 'Your Song' into a microphone while surrounded by actors posing as paparazzi taking my photograph. It is still shown on television on occasion. I appear enraged, as if I'm about to hit someone - a reasonably accurate picture of how I felt, but not the best delivery for a beautiful ballad about growing love.

Back in home, however, there was clearly a buzz. We played the Krumlin Festival in Yorkshire in August, which was supposed to be a disaster. It was in the middle of the moors, in a field. It was bitterly cold, storming outside, and absolutely chaotic. The stage was still being built when the event was due to begin, giving the bands that were supposed to perform time to argue about the running order. I couldn't be bothered getting involved, so we just went on, handed out brandy to the audience, and tore the place apart while Atomic Rooster and The Pretty Things argued over who was the biggest star backstage. I started seeing famous faces in the crowds at our London gigs, which suggested that word was spreading in the music industry that we were worth checking out. A few weeks before we played Krumlin, The Who's Pete Townshend and Jeff Beck saw our gig at the Speakeasy club, which had replaced the Cromwellian and the Bag O' Nails as

London's major music industry hangout. We were invited to perform 'Border Song' on Top of the Pops; our participation didn't improve the single's sales, but Dusty Springfield presented herself to us in the dressing area and offered to mime backing vocals during our performance. My mouth simply hung open. I'd gone to see her live with The Springfields when I was still in school, and I'd stayed around outside the stage door afterwards, just to catch another glimpse of her: she passed past in a lilac blouse and mauve skirt, looking wonderfully chic. In the early 1960s, I joined her fan club and hung posters of her on my bedroom wall.

The only thing standing in our way was Dick, who had decided we should go to America and play. He'd sold the album to a US label named Uni - a part of MCA - and kept gushing about how excited they were about it, how they wanted us to play some club shows. I told him I didn't see the point. Something was starting to happen in the United Kingdom. The shows were fantastic, the album was doing well, and Dusty Springfield liked me. Bernie and I were working on demos for the forthcoming album while creating song after song. Why risk losing momentum by departing immediately for America, where no one knew who I was?

The more I fought, the more insistent Dick became that we go. But then I received a lifeline. Jeff Beck had asked me to his rehearsal facility in Chalk Farm after the Speakeasy event to jam. His representative then scheduled a meeting at DJM. Jeff wanted to employ me, Dee, and Nigel as his supporting band for an upcoming American tour. I'd be given a solo spot throughout the show to perform my own music. It appeared to be a fantastic bargain. Jeff Beck was one of the most talented guitarists I'd ever seen. Beck-Ola, his previous album, was a big success. We were only to receive 10% of the nightly revenue, but 10% of Jeff Beck's earnings was still a lot more than we were making presently. And the most crucial aspect was the exposure. These would be large crowds, and I'd be performing my songs in front of them - not as an obscure artist, but as a member of Jeff Beck's band; not as a support act that everyone could ignore, but in the middle of the main set.

I was about to inquire where they wanted to sign when Dick ordered Beck's agency to stuff their 10%. What was he up to? I tried to capture his eye in order to signal without saying anything that he should think about shutting up right away. He didn't even bother to glance at me. The representative stated that the agreement was non-negotiable. Dick shook his head.

'I promise you today, Elton John will earn double as much as Jeff Beck in six months,' he claimed.

What? Dick, you utter moron. What was the point of saying that? It sounded suspiciously like a comment that would haunt me for the remainder of my career. I could imagine myself in five years as The Guy Who Was Going To Earn Twice What Jeff Beck Does, still trudging around the clubs. The agent quickly vanished, undoubtedly in a rush to notify the rest of the music industry that Dick James had lost his marbles, but Dick was utterly unapologetic. I didn't require Jeff Beck. I should travel to America by myself. Elton John's tunes were fantastic. The band was incredible live. The US record label was there for us every step of the way. They were going to go to great lengths to promote us. I'd like to thank him for this one day.

I discussed it with Bernie back at Frome Court. He proposed that we consider it a holiday. We could go to places we'd only seen on TV or in movies, such as 77 Sunset Strip and the Beverly Hillbillies' mansion. We could take a trip to Disneyland. We could go record shopping together. Besides, the US record label was planning to go all out. A limousine would most likely meet us at the airport. Perhaps a Cadillac. It's a Cadillac!

We stood blinking in the Los Angeles sun, a tiny cluster of us - myself and Bernie, Dee and Nigel, DJM's manager Steve Brown and Ray Williams, our roadie Bob, and David Larkham, who'd designed the covers for Empty Sky and Elton John. We were puzzled by jet lag and couldn't figure out why a bright red London bus was parked outside LAX Airport. A bright red London bus with my name written on the side: ELTON JOHN HAS ARRIVED. A bright red

London bus that our ecstatic American publicist, Norman Winter, was pressing us to board. Bernie and I exchanged a horrified look: oh, for fuck's sake, isn't this our limo?

You have no idea how slow a London Routemaster bus travels until you ride one from LAX to Sunset Boulevard. It took us two and a half hours, partially because the contraption could only go about forty miles per hour, and partly because we had to take the scenic route because they wouldn't let us on the freeway. Bernie was progressively sliding down in his seat until he couldn't be seen from outside the window, probably in case Bob Dylan or a member of The Band happened to drive by and laugh at him.

This was not how I had anticipated our arrival in California. I could as well have been on the 38 to Clapton Pond if it hadn't been for the fact that I could see palm trees out the window and the bus was packed with Americans - the personnel of Uni Records. It was my first taste of the distinction between British and American record labels. In Britain, no matter how much your label adores you or how enthusiastically they are working on your album, it is always tempered by a certain reserve, a national inclination to understatement and dry humor. That was certainly not the situation in America: it was non stop excitement, a whole different kind of energy. Nobody had ever talked to me like Norman Winter - 'this is going to be huge, we've done this, we've done that, Odetta's coming to the show, Bread's coming to the show, The Beach Boys' coming to the show, it's gonna be fantastic'. No one had ever talked to me as much as Norman Winter was talking: his mouth hadn't stopped moving since he'd introduced himself in the arrivals room, as far as I could tell. It was both startling and strangely invigorating.

And everything he mentioned was totally accurate. Norman Winter and his promotions team had done everything: gotten LA record stores to carry the CD and display posters, set up interviews, and invited a slew of celebrities to watch the show. Someone had persuaded Neil Diamond, my Uni labelmate, to come onstage and introduce me. It seemed absurd that I was headlining over David Ackles.

'But David Ackles is on Elektra,' Bernie protested, recalling the hours we'd spent in Frome Court listening to his debut album and discussing the unrivaled West Coast hipness of the label that had released it: Elektra, run by the great Jac Holzman, home to The Doors and Love, Tim Buckley and Delaney and Bonnie.

It was amazing work from a dedicated and committed team who had used all of their knowledge to generate buzz. They had miraculously converted an unknown artist's show at a 300-capacity venue into an event. And it surely had a tremendous impact on me. Previously, I had reservations about performing in America. I was afraid at this point. When everyone else went on a day trip to Palm Springs, coordinated by Ray, I prudently chose to stay at the hotel alone in order to focus on the vital matter of stressing about the gig. The more I panicked, the angrier I became. How dare they all go to Palm Springs and have fun when they could have stayed at the hotel with me, worrying themselves sick? In the lack of somebody to shout at, I called Dick James in London and yelled at him. I was returning to England. Now. They could shove their gig, their star-studded guest list, and Neil Diamond's onstage introduction up their asses. It took all of Dick's avuncular persuading skills to keep me from packing my suitcase. I chose to stay, dividing my remaining time before the gig between record shopping and light sulking whenever Palm Springs was mentioned.

I recall two specific details from our first performance at the Troubadour. The first was that the ovation as I stepped onstage had an unusual feel to it: it was followed by a shocked mutter, as if the crowd had expected someone else. I think they were in some ways. The album cover for Elton John is dark and solemn. The musicians in the rear are dressed casually and hippy-style, whereas I'm dressed in a black T-shirt and a crocheted waistcoat. And that's exactly who they expected to see: a brooding, introspective singer-songwriter. But a few weeks before I left for America, I went shopping for new clothes at Mr Freedom in Chelsea, where there was a real buzz: the designer Tommy Roberts was letting his imagination run wild, creating clothes that looked like they'd been drawn by a cartoonist. The material in the window was so absurd that I stood on the sidewalk outside for a long time, trying to work up the confidence to go in. Once I did, Tommy Roberts was so nice and eager that he pushed me into purchasing clothing that not even Tony King would have considered wearing in public. I felt different wearing them, as if I was expressing a piece of my personality that I'd kept buried, a desire to be outrageous and over-the-top. I suppose it all started when I was a youngster and happened upon a photo of Elvis in a barbershop in Pinner: I liked the sensation of surprise, of seeing a celebrity who made you wonder what the hell was going on. Mr Freedom's garments were outrageous not because they were seductive or scary, but because they were larger than life, more fun than the world around them. They were fantastic. I put them all on at once before going onstage at the Troubadour. Instead of a contemplative hippy singer-songwriter, the audience was greeted by a man dressed in bright yellow dungarees, a long-sleeved T-shirt with stars on it, and a pair of heavy workman's boots with a giant set of blue wings emerging from them. This was not how sensitive singer-songwriters in America seemed in 1970. This was not how any rational person in America looked in 1970.

The second thing I recall vividly is looking out into the crowd when we were playing and realizing, after a bad start, that Leon Russell was in the second row. I hadn't noticed any of the supposed galaxy of stars, but he was impossible to miss. He had a massive mane of silver hair and a long beard framing a cruel, emotionless face. I couldn't take my gaze away from him, even though gazing at him made my stomach drop. The gig had been going well up until that point, with Dee and Nigel sounding tight and us starting to relax and extend out the tunes a little. Now I was as nervous as I had been at the motel on the day of the Palm Springs trip. It was like one of those horrible nightmares when you're back in school, taking a test, then discover you're not wearing any trousers or underpants: you're playing the most crucial gig of your career, then see your idol in the audience, stony-faced, gazing at you.

I had to force myself to calm down. I needed to do anything to distract myself from the thought that Leon Russell was observing me. I stood up and kicked my piano stool away. I stood there with my knees bowed, hitting the keys like Little Richard. I knelt on the floor, one hand balancing and the other playing, my head under the piano. Then I jumped up, leapt forward, and performed a handstand on the keyboard. They, too, had not expected that, judging by the uproar in the audience.

Following that, I stood bewildered in the stench of the crowded dressing room. It had gone extremely nicely. Everyone in the United Kingdom was overjoyed. Norman Winter was speaking at a rate and intensity that suggested he'd been at his most relaxed and laconic on the flight from LAX. Uni Records personnel kept bringing more folks over to shake my hand. Journalists. Celebrities. Quincy Jones is a musician. The wife of Quincy Jones. The children of Quincy Jones. He appeared to have arrived with his entire family. I couldn't take in anything.

Then I went completely still. I could see Leon Russell in the doorway somewhere over the shoulder of one of Quincy Jones' countless relatives. He began forcing his way through the mob towards me. His expression was as cold and harsh as it had appeared from the stage: he didn't look like a man who'd just had the best night of his life. Shit. I've been discovered. He's going to tell everyone I'm a liar. He'll tell me I can't play the piano.

He shook my hand and inquired how I was. His voice had a sweet drawl from Oklahoma. Then he informed me I'd just finished a wonderful show and asked if I wanted to join him on tour.

The days that followed felt like a bizarre, feverish dream. We played additional Troubadour performances, all of which were sold out and great. More celebs arrived. Each night, I rummaged deeper into my Mr Freedom clothing bag, pulling out more and more outrageous items, until I found myself in front of an audience of rock stars and Los Angeles tastemakers wearing a pair of tight silver hot pants, bare legs, and a T-shirt with ROCK AND ROLL emblazoned across it in sequins. As if we were old acquaintances, Leon Russell reappeared backstage and told me his own formula for a sore throat treatment. Uni Records took us all to Disneyland, and I filled my arms with albums at Tower Records on Sunset Strip. Robert Hilburn, the LA Times' music editor, wrote a review for the paper. 'Rejoice,' it began. 'Rock music, which has been quite uninteresting recently, has a new star. He's Elton John, a 23-year-old Englishman whose Troubadour debut on Tuesday night was spectacular in nearly every way.' The fucking hell. Bob Hilburn was a big deal: I knew he'd be there, but I had no idea he'd write that. Ray Williams was inundated with offers from American promoters once it was released. We decided to remain longer and play more shows in San Francisco and New York. I went through interview after interview. The Elton John record was playing nonstop on FM radio. KPPC, a Pasadena radio station, ran a full-page advertisement in the Los Angeles Free Press praising me for coming to America.

Everyone understands that celebrity, especially unexpected fame, is a hollow, shallow, and deadly thing, with its dark, alluring powers being no substitute for true love or true friendship. On the other hand, if you're a terribly shy person in desperate need of a confidence boost - someone who spent a lot of their childhood trying to be as invisible as possible so they didn't provoke one of your mum's moods or your dad's rage - being hailed as the future of rock and roll in the LA Times and feted by a succession of your musical heroes will undoubtedly do the trick. As proof, on the night of August 31, 1970, I saw Elton John, a twenty-three-year-old virgin, a man who'd never talked anyone up in his life. I'm in San Francisco, where I'll be performing in a few days. I'm spending the evening at the Fillmore, watching the British folk-rock band Fairport Convention - fellow Krumlin Festival survivors - and meeting the venue's owner, legendary promoter Bill Graham, who wants me to play at his New York concert hall, the Fillmore East. But I'm not paying attention to the Fairport Convention or Bill Graham. Because I've determined that tonight will be the night I seduce someone. Or I can let myself be seduced. Either one or the other will suffice.

I'd discovered that John Reid was in San Francisco at the same time as me, celebrating Motown Records' tenth anniversary. I'd stopped in on him at EMI a number of times since meeting him through Tony King. Whatever meager signals I was attempting to emit - if I was attempting to emit any signals at all - went entirely unnoticed. He seemed to believe I was simply there to raid his stack of soul singles or to offer him copies of my own records. But that was back then. I found out where he was staying and called him, boosted by the events of the previous week. I told him what had transpired in LA as quickly as I could and then proposed we meet up as casually as possible. I was staying at the Miyako, a charming Japanese-themed hotel close to the Fillmore. Could he come over for a drink one night?

The performance was completed. I went backstage to say hello to Fairport, had a few drinks and a little chat, then excused myself and returned to the Miyako alone. I hadn't been in my room long when the phone rang: Mr Reid is waiting for me in reception. Oh God. That's all there is to it.

CHAPTER 4

After that night in San Francisco, things went rapidly. A week later, I was doing interviews in Philadelphia when I got a phone call from John, who'd returned to England, telling me that he'd run into Tony King at the BBC. He'd told Tony about what had transpired and our plans. Tony had progressed from perplexed - 'Reg? Is Reg gay? You're moving in together, as in moving in together?' he exclaimed, amused by my desire for the relationship to remain low-key. 'What do you mean, Reg prefers to keep it quiet? He's on your side! Everyone who has stepped into a gay club in London has heard about you! He should hang a fucking neon sign out the window that says, 'I AM GAY.'

I wanted to keep it a secret since I didn't know how others would react if they found out. I didn't have to be concerned. None of my friends or coworkers seemed concerned. Bernie and the band, as well as Dick James and Steve Brown: They appeared to be relieved that I'd finally had sex. Outside of those circles, no one appeared to consider the concept that I was anything other than heterosexual. When you consider what I was wearing and performing onstage, it seems absurd that no one even raised an eyebrow, but it was a different world back then. Homosexuality had just been decriminalized in the United Kingdom for three years, and the general public's knowledge or understanding of the matter was limited. When we visited the United States, all of the great groupies from that era - the Plaster Casters and Sweet Connie from Little Rock - would show up backstage, much to the joy of the band and road crew. 'Hold on, what are you doing here?' I'd wonder. You're not here for me, are you? Surely someone has informed you? Even if they haven't, I was just carried onstage by a bodybuilder while wearing half the world's supply of diamanté, sequins, and marabou feathers - does it not indicate something to you?' Evidently not. To avoid their gaze, I grew pretty skilled at slipping away and shutting myself in the toilet.

If anyone I knew thought it was strange that I was moving in with John so soon, they didn't say anything. And, as it turned out, the speed with which my connection with John developed was only the beginning of my personality. I was the type of person who met someone, fell head over heels, and instantly began planning our future together. I couldn't tell the difference between a crush and true love, so I could see the white picket fence and an eternity of connubial happiness before I'd even spoken to someone. When I became renowned, this became a terrible dilemma for both me and the object of my emotions. I'd insist they gave up their own life to follow me on tour, which always ended in disaster.

But that was in the distant future. I was truly in love with John - that deep, guileless, naive first love. And I'd just recently discovered sex. Moving in together seemed to make sense. My current living situation was far from ideal given the circumstances. It's hard to have a genuine sexual relationship with someone if you're living in your mother's spare room and your co-writer is sleeping in the bunk bed beneath yours.

When I returned from America, we began looking for a shared apartment to rent. We found one in the Water Gardens, near Edgware Road, with one bedroom, one bathroom, a living room, and a kitchen. Bernie momentarily relocated to Steve Brown's home. He'd also fallen in love in California, with Maxine, a girl he'd met on the renowned day trip to Palm Springs. It's no surprise he was eager to leave.

My mother and Derf were the last people I told. I put it off for a few weeks after I'd moved out. I was probably psyching myself up. I finally decided the night John and I were due to see Liberace at the London Palladium was the ideal time. We got tickets, but I told John to go alone since I needed to call Mum that night. I was worried, but the phone call went smoothly. When I told Mum I was gay, she looked unsurprised: 'Oh, we know. That's something we've known for a long time.' I attributed her knowledge of my sexuality to the intangible mystic power of a mother's intuition at the time, but with the benefit of hindsight, she and Derf probably had an inkling what was going on when they helped move my belongings into the Water Garden and discovered that I was living in a one-bedroom flat with another man.

Mum wasn't delighted with the news that I was gay - she mumbled something about condemning myself to a life of loneliness, which didn't seem to make much sense given that I was in a relationship - but she hadn't abandoned me or refused to accept it. And, strangely, when John returned home, I noted that he appeared to have had a much more stressful evening than I had. Liberace had unexpectedly declared midway through the act that he had a very special guest in the crowd, a fantastic new vocalist who was destined to be a big star: '... and I know he's here today, and I'm going to make him get up and wave to you all, because he's so fabulous...' 'Elvis Presley!' Liberace had been increasingly solicitous, supposing that my hesitation to make myself known was due to shyness - 'Come on now, Elton, don't be timid, the public wants to meet you. Ladies and gentlemen, don't you want to meet Elton John? 'I tell you, this guy's gonna be huge - let's give him a big hand and see if we can't get him to say hello,' said the announcer, as a huge spotlight circled the stalls in vain. Liberace had gone on like this for about three weeks, according to John's account, during which time the audience had grown restless, then openly angered at my churlish unwillingness to present myself. Meanwhile, the one of them who truly knew where Elton John was had grown frightened that he might become the first person in history to literally die of shame. Liberace eventually gave up. He was still smiling, according to John, but the manner he started into Liszt's Hungarian Rhapsody implied murderous rage.

Despite the fact that I ruined a Liberace concert by coming out to my parents, everything was perfect. I was finally able to be myself, to have no fear of myself, and to have no fear of sex. When I say John taught me how to be debauched, I mean it in the kindest possible sense. As Tony had mentioned, John was well-versed in the LGBT scene, including clubs and bars. We'd go to the Vauxhall Tavern to watch Lee Sutton, the legendary drag queen - 'The name is Lee Sutton, DSM, OBE - Dirty Sex Maniac, On the Bed with Everybody' - and the Sombrero club on Kensington High Street. We'd have dinner parties and other musicians would come over. Neil Young returned home with us one night after seeing him perform live and, after a few beers, decided to perform his new album in its entirety for us at 2 a.m. The nerve-jangling sound of my friend Kiki Dee drunkenly walking into a glass door while holding a tray containing every champagne glass we owned had already alerted the adjoining flats to the fact that an impromptu party was taking place, and the delight of the adjoining flats at Neil Young performing his forthcoming album was audible. So that's how I first heard Neil Young's iconic 'Heart Of Gold,' given in an unusual arrangement of solo piano, voice, and a neighbor banging on the roof with a broom handle and loudly urging Neil Young to quiet up.

My career gained significant traction. We weren't as popular in the UK as we were in the US, but the band and I had returned from America with a renewed feeling of purpose. We'd been confirmed and certified by so many folks over there that we felt we'd hit on something big. The news of what happened in Los Angeles had reached Britain, and the press was suddenly fascinated. Friends, a hippy magazine, dispatched a journalist to interview me. I played him two tracks from the next album, Tumbleweed Connection, and he went as crazy as Robert Hilburn in the subsequent article: 'I think he will possibly become the finest, and almost certainly the most popular songwriter in England, and eventually the world, along with his lyricist.' We opened for Fotheringay, a band created by Fairport Convention's former lead singer Sandy Denny, at the Royal Albert Hall. They, like the audience at the Troubadour, expected a sensitive singer-songwriter - the perfect complement to what they did, which was melancholy folk music - but instead got rock 'n' roll with Mr Freedom clothes and handstands on the piano keyboard. They couldn't keep up with us because we were so high on adrenaline and confidence. Of course, I felt terrible as the adrenaline went off and I realized what we'd done. Sandy Denny, an incredible vocalist, was one of my heroes. It was supposed to be their big show, and I'd destroyed it for them. I dashed home, humiliated, before they took the stage.

But it felt like the proper time. The sixties were finished, The Beatles had split up, and a new wave of artists, including myself, Rod Stewart, Marc Bolan, and David Bowie, were all breaking out at the same time. We were all quite diverse musically, but in some respects we were like birds of a feather. We were all working-class Londoners who had spent the 1960s with our noses pressed against the glass, toiling on the same club circuit, never really getting anywhere. And we were all acquainted. Our paths have met backstage at r'n'b clubs and at Roundhouse shows. I was never close to David Bowie. I liked his music, and we socialized a few times, going to the Sombrero with Tony King and having dinner in Covent Garden while he was rehearsing for the Ziggy Stardust tour, but he was always distant and aloof, at least when I was around. I honestly don't know what the issue was, but there was certainly one. Years later, he'd always make snide statements about me in interviews, the most famous being 'the token queen of rock and roll,' though to be fair, he was completely out of his mind on coke at the time.

But Marc and Rod were my favorites. They couldn't be more dissimilar. Marc appeared to be from another planet: he had an unearthly quality to him, as if he was passing through Earth on his way somewhere else. It was evident in his music. When we moved into the Water Garden, 'Ride A White Swan' was never off the radio, and it didn't sound like anything else; you couldn't figure out where he was coming from. That's how he was in person. He was larger than life, straight yet campy, and wonderfully loving and gentle all at once. He obviously had a great ego, but he never seemed to take himself seriously. He managed to be both perfectly charming and fully, blatantly full of shit. With a straight face, he'd say stuff like, 'Darling, I sold a million records this morning.' Marc, no one in music history, let alone you, has ever sold a million copies in a single morning. But something about him was so enticing and lovable that you'd never say it out loud. You'd find yourself agreeing with him instead: 'A million, Marc? Congratulations! 'How wonderful!'

I'd heard about Rod for years because of his connection with Long John Baldry, but it wasn't until he covered 'Country Comfort,' one of the new songs I'd played the journalist from Friends, that I truly got to know him. He modified the lyrics, which I lamented in the press: 'He sounds like he made it up as he went along!' He couldn't have sang "The Camptown Races' ' without deviating from the original!' That established the tone for the rest of our friendship. We have a lot in common. We both enjoy football and art collecting. We both grew up in low-income homes after the war, so neither of us has ever been shy about enjoying the fruits of our success. But it's our sense of humor that we really have in common. Rod has a rather goofy sense of humor for a man with a well-documented lifelong love with leggy blondes. When we started giving ourselves drag names in the 1970s, he happily joined us. I played Sharon, John played Beryl, Tony played Joy, and Rod played Phyllis. We've spent nearly fifty years continually making fun of one other and attempting to outdo each other. Rod could be counted on to send me a present when the press was speculating about my hair falling out and whether or not I'd started wearing a hairpiece. It was one of those old-fashioned, helmet-shaped hair dryers that old women used to sit under in salons. I sent him a Zimmer frame decked out in fairy lights to thank him for his thoughtfulness. Even today, if I find he has a better-selling CD than mine, I know it's only a matter of time before I get an email: 'Good day, Sharon. I'm simply writing to express my regret that your record isn't even in the Top 100, sweetheart. What a shame, love, Phyllis, when mine is doing so well.'

It peaked in the early 1980s, when Rod was playing at Earls Court. They had advertised the show by flying a blimp with his face on it over the venue. I was in London at the time and could see it from my hotel room window. It was simply too fantastic a chance to pass up. So I phoned my boss, and he paid someone to shoot it down: it supposedly landed on top of a double-decker bus, and was last seen headed towards Putney. The phone rang about an hour later. Rod was muttering about the disappearance.

'Where has my fucking balloon vanished? Wasn't it you who did it? You pig! 'You scumbag!'

A year later, I was performing at Olympia, and the promoters had erected a massive banner across the street. It was inexplicably cut down shortly after it was erected. The phone call informing me of the sabotage came from Rod, who appeared unusually well informed about what had occurred.

'It's really bad about your banner, love. It wasn't even up for five minutes, according to what I heard. I'm guessing you didn't even get to see it.'

I went back to America for another tour not long after we moved into the Water Gardens. It's a big country, and most of the people don't care if the LA Times proclaimed you the "future of rock and roll." You must put yourself out there and demonstrate your abilities. In addition, we had a new album to promote: Tumbleweed Connection, which was recorded in March 1970 and released in the UK in October. That's how it was back then. You didn't make an album in three years. You recorded quickly, got it out quickly, kept the momentum rolling, and kept things interesting. It was ideal for the way I operated. I despise squandering time in the studio. I think it's a hangover from my days as a session musician or recording demos at DJM in the middle of the night: you were always working against the time.

As a result, we crisscrossed the United States, generally as a support act for Leon Russell, The Byrds, Poco, The Kinks, and Eric Clapton's new band Derek And The Dominos. That was the notion of my booking agent, Howard Rose, and it was a brilliant move: don't play first, play second, and make people want to come back and see you in your own right. Every artist we funded was extremely gracious and generous to us, but it was difficult work. We'd go onstage every night with the objective of stealing the show. We'd go down big and believe we'd blasted the headliners offstage, but every night, the headliners would come out and outplay us. People talk about Derek And The Dominos being a terrible mess, high on drugs and liquor, but you'd never know if you'd seen them live that autumn. They were incredible. I took mental notes regarding their performance from the side of the stage. Although Eric Clapton was the headliner, it was their keyboard player, Bobby Whitlock, who I kept a close eye on. He was from Memphis, learnt his trade at Stax Studios, and played soulful, Deep Southern gospel music. When I was in Bluesology, touring with them or Leon was like touring with Patti LaBelle or Major Lance: you watched and learnt from somebody who had more experience than you.

Even though we still had a long way to go, it was evident on that tour that the word was getting out. We had supper with Danny Hutton of Three Dog Night in Los Angeles, and he casually mentioned that Brian Wilson wanted to see us. Really? I had loved The Beach Boys in the 1960s, but their success had waned, and Brian Wilson had become a mysterious, mythic character - according to some slanderous gossip, he was said to have become a recluse, or gone insane, or both. Oh no, Danny informed us, he's a tremendous fan and would love for you to come visit.

So we drove up to his Bel Air home, a Spanish-style mansion with an intercom system at the entrance. Danny buzzed it, announcing that he was with Elton John. The other end was deafeningly silent. Then there came a voice, clearly The Beach Boys' genius, singing the chorus of 'Your Song': 'I hope you don't mind, I hope you don't mind'. The main door opened as we approached, revealing Brian Wilson himself. He looked fine - possibly a touch chubbier than on the cover of Pet Sounds, but nothing like the recluse freak about whom everyone gossiped. We exchanged greetings. He nodded and glanced at us. He then sang the chorus of 'Your Song' once more. He invited us to come upstairs and meet his children. It came out that his children were sound asleep in their beds. He jolted them awake. 'Hello, this is Elton John!' he exclaimed. His daughters were understandably perplexed. 'I hope you don't mind, I hope you don't mind,' he sang to them as the chorus of 'Your Song'. He then sang the chorus of 'Your Song' to us once more. The novelty of hearing the chorus of 'Your Song' sung to me by one of pop history's great geniuses had worn off by this point. I had the sinking feeling that we were in for a long and unpleasant evening. I glanced to Bernie, and a look passed between us that combined dread, perplexity, and the fact that we were both desperately trying not to laugh at the absurdity of the scenario we found ourselves in, a look that said: what the fuck is going on?

During the later months of 1970, we became increasingly accustomed to wearing this style. I was invited to a party at Mama Cass Elliot's house on Woodrow Wilson Drive in Los Angeles, which was famous as the leading hangout for Laurel Canyon musicians, where Crosby, Stills, and Nash had formed, and David Crosby had shown off his new discovery, a singer-songwriter named Joni Mitchell, to his friends. They were all present when I arrived. It was insane, like the record sleeves in Frome Court's bedroom had come to life: what the fuck is going on?

We passed Bob Dylan on the Fillmore East steps, and he stopped, introduced himself, and told Bernie he admired the lyrics of a Tumbleweed song called 'My Father's Gun': what the fuck is going on?

We were sitting backstage after a show in Philadelphia when the dressing room door unexpectedly opened and five men walked in. The Band couldn't have been mistaken for anyone else: they looked like they'd just stepped off the cover of the album we'd listened to over and over in England. Robbie Robertson and Richard Manuel began telling us that they'd flown in by private plane from Massachusetts just to see the show, while I pretended that The Band flying in from Massachusetts to see me perform was a perfectly normal state of affairs, and occasionally stole a glance at Bernie, who was similarly engaged in a desperate attempt to play it cool. We were dreaming about attempting to compose songs like them a year ago, and now they're here in front of us, asking us to play them our new album: what the fuck is going on?

Not only did The Band want to meet us. Albert Grossman and Bennett Glotzer were their managers. They were legendary figures in the American music industry, particularly Grossman, a renowned tough guy who had handled Bob Dylan since the early 1960s. He had responded to another client, Janis Joplin, being hooked to heroin by taking out a life insurance policy on her. They must have discovered that I was now without a manager. Ray Williams was a lovely man, I owed him a lot, and he was incredibly loyal - he'd even named his daughter Amoreena, after another Tumbleweed Connection song - but after our first trip to America, I'd discussed it with the rest of the band, and no one thought he was the right person to look after us. But Grossman and Glotzer were not, as I discovered the instant I met them. They looked like characters from a movie, one that had been ridiculed for its utterly ludicrous portrayal of two aggressive, motor mouthed American showbiz executives. Nonetheless, they were genuine people, and their combined efforts to win me over succeeded in frightening me to death. They were not going to leave me alone as long as there remained a vacancy.

'I'll follow you around until you sign for me,' Glotzer said.

He wasn't kidding. There seemed to be no way to get rid of him other than to file a restraining order. The appeal of isolating myself in the toilet proved too strong to refuse once more.

It could have been while I was hiding from Bennett Glotzer that I considered hiring John to manage me. The more I thought about it, the more it made sense. John was young, ambitious, and pumped up on adrenaline. He'd grown up in working-class Paisley in the 1950s and 1960s, which had made him tough enough to deal with whatever the music business threw at him. We were already together, so he'd have my best interests at heart. He was a natural hustler with the gift of gab who excelled at his work. He wasn't simply knowledgeable about music; he was also wise about it. Earlier in the year, he persuaded Motown to release a three-year-old album track by Smokey Robinson And The Miracles as a single, then watched as 'Tears Of A Clown' went to No. 1 on both sides of the Atlantic. It sold so many copies that Smokey Robinson had to postpone his retirement from music.

Everyone, including John, thought it was an excellent idea. He left EMI and Motown at the end of the year, got a desk in Dick James' office - initially, he was effectively an employee of DJM, paid to function as a kind of liaison between me and the company - and that was the end of it. To commemorate the occasion, we traded in my Ford Escort for an Aston Martin. It was the first truly costly item I purchased, the first indication that I was genuinely making money from music. We acquired it from The Bee Gees' Maurice Gibb, and it was a real pop star's car: a purple DB6, flamboyant and magnificent. And extremely inconvenient, as we discovered when John had to meet Martha And The Vandellas at Heathrow Airport. It was one of his final jobs for Motown, and we proudly brought the Aston Martin with us. Martha and The Vandellas appeared impressed until they discovered they needed to crawl into the back of the car. The designers had clearly spent far more work on its graceful lines and poetic curves than on whether the back seats could accommodate a legendary soul trio. They got in some way. Perhaps the legendary Charm School in Motown taught contortionism. I checked my rear-view mirror as I drove back along the A40. Back then, it was like riding the Tokyo subway during rush hour. Wait a minute, Martha And The Vandellas were squeezed into the rear of my Aston Martin. That would have seemed unusual a year ago, when I was driving a Ford Escort with a back seat empty of Motown legends. Strange was becoming a relative concept after the year I'd experienced.

I didn't have much time to consider how my life had changed. I was overworking myself. We spent 1971 touring back and forth between America and the United Kingdom, then down to Japan, New Zealand, and Australia. We were now headlining, but we still took Howard Rose's advice and played venues that were somewhat smaller than we could fill, or performed one night in a place where we could have sold out two. In Britain, we did the same thing: we kept performing at universities and rock clubs long after we could have packed theaters. It's a very wise thing to do: don't be greedy, grow your career gradually, and it's very Howard. He was so clever and full of wise counsel that he is still my agent today. When I first arrived in America, I was really fortunate in the folks I worked with. Young British artists may easily fall prey to a swarm of sharks over there, but I had individuals go out of their way to make me feel like part of the family, including not only Howard, but also my publisher David Rosner and his wife Margo.

I was in the studio whenever I wasn't onstage. In America, I released four albums in 1971: Tumbleweed Connection in January, the soundtrack to a movie called Friends in March (which was only a minor hit, but did better than the film, which was a complete flop), a live album we'd recorded the previous year, 11-17-70, in May, and Madman Across the Water in November. Madman was recorded in four days. It was intended to be five, but Paul Buckmaster caused us to lose a day. He remained up the night before the sessions to finalize the arrangements - I presume with some drug assistance - and then managed to spill a bottle of ink all over the lone score, ruining it. I was enraged. It was an expensive error, and we didn't work together again for decades. But I was equally pleased when he rewrote the entire music in twenty-four hours. Even when Paul messed up, it was in a way that reminded you that he was a genius.

I also enjoy Madman Across the Water. It was a considerably larger hit in America than in the UK at the time, peaking at number ten abroad but only number 41 at home. It's not particularly commercial; there were no big hit singles, and the songs were considerably longer and more complicated than I'd previously composed. Some of Bernie's songs read like a diary from the previous year. One song, 'All The Nasties,' was about me, and I wondered aloud what would happen if I came out publicly: 'If they should ask - what would I tell them? Will they berate me behind my back? Perhaps I should let them'. Nobody appeared to care about what I was singing about.

Something else happened during the Madman sessions. Gus Dudgeon hired Davey Johnstone, an acoustic guitarist, to play acoustic guitar and mandolin on a few tracks. I loved him because he was Scottish, lanky, and direct, and he had excellent musical taste. I approached Gus and asked him what he thought about Davey joining the band. I'd been considering adding a guitarist to the trio for a while. It was a horrible idea, according to Gus. Davey was a fantastic musician, but he only played acoustic: as far as Gus was aware, he'd never even touched an electric guitar. He was in Magna Carta, a band that specialized in bucolic folk, and there wasn't much of it in Elton John's repertoire.

It was a pretty convincing argument. I ignored it and nevertheless offered Davey the job. If there was one thing I'd learned over the last few years, it was that sometimes a gut instinct is the most essential thing. You can work as hard as you want and prepare as meticulously as you want, but there are times when it's all about a gut feeling, trusting your intuition, or fate. What if I hadn't replied to the Liberty advertisement? What if I'd gotten through the audition but wasn't given Bernie's lyrics? What if Steve Brown had not arrived at DJM? What if Dick hadn't been so confident that I should go to America, even though it seemed such a ridiculous idea?

So Davey came with us to France to record the second album at the Château d'Hérouville. It was the first time I'd attempted to record an album with my touring band rather than crack session musicians; the first time Davey had picked up an electric guitar; the first time we'd had the funds to record abroad, in a residential studio - but I was in a really confident mood. I'd legally changed my name to Elton John just before we left for France. Hercules John Elton. I'd always thought middle names were a little ludicrous, so I got mine from the rag and bone man's horse in the sitcom Steptoe and Son. Basically, I was tired of making a scene in stores when the cashier knew me but not the name on my checkbook. But it felt more symbolic than practical, like if I was finally, legally, leaving Reg Dwight behind and really becoming the person I was destined to be. As it turned out, it wasn't quite that straightforward, but it felt nice at the time.

Even though it came with a reputation, I was intrigued by the prospect of working at the Château. The locals had apparently become wary of the studio's clientele after The Grateful Dead had stayed there, offered to play a free concert for the villagers, and then took it upon themselves to expand the minds of rural France by spiking their audience's drinks with LSD. But it was a gorgeous house, an eighteenth-century mansion - we named the record Honky Château after it - and I was delighted about having to write songs on the spot.

I'm not a musician who constantly hears melodies in his thoughts. When inspiration comes, I don't run to the piano in the middle of the night. When I'm not composing songs, I don't even think about it. Bernie writes the lyrics and offers them to me. I read them, play a chord, and then something else takes over, something emerges through my fingers. You can call it the muse, God, or luck, but I have no idea what it is. I can already tell where the music is going to go. A song may only take as long to write as it does to listen to. 'Sad Songs (Say So Much)' was the same way: I sat down, read the lyrics, and played it exactly as you hear on the record. It can take a little longer at times. I give up after approximately forty minutes if I don't like what I've done and move on to something else. Bernie has penned certain words that I've never been able to put to music. He wrote a fantastic lyric called 'The Day That Bobby Went Electric' about hearing Dylan sing 'Subterranean Homesick Blues' for the first time, and I just couldn't produce a music that felt right; I tried four or five times. But I've never experienced writer's block, and I've never sat down with one of Bernie's lyrics and nothing came out. I'm not sure why. I don't know how to explain it, and I don't want to. Actually, I enjoy the fact that I can't explain it. It's the spontaneity that makes it so lovely.

So Bernie brought his typewriter to the Château, and we set up instruments in both the dining room and the studio. Bernie would scribble his lyrics and leave them on the piano for me. I'd get up early, go to the dining room, see what he'd come up with, and write songs as I ate. I had three finished by the time the band wandered downstairs looking for something to eat the first morning we were there: 'Mona Lisas and Mad Hatters,' 'Amy,' and 'Rocket Man'.

Davey took up his guitar and requested me to perform 'Rocket Man' again when he was sure that this wasn't an elaborate hoax on the new boy and that I had actually created three songs while he was sleeping. He didn't perform a solo or anything else that a conventional lead guitarist might do. He played weird, lonely sounds that wandered around and away from the tune using a slide. It was fantastic. As I previously stated, sometimes a gut instinct is the most important thing; other times, you must trust fate.

The rest of the band was so used to performing together that there was practically a telepathic connection between us: they just knew what to do with a song without being instructed. It was great, sitting in the Château's dining room with my friends, hearing a song take shape around us, trying out ideas and knowing right away that they were the perfect ones. There have been times in my life when music was an escape, the only thing that worked when everything else looked broken, but I had nothing to flee from at the time. I was 24, successful, settled, and in love. Furthermore, we had a day off tomorrow, and I was planning on traveling to Paris and completely looting the Yves Saint-Laurent store.

CHAPTER 5

In 1972, John and I relocated from London to Virginia Water in Surrey, where we purchased a three-bedroom cottage with its own swimming pool and a games area built in what had been the attic. I named it Hercules after my middle name. Bernie and Maxine, who had married in 1971, lived close; Mum and Derf, who had also finally married, moved just down the road and kept a watch on the bungalow while we were gone. That part of England is known as the stockbroker belt, which sounds boring and suburban, but it wasn't. For one thing, Keith Moon lived 10 minutes away, which clearly added to the volatility of my everyday life. Keith was fantastic, but his pharmaceutical diet seemed to have left him with no notion of time. He'd show up unannounced at 2:30 a.m., absolutely out of his mind - typically with Ringo Starr, another neighborhood resident - and appear genuinely astonished that he'd gotten you out of bed. Or he'd appear out of nowhere in your driveway at 7 a.m. on Christmas Day, in a Rolls-Royce convertible with the top down and thunderous loudness of The Shadows' Greatest Hits playing. 'Dear young man! Take a look at the new automobile! Come take a whirl! No, now! There's no need to remove your dressing gown!'

But the most intriguing individual I met in Virginia Water had nothing to do with music. I met Bryan Forbes when I went into the little bookshop he owned to hunt for something to read. He approached me and introduced himself, saying he felt he remembered me. That didn't seem unlikely; by this point, my onstage flamboyance had permeated my everyday clothing, so my idea of dressing down for an afternoon of shopping in a Surrey commuter town included a bright orange fur coat and a pair of eight-inch platform boots. But it turned out he didn't recognize me at all: as the talk went, it became clear that he mistook me for one of The Bee Gees.
We got along great after we determined that I wasn't a Gibb brother. Bryan was enthralling. He'd been an actor before becoming a screenwriter, novelist, and director, and he'd go

on to become a studio executive. He was married to actress Nanette Newman, and the two appeared to know everyone: Hollywood giants, writers, and TV stars. If you were in America and professed a long-held ambition to see David Niven or Groucho Marx, Bryan could make it happen, which is how I got up with a Marx Brothers film poster inscribed 'to John Elton from Marx Groucho': he couldn't understand why my name was, as he put it, 'the wrong way round'. It's interesting, I thought about Groucho years later at Buckingham Palace, when I got my knighthood, because that's how Lord Chamberlain announced to the Queen: 'Sir John Elton'.

One summer Sunday afternoon, John and I were having a snack outside the bungalow when we observed a sixty-something lady who resembled Katharine Hepburn cycling up our drive. 'I'm staying with Bryan Forbes - he said it would be OK if I used your pool,' Katharine Hepburn replied, and John and I just nodded, dumbfounded. She arrived five minutes later in a swimsuit, moaning about a dead frog in the pool. When I was debating how to pull it out - I'm a little squeamish about such things - she just jumped in and grabbed it with her hand. I wondered how she could tolerate touching it.

'Character, young man,' she said firmly.

If you were invited to the Forbes residence for lunch, you may find yourself sitting between Peter Sellers and Dame Edith Evans, listening to their stories, or you might arrive to find the Queen Mother among the other guests. Bryan was acquainted with the Royal Family because he was president of the National Youth Theatre, of whom Princess Margaret was a sponsor. Princess Margaret was discovered to like music and the company of musicians. After a performance at the Royal Festival Hall, she invited me and the band back to Kensington Palace for supper, which turned out to be really embarrassing. Not because of Princess Margaret, who was genuinely nice to everyone, but because of her husband, Lord

Snowdon. Even though everyone knew the marriage was in danger - there were constant rumors in the press about one or both of them having an affair - nothing could have prepared us for his visit. He walked in midway through the meal and genuinely shouted 'Where's my fucking dinner?' at her. They had a major argument, and she sobbed her way out of the room. We were just sitting there, dumbfounded, not knowing what to do. How strange can life in the Elton John Band get? Other musicians unwind after a performance by consuming weed, seducing groupies, or destroying hotel rooms; we end up witnessing Princess Margaret and Lord Snowdon yell at each other.

But it wasn't just who Bryan knew; it was also what he knew, and the fact that he was a natural teacher: patient and generous with his time, sophisticated in his preferences but absolutely unpretentious, eager for others to love what he loved. He taught me about art and influenced me to begin collecting. Then there were surrealist painters like Paul Wunderlich, who collected art nouveau and art deco posters, which were popular in the early 1970s. I started collecting Tiffany lights and Bugatti furniture. Bryan got me interested in theater and gave me reading recommendations. We got extremely close and began going on vacation together: John and I, Bryan and Nanette, and their daughters Emma and Sarah. We would rent a property in California for a month and invite friends to visit.

Nanette proved to be an excellent shopping companion, something I'd grown to enjoy since I began earning a little money. Actually, that's not entirely correct. Since I was a child, I've had a strong desire to go shopping. Growing up in Pinner, I remember the shops: the different-colored cotton reels in the wool shop where my grandmother used to get her knitting supplies; the smell of fresh peanuts as you walked into Woolworths; and the sawdust on the floor of Sainsbury's, where Auntie Win worked on the butter counter. I'm not sure why, but something about those locations captivated me. I've always loved collecting things, and I've always preferred giving gifts to receiving them. When I was a kid, my favorite part of Christmas was deciding what I was going to get my family: aftershave for my father, a rain cap for my grandmother, maybe a little vase for my mother from the kiosk outside Baker Street station that I used to pass on my way to the Royal Academy of Music.

Of course, success allowed me to follow my desire on a little larger scale. We'd return from LA with so much stuff that the over baggage fee would be equal to the cost of the ticket home. When I heard that my auntie Win was feeling bad, I'd call a dealership and request that they bring her a new car to cheer her up. Therapists have told me that it's obsessive, addictive behavior or that I'm attempting to buy people's affection by giving them things throughout the years. With all due respect to members of the psychiatric profession who have stated such things to me, I believe it is nonsense. I'm not looking to buy people's affection. I simply enjoy making others feel included or letting them know I'm thinking about them. I enjoy watching people's reactions when you treat them to something.

I don't need a doctor to convince me that money isn't a substitute for love or personal pleasure. I've spent enough unhappy, lonely nights in gorgeous mansions to have figured it out for myself a long time ago. And I strongly advise against going shopping in the sad aftermath of a three-day cocaine binge, unless you want to wake up the next day confronted with bags and bags of crap you don't remember buying. In my situation, I awoke the next morning to a phone call alerting me that I had purchased a tram. It's not a toy tram. A genuine tram. The voice on the other end of the phone is now informing you that a Melbourne W2 class drop-center combo tram must be shipped from Australia to Britain, where it can only be delivered to your house by hanging it from two Chinook helicopters.

So I'd be the first to say that I've made some really hasty judgments while holding a credit card. I'm sure I could have gotten by without a tram in my garden, or the full-scale fiberglass model of a Tyrannosaurus rex that I volunteered to take off Ringo Starr's hands at the end of a long night. Ringo was attempting to sell his home at the time, and the sight of a full-scale fiberglass Tyrannosaurus rex in the garden was supposedly proving to be a stumbling block for prospective buyers. But I've always found collecting things strangely soothing, and I've always enjoyed learning about things by collecting them, whether it's records, photography, clothes, or art. And that has never changed, no matter what has happened in my personal life. It's soothing and pleasurable when I'm lonely and adrift, and it's comforting and enjoyable when I'm loved, pleased, and established. Many individuals share that sentiment: the globe is full of model railway aficionados, stamp collectors, and record collectors. I'm just fortunate enough to be able to follow my interests in greater depth than most individuals. I worked hard to acquire that money, and if people believe the way I spend it is extravagant or ridiculous, I'm afraid that's their problem. I don't feel any remorse about it. If it's an addiction, I've been addicted to far more destructive things in my life than buying crockery and photographs. It brings me joy. I have 1,000 candles in a closet in my Atlanta house, which I assume is excessive. But I'll tell you something: it's the best-smelling closet you've ever been in.

My shopping habit wasn't the only thing that had been amplified. Everything seemed to be getting bigger, louder, and more out of hand. Bernie and I didn't intend for 'Rocket Man' to be a great smash single - we regarded ourselves as album artists - but that's exactly what it became: it was Number Two in the UK, considerably higher than any of our previous singles, and went triple-platinum in the US. We'd discovered a new type of commerciality, and its success had influenced our audience. Screaming girls began to appear in the front rows and outside the stage entrance, clinging to the car as we attempted to go. It felt strange, like if they'd gone to see The Osmonds or David Cassidy but had made a wrong turn and wound up at our show instead.

I worked really hard, perhaps too hard, but there seemed to be an unstoppable momentum behind me that carried me on no matter how fatigued I was, that propelled me through any kind of setback. In the summer of 1972, I had glandular fever just before we went into the studio to record Don't Shoot Me, I'm Only the Piano Player. I should have canceled the sessions to rest, but instead I went to Château d'Hérouville and plowed through them, running on adrenaline. Listening to the CD, you'd never guess I was sick: the guy singing 'Daniel' and 'Crocodile Rock' doesn't sound sick. I was back on tour a few weeks after we finished. I kept pushing the live show, attempting to make it more ridiculous and over-the-top. I began hiring professional costume designers - first Annie Reavey, then Bill Whitten and Bob Mackie - and encouraged them to do whatever they wanted, no matter how outlandish: more feathers, more sequins, brighter colors, larger platforms. You made an outfit consisting of multicolored balls tied to elastic pieces that glow in the dark? How many balls are there? Why not include some more? Will I be able to play the piano? Let me take care of that.

Then I had the brilliant idea of bringing 'Legs' Larry Smith, formerly of The Bonzo Dog Doo-Dah Band, on tour with us. Legs was a drummer, but tap dancing was his true gift. We got him to come to the studio and tap-dance on a song called 'I Think I'm Going To Kill Myself' when we were creating Honky Château, and now I got him to tap-dance onstage as well. As the tour progressed, his routine became increasingly complicated. Legs appeared onstage wearing a crash helmet and a wedding gown with a long train. Then he began to go onto the stage, flanked by two dwarfs dressed as US Marines, while confetti fell from the ceiling. Then he devised a skit in which he and I mimed to 'Singing In The Rain,' replete with dialogue. Larry would lean against my piano and moan, 'Gee, Elton, I wish I could play like you. I'm sure you get all the boys.' No one even raised an eyelid.

I even requested Larry to come with me when I was asked to do the Royal Variety Performance, which caused quite a stir.

Bernard Delfont, the show's organizer, was perplexed by the idea of a man in a wedding train and a crash helmet tap-dancing in front of the Queen Mother. I told him to fuck off and that I wasn't going to play unless Larry got on, and he eventually succumbed. Apart from the fact that I got to share a dressing room with Liberace, I thought it was the nicest part of the evening. He'd evidently forgotten or forgiven me for missing his London Palladium concert a couple of years prior and was really divine, like a live essence of showbiz. He arrived with trunk after trunk of clothing. I thought I looked quite wild with multicolored lurex pinstripes, matching platform shoes, and a top hat, but in comparison to his side of the changing room, mine looked like a particularly dowdy area of Marks and Spencer. He wore a suit that was covered in tiny bulbs that illuminated when he sat at the piano. He signed an autograph for me in the shape of a piano, then spent the rest of the afternoon telling me incredible stories in an impossibly camp accent. The hydraulic platform that brought him up through the stage had broken midway through his big entrance, he added, and he'd played for forty minutes with only his head visible to the crowd.

I'd grown increasingly preoccupied with making a huge entry onstage myself, because it was the only moment when I wasn't locked behind the piano. It peaked when we performed at the Hollywood Bowl in 1973. A large portrait of myself in a top hat and tails surrounded by dancing females hung over the stage. Tony King took the stage first and presented Linda Lovelace, the biggest porn star in the world at the moment. The Queen, Batman and Robin, Frankenstein's Monster, and the Pope then proceeded down a lit stairway lined by palm trees at the back of the stage. To the sound of the Twentieth-Century Fox theme, I finally appeared, clad in what I dubbed the Incredible Cheese Straw Outfit: it was entirely covered in white marabou feathers - the trousers as well as the jacket - and came with a matching hat. The lids of five grand pianos sprung open as I dropped, spelling out ELTON.

For others who thought this was too modest and understated, 400 white doves were supposed to flutter out of the grand pianos. I'm not sure if they were sleeping or too scared to come out, but none of them appeared. As I jumped on top of my own piano, I was unexpectedly joined onstage by John Reid - who, judging by his enraged expression, seemed to have taken the doves' absence as a personal insult, as if they'd done it deliberately to challenge his managerial authority - and a more sheepish-looking Bernie, frantically grabbing doves and throwing them into the air.

Dance routines, marabou feathers, and doves flying - or not, depending on the scenario - out of grand pianos with my name on the lids: the band didn't like it, and neither did Bernie. He believed it was detracting from the music. I thought I was shaping myself into a personality unlike anyone else in rock. And, furthermore, I was having a good time. We'd have these ridiculous disagreements about it. Backstage at the Santa Monica Civic, the biggest songwriting team of the era was arguing about whether it was a good idea for me to go onstage with a lighted figure of Father Christmas hanging in front of my willy. Bernie had a point every now and again. The outfits had a direct impact on the music. I had a set of spectacles constructed in the shape of the word ELTON, complete with lights. My nostrils were squished by the weight of the spectacles and the battery pack that powered the lights, making it sound like I was singing while clutching my nose. To be fair, that did probably lessen the emotional impact of his meticulously penned lyrics.

The Hollywood Bowl gig was a big success, serving as a sort of debut for my upcoming album, Goodbye Yellow Brick Road. Its creation had been somewhat traumatic, at least by my standards. We had relocated to Dynamic Sounds Studios in Kingston, Jamaica: it was considered quite cool back then to record an album somewhere other than Europe. Dynamic Sounds looked like an obvious choice. Bob Marley had made a recording there. Cat Stevens had done the same. It was the location of The Rolling Stones' Goats Head Soup. However, when we arrived, we discovered that the studio was connected to a record-pressing plant, and the pressing plant workers were on strike. They would open the windows of the minivan that carried us from our hotel and spit crushed fiberglass at everyone inside with blowpipes, causing you to break out in a rash. Nothing worked after you got into the studio. When you request a new microphone, someone will nod slowly and suggest, 'We can get one in maybe... three days?'There was no hope. I'm not sure how The Rolling Stones recorded an album there. Maybe Keith was so high that waiting three days for a working microphone felt like twenty minutes.

We eventually gave up, returned to the hotel, and booked recording sessions at the Château d'Hérouville. While we waited for an aircraft out of there, the band sat by the pool, apparently engaged in some sort of deliberate world record effort involving marijuana intake. We had so many songs by the time we arrived at the Château that Goodbye Yellow Brick Road became a double CD. When it was released, it took off in ways that none of us could have predicted. In many ways, it's a very bleak record. Songs about despair and disappointment, alcoholics, prostitutes, and murderers, and a song about a sixteen-year-old lesbian who dies in a subway. But it kept selling and selling and selling till I couldn't figure out who was buying it anymore. I don't say it lightly: I had no idea who was going to buy it. The American record company insisted on releasing 'Bennie And The Jets' as a single, and I battled them tooth and nail: it's a really strange song, it doesn't sound like anything else I've done, it's five minutes long; why don't you just put out 'Candle In The Wind,' as we did in the UK? Then they told me it was being played on all of Detroit's black radio stations. When they launched it, it raced up the Billboard Soul Chart: it was surreal to see my name among Eddie Kendricks', Gladys Knight's, and Barry White's singles. I may not have been the first white artist to do so, but I am positive I was the first Pinner artist to do so.

I was so successful that I toured America on the Starship, an ancient Boeing 720 passenger plane converted into a luxury flying tour bus for the rock and roll elite of the 1970s. There were gruesome stories about the parties Led Zeppelin threw on it. I was more concerned with what they'd done on the inside than with what they'd done on the outside. The object was purple and gold in color. It resembled a massive Milk Tray box with wings. We may have it repainted to our specifications. It was completely repainted in red and blue with white stars. Much more refined.

The Starship featured an orange and gold foil-decorated bar with a long mirror behind it, an organ, dining tables, sofas, and a TV with a video recorder, on which my mother insisted on viewing Deep Throat - 'Everyone's talking about it, aren't they? So, what's the deal?' - while she ate her lunch. Whatever nasty deeds Led Zeppelin had been up to on board, I'm pretty sure they never kept themselves amused for an hour watching a middle-aged lady shriek with dread while Linda Lovelace did her thing: 'Oh gawd, no, what's happening now? Oh! I'm unable to look! What is she doing?'

There was a bedroom in the back with a shower, a fake fireplace, and plexiglass bedside tables. You could hide out there and have sex. Or sulk, like I was doing one night when my American publicist, Sharon Lawrence, was knocking on the door and pleading with me to come out: 'Come back to the bar, we've prepared a surprise for you,' I told her. She kept returning. I was constantly telling her to fuck off. She eventually fell into tears, saying, 'You have to come to the bar!' You have no choice! You have no choice!' - so I angrily opened the door and did as she asked, huffing and eye-rolling and muttering 'for fuck's sake, can't you leave me alone' along the way. When I arrived at the bar, Stevie Wonder was seated at the organ, ready to perform for me. He began singing 'Happy Birthday'. I'd have prayed for the ground to open and engulf me if I hadn't been flying at 40,000 feet.

From the outside, everything appeared to be in order: the tours were becoming larger and more spectacular, and the recordings were selling so well that journalists began to refer to me as the world's biggest pop artist. John had entirely taken over my management: the contract he had signed with

DJM in 1971 had expired, and he had moved out of his offices and established his own management firm. We had also founded Rocket Records with Bernie and Gus Dudgeon, not to release my records, but to locate talent and give them a chance. We were sometimes better at finding talent than developing it - we couldn't make Longdancer a success despite the fact that their guitarist, a youngster named Dave Stewart, certainly had something about him, as he proved years later when he created Eurythmics. But we also had some successes. We signed Kiki Dee, whom John and I had known for years: she had been Motown's only white British artist when John worked there. She'd been releasing singles since the early 1960s, but she'd never had a hit until we published her rendition of 'Amoureuse,' a song by a French singer named Véronique Sanson that had flopped in the UK but that Tony King had discovered and recommended to Kiki.

But things were going wrong behind the surface. We spent the first several weeks of 1974 recording at the Caribou Ranch, a Rocky Mountain facility that inspired the title of our new album, Caribou. It could be difficult to sing at such a high altitude, which is how I ended up throwing a tantrum while we were recording "Don't Let The Sun Go Down On Me." After declaring that I despised the song so much that we were going to quit recording it and send it to Engelbert Humperdinck - 'and if he doesn't want it, tell him to send it to Lulu!' She can make it a B-side!' - I was dragged back into the vocal booth and finished the take. Then I yelled at Gus Dudgeon that I despised it even more now that it was finished and that if he placed it on the album, I was going to kill him with my bare hands. Aside from that, it was fantastic up at Caribou. The studio was far more luxurious than the Château. You stayed in gorgeous log cabins filled with antiques - the bed I slept in was said to have belonged to Grover Cleveland, a nineteenth-century US president. There was a movie screening room, and singers passing through Denver or Boulder would stop by. Stevie Wonder showed up one day, clearly forgiven for the incident on the Starship, and got out a snowmobile, insisting on driving it himself. To answer your question, no, I have no idea how Stevie Wonder managed to pilot a snowmobile over the Rocky Mountains of Colorado without killing himself or anyone else, but he did.

We were wrapping up one night when I strolled into a room at the back of the studio and noticed John tinkering with something on a table. He was carrying a straw and some white powder. When I asked what it was, he said it was cocaine. When I asked what it did, he replied, 'Oh, it simply makes you feel nice.' So I inquired if I might have some, and he agreed. I retched at the first line I snorted. I despised the strange combination of numbness caused by the drug and a powdery dryness from whatever junk the coke had been cut with in the back of my throat. No matter how many times I swallowed, I couldn't get rid of it. I went to the bathroom and puked. I then went back into the room where John was and requested another line.

What in the world was I doing? I tried it, I didn't like it, and it made me puke - hello? Talk about God's way of asking you to stop there. It's difficult to imagine a stronger signal that this was a horrible idea unless it started raining brimstone and I was visited by a plague of boils. So why didn't I stop there? Partly because vomiting didn't stop the coke from affecting me, and partly because I liked how it made me feel. That surge of self-assurance and happiness, the feeling that I could instantly open up, that I wasn't shy or afraid, that I could talk to anyone. Of course, that was all nonsense. I was full of energy, inquisitive, witty, and thirsty for knowledge: I didn't need a drug to make me talk to others. Cocaine gave me much too much confidence for my own benefit. If The Rolling Stones hadn't shown up in Colorado and invited me to join them onstage, I could have just performed 'Honky Tonk Women,' waved to the crowd, and walked away. Instead, I thought that because things were going so well, I'd stay on and jam along to the rest of their concert, without first asking the Stones whether they needed an auxiliary keyboard player. For a time, I assumed Keith Richards was staring at me because he was blown away by the brilliance of my spontaneous contributions to their work. After a few songs, it eventually dawned on me that the expression on his face was not indicative of great musical pleasure. Actually, he appeared to be prepared to perpetrate heinous violence on a musician who had overstayed his welcome. I hurriedly scurried away, observing that Keith was still staring at me in a way that suggested we'd be talking about this later, and decided it might be best if I didn't stay for the after-show party.

But there was more to cocaine than just how it made me feel. Cocaine has a particular allure to it. It was trendy and exclusive. It felt like I was joining an elite small circle that covertly participated in something edgy, risky, and unlawful. Surprisingly, that actually appealed to me. I'd achieved success and popularity, but I'd never felt cool. Even in Bluesology, I was the nerd, the one who didn't look like a pop star, who couldn't pull off the cool clothes, who spent all his time in record stores while the rest of the band was out getting stoned and doing drugs. And cocaine seemed cool: the cleverly coded talks to figure out who had some or wanted some - who was in the clique and who wasn't - the secretive excursions to club and bar restrooms. Of course, that was also nonsense. I was already a member of a club. Other artists have shown me nothing but kindness and love since the start of my solo career. From the moment I arrived in LA, musicians I liked and revered - folks who were formerly just fabled names on album jackets and record labels - rushed to offer friendship and support. But, by the time it arrived, my triumph had come so quickly that, despite the warm greeting, I couldn't help but feel a little out of place, as if I didn't quite belong.

As it turned out, doing a line of coke and then returning for another was very me. I was never the type of drug addict who couldn't get out of bed without a line or who required it every day. But once I got started, I couldn't stop until I was confident there was no cocaine in the area. I immediately understood that I needed to hire someone - a PA or a roadie -

to watch after my cocaine for me: not because I was too grand or too terrified to be the stash holder, but because if you left me in charge of that evening's supply of cocaine, there would be none left by teatime. My appetite for the thing was incredible, drawing attention in the circles I was in. Given that I was a rock star spending a lot of time in 1970s Los Angeles, this was no small effort. You'd think this would have given me pause for thought, but as we'll see, the next sixteen years were full of experiences that would have given any sane human being pause about their drug use. That was the issue. I was no longer a rational human being since I was high on coke. You may tell yourself that you're alright, citing the fact that your drug usage isn't impacting your career as proof. But you can't think rationally after consuming so much cocaine. You become irrational and irresponsible, consumed with oneself, a law unto yourself. It's your choice between the two. It's a filthy fucking drug.

I'd made the worst decision of my life, although I wasn't aware of it at the time. In contrast, the issues in my relationship with John were staring me down. I have stated that I was really ignorant about gay relationships. I had no idea John thought it was totally acceptable to have sex with other people behind my back. Open relationships are far more prevalent among homosexual men than among heterosexual couples, but that wasn't what I was looking for. I was madly in love. When he discovered this, it didn't stop him from being promiscuous; instead, it caused him to be dishonest about it. This resulted in some quite humiliating incidents. John went missing during a party at filmmaker John Schlesinger's house in Los Angeles. I went upstairs to check for him and discovered him in bed with someone. My mother called me while I was on tour to inform me she'd gone to the house in Virginia Water and discovered John was throwing a sex party while I was gone. I'd confront him, there'd be a big fight, everything would quiet down, and then he'd go out and do it all over again. Worse, he'd come up with some new variation on sleeping around that appeared designed to make me further crazier. I discovered he'd gone to a movie premiere, picked up a famous TV actress, and begun an affair with her. Her. So he was now fucking ladies as well. What was I expected to do about that turn in our relationship?

It went on and on and on, and it was excruciatingly painful. I seemed to spend half my life crying over his behavior, yet it made no difference. So why didn't I abandon him? It was partly motivated by love. I'd fallen head over heels for John, and when you're like that with someone who cheats, you'll create an excuse for them, deceive yourself that this time they truly mean it and everything will be fine from now on. And, in his own unique way, John adored me. If left to his own devices, he was absolutely unable to keep his dick in his pants.

I stayed because I was afraid of him. John had a volatile temper that could easily turn violent, especially if he'd been drinking or doing coke. His rages could be amusing at times. I'd contact the offices of Rocket and ask to speak to him: 'Oh, he's not here. He became enraged and attempted to throw an electric typewriter down the stairs. However, it was still plugged in, so that didn't work. This enraged him even more, so he fired everyone and walked out. We're just debating whether or not to return home.' But, for the most part, they weren't hilarious. I saw John threaten someone with a shattered glass at a party given by Rod Stewart's manager, Billy Gaff. After an altercation about parking, he struck a doorman outside a hotel in San Francisco. At the launch of Goodbye Yellow Brick Road, he struck a sound engineer in front of a room full of American media. When we were traveling in New Zealand in 1974, he flung a glass of wine in the face of the local record label publicity guy when the whisky ran out at the party they'd given for me. He punched a female reporter from a local newspaper in the face as she tried to intervene. Later that night, at another party, I got into a dispute with another local writer about the earlier event, which I hadn't witnessed. John flew across the room, knocked him to the ground, and began kicking him.

We were both arrested and charged with assault the next morning. I was acquitted, charged $50 in costs, paid up, and left New Zealand as soon as possible. I left without John, who had his bail application denied and was later sentenced to 28 days in Mount Eden prison. I returned home without him. His actions were completely inexcusable, but it was an era when the line between tough-guy rock manager and thug was frequently blurred - look at Peter Grant and Led Zeppelin - and as I waited in on a Saturday night for his weekly call from prison, I somehow managed to construct a version of events in my head where he was the injured party, acting nobly in my defense, aided by his claim that the female journalist had called him a po

It wasn't until John punched me that I realized what was going on. It happened the night we had a costume party at Hercules. I can't even remember what the dispute was over, perhaps the latest episode in John's long list of cheating, but it started before the visitors arrived and grew increasingly heated. There was yelling, doors were slammed, and a lovely art deco mirror gifted to us by Charlie Watts of The Rolling Stones was smashed. Then John hauled me into the restroom and smacked me across the face. I stumbled backwards. I didn't retaliate because I was so shocked. I gazed in the bathroom mirror as he rushed away. My nose was bleeding, and I had a cut on my face. I washed up, and the party continued as if nothing had occurred. Everyone had a good night - Derf dressed up as Shirley Eaton in Goldfinger, and Tony King arrived completely covered in gold paint. But something had happened, and it felt to me as if a switch had finally been turned off. I couldn't justify John's behavior any longer. I couldn't stay with someone who had assaulted me.

I doubt John anticipated me to inform him it was all over. I think he was still in love with me even when he moved out, to a house on Montpelier Square in Knightsbridge, and I begged my parents and Derf to help me find a place to live on my own - I literally didn't have time to go house-hunting myself. I had the impression that if I had asked him to return, he would have done so without hesitation. But I didn't want him to come back. I wanted him to remain my manager, but everything else in our relationship had altered. The balance of power shifted: he had previously been the dominant personality, but when we split up, I became more confident and forceful. He managed other acts besides musicians, such as comedians Billy Connolly and Barry Humphries, but our business relationship remained strong because I knew how astute he was and how good his ear was for music. He said he wanted to play me something by one of his new clients that was going to be a tremendous hit all over the world one morning at the offices on South Audley Street. I shook my head in disbelief as we listened to the music.

'You're not actually going to release that, are you?'

He frowned. **'What's wrong with it?'**
'Well, for one thing, it's about three hours long. For another, it's the campest thing I've ever heard in my life. And the title's absolutely ridiculous as well.'

John was completely unfazed. **'I'm telling you now,' he said, lifting the test pressing of 'Bohemian Rhapsody' off the turntable, 'that is going to be one of the biggest records of all time.'**

But, if Queen's most renowned song flew over my mind at first, I immediately recognized Freddie Mercury. I fell in love with him the moment I met him. As was customary, he was given a drag name: Melina, after the Greek actress Melina Mercouri. He was simply fantastic. Exceptionally astute and daring. Kind, generous, and caring, but also ridiculously funny. You'd spend the entire night roaring if you went dancing with him and Tony King - they were terrific buddies. Nobody was spared, not even Queen's other members: "Have you seen the guitarist, darling?" Miss May? Have you seen what she dresses like onstage? Clogs! Those clogs! 'How did I wind myself onstage with a clog-wearing guitarist?'

And not Michael Jackson, whom Freddie dubbed Mahalia, a moniker I doubt Michael found as amusing as Freddie did. He'd provoked Freddie's fury by attempting to pique his interest in his animal collection, and Freddie had turned repeating the story into a tour-de-force performance that rivaled anything he performed on stage. 'Oh, sweetie! That horrible llama! I traveled all the way to California to see Mrs Jackson, and she walked me out into the garden, where I saw the llama. Then she begs me to assist her in getting it back into its pen! I was wearing a white suit and was drenched in mud, so I had to yell at her, "For fuck's sake, Mahalia, get your fucking llama away from me!" 'Oh, honey, that was a nightmare,' he'd add, shivering for comedic effect.

CHAPTER 6

I first met John Lennon through Tony King, who had relocated to Los Angeles to become Apple Records' US general manager. In fact, I first met John Lennon while he was dancing with Tony King. There was nothing strange about that, except that they weren't in a nightclub, there was no music playing, and Tony was dressed as Queen Elizabeth II. They were at Capitol Records in Hollywood, where Tony's new office was, filming a TV commercial for John's upcoming album Mind Games, and this was the main concept, for reasons best known to John.

I was immediately drawn to him. It wasn't only the fact that he was a Beatle and hence one of my idols. For fuck's sake, he was a Beatle who thought it would be a good idea to advertise his new record by dancing about with a man dressed as the Queen. We're going to get along like a house on fire, I reasoned. And I was correct. I felt like I'd known him my entire life as soon as we started talking.

When I was in America, we started spending a lot of time together. He'd divorced Yoko and was now living in Los Angeles with May Pang. I know that time in his life was supposed to be very troubled, unpleasant, and gloomy, but to be honest, I never saw that in him. I heard rumors about him going insane one night and breaking up record producer Lou Adler's house, about some sessions he'd done with Phil Spector that went absolutely out of control. Some of the folks he was hanging out with seemed gloomy to me: Harry Nilsson was a nice guy, a fantastic singer and songwriter, but one drink too many and he'd transform into someone else, someone you had to be careful around. And, as poor old Dr. John would tell you, John and I did use a lot of drugs together and had some wild evenings out. We saw him at the Troubadour, and he brought John onstage to jam with him. John was so enraged that he began playing the organ with his elbows. It was up to me to remove him offstage.

In fact, you didn't even have to leave the house to have a wild night with John. We were holed up in my suite at the Sherry-Netherlands hotel in New York one evening, determinedly working our way through a quantity of coke, when someone knocked on the door. My first instinct was that it was the cops: if you've had a lot of cocaine and someone abruptly knocks on your door, your first assumption is always that it's the cops. John motioned to me to see who it was. I peered through the spyhole. My reaction was a strange mix of relief and skepticism. 'John,' I said quietly. 'It's Andy Warhol,' he says.

John furiously shook his head and swiped his finger across his throat. 'There's no way. 'Don't respond,' he growled.

'What?' I replied in hushed tones. 'What do you mean you don't respond? Andy Warhol is an artist.'

There was more pounding. John sighed and rolled his eyes. 'Does he have that fucking camera with him?' he inquired.

I nodded once again through the spyhole. Andy carried his Polaroid camera with him everywhere.

'Right,' John said. 'And do you want him coming in here shooting shots of you with coke icicles dripping from your nose?'

I had to admit that I didn't. 'Then don't fucking answer it,' John said quietly, and we crept back to whatever we were doing, attempting to ignore the world's most renowned pop artist's relentless knocking.

But I never met the nasty, scary, destructive side of John that everyone talks about, the stinging, sardonic wit. I'm not attempting to construct some saintly postmortem portrayal of him; I certainly knew that side of him existed, but I'd never seen it firsthand. All I ever saw from him was kindness, gentleness, and fun, so I took my mother and Derf to meet him. When John went to the bathroom, Derf thought it would be a great joke to pull his false teeth out and put them in John's drink: there was something infectious about John's sense of humor that made people do things like that. He was hilarious, Jesus. I just laughed and laughed and laughed whenever I was with him - or, better still, him and Ringo.

We became so close that when his ex-wife Cynthia brought their son Julian to meet him in New York, he invited me and Tony to accompany them. We traveled to America on the SS France, a beautiful old ship that was on its final voyage from Southampton to New York. The majority of my band and their partners also attended. The other passengers were quite snobbish towards us, these rich, enormous American women saying things like, 'He's supposed to be famous, but I've never heard of him,' whenever I walked past them, but to be fair, I had dyed my hair bright green and brought suitcases full of Tommy Nutter suits that were so loud they could permanently damage your hearing. I couldn't complain about attracting attention, positive or negative. They disliked me even more after I won the bingo one day, not least because I became overly exuberant and yelled 'BINGO!' at the top of my lungs. I eventually learnt that the correct method to announce that you'd won on board the SS France was to sweetly and demurely mumble the word 'house'. That's not how you learn to play bingo in Pinner, sweetie.

I didn't mind. I was having a great time playing squash and going to horrible cabaret concerts that usually finished with a boisterous song of 'Hava Nagila'. Midway through the trip, I received a ship-to-shore call informing me that my latest album, Caribou, issued in June 1974, had gone platinum. And I was working on the sequel. Bernie had written a collection of songs about our early years together that were all in order and told our tale. They had lovely lyrics. Songs about songwriting attempts. tunes about how no one wants to hear our tunes. A song about my idiotic failed suicide attempt at Furlong Road, as well as a song about the strange friendship we'd formed. 'We All Fall In Love Sometimes,' the latter was titled. It brought tears to my eyes because it was true. I wasn't physically in love with Bernie, but I loved him like a brother; he was the best friend I'd ever had.

The lyrics were even easier to make music for than normal, which was fortunate because they only allowed me to use the music room for a couple of hours a day during lunch. The ship's classical pianist occupied it the remainder of the time. When I arrived, she would leave with a great display of exhausted generosity, then proceed to the room just above it and strike up again. She'd occasionally be accompanied by an opera singer, who was the star attraction at the aforementioned horrible cabaret. So I'd try to drown them out for two hours. Captain Fantastic and the Brown Dirt Cowboy was written in this manner. Every day over lunch break, I'd write a song - or maybe two - to the music of an irritated pianist hammering away at the ceiling. And I'd have to keep them in mind. I didn't bring a recording recorder.

We stayed at the Pierre hotel on Fifth Avenue in New York. John Lennon, who was in the suite above mine, summoned me. He wanted to show us the preliminary mixes of his next album. Furthermore, he requested that I perform on two of the songs, 'Surprise Surprise' and 'Whatever Gets You Through The Night'. The second tune sounded like a hit, and it sounded even better when we got to the Record Plant East studio, just off Times Square, a couple of nights later. The overdub engineer was Jimmy Iovine, who went on to become one of the world's largest music moguls, although John produced it himself and worked rapidly. Because of Sergeant Pepper and 'Strawberry Fields,' everyone thinks of John as someone who spent hours in the studio exploring, but he was quick and easily bored, which was perfectly up my alley. By the time we were done, I was confident it would be number one. John wasn't: Paul had number one solo singles, George had number one solo singles, and Ringo had number one solo singles, but he didn't. So I proposed a wager: if it reached Number One, he had to join me onstage. I just wanted to watch him play live, something he hadn't done much of since

The Beatles broke up; a couple of appearances at benefit concerts and that was all.

To his credit, he didn't try to back out of the wager after 'Whatever Gets You Thru The Night' hit Number One, not even after Tony took him to a gig in Boston to see what he was getting himself into. When I got onstage for the encore wearing something that looked like a little heart-shaped chocolate box with a tunic attached to it, John looked at Tony and said, 'Fucking hell, is this what rock and roll's all about nowadays, then?'

But John agreed to play with us at Madison Square Garden on Thanksgiving 1974 if we made sure Yoko didn't come: they were still estranged. Of course, Yoko showed there anyhow, which is very Yoko, but Tony made sure her tickets were out of the way of the stage. She sent John a gardenia before the show, which he wore in his buttonhole onstage. I'm not sure if that was what made him nervous before he walked out, or if it was just because he didn't know what to expect. But, in any case, he was afraid. He puked before the show. He even tried to get Bernie to join him onstage, but to no avail: Bernie had always despised the spotlight, and not even a desperate Beetle could persuade him otherwise.

In my whole career, I've never heard a crowd make as much noise as they did when I introduced him. It simply kept going and going. But I knew just how they felt. I was as excited as they were, as was the rest of the band. Having someone like that share a stage with you was certainly the peak of our careers up to that time. The three songs whizzed by, and he was gone. He returned for an encore, this time with Bernie, both of them playing tambourines on 'The Bitch Is Back'. It was fantastic.

Yoko returned backstage after the show. Myself, John, Yoko, Tony, and John Reid all ended up back at the Pierre hotel. We were sitting in a booth enjoying a drink when Uri Geller appeared out of nowhere, came up to our table, and began bending all the spoons and forks on it. Then he started his mind-reading act. It had been an odd day. But, in the end, it led to John reconnecting with Yoko, having Sean - my godson - and retiring to the Dakota Building to live a life of domestic tranquility. I was happy for him, even though there were better places to find domestic satisfaction than the Dakota. The architecture of that structure has a somewhat evil feel about it. The mere sight of it gave me the shivers. There's a reason Roman Polanski opted to film Rosemary's Baby there.

It turned out that recording Captain Fantastic was as simple as writing it. We went back to Caribou in the summer of 1974 and taped the songs in the sequence they appear on the album, as if we were recounting the narrative as we went along. We'd also released two singles: a rendition of 'Lucy In The Sky With Diamonds' on which John played guitar and sang backup vocals, and 'Philadelphia Freedom,' one of the few songs I ever commissioned Bernie to write. Normally, I just let him write lyrics about whatever he wanted - we'd learned we couldn't really write to order back when we kept failing miserably at writing singles for Tom Jones or Cilla Black - but Billie Jean King had asked me to write a theme song for her tennis team, the Philadelphia Freedoms. I couldn't say no since I adored Billie Jean. We'd met a year ago at a party in LA, and she'd quickly become one of my best friends. It may seem strange, but she and John Lennon reminded me of one other. They were both extremely determined, kind, and loved to laugh. They both believed that they could utilize their celebrity to make a difference. Billie was a big pioneer for feminism, lesbian rights, and women's rights in sport in general, not just tennis. All today's major female tennis players should go on their knees and thank her, because she was the one who had the guts to turn back when she won the US Open and say, 'You have to offer women the same prize money as men, or I'm not playing next year'. I adore her to the moon and back.

Bernie was obviously uninterested in writing about tennis - it's not exactly the ideal theme for a pop song - so he instead wrote about the city of Philadelphia. That worked nicely because the tone of the song was influenced by the music coming out of the city at the time: The O'Jays, MFSB, Harold Melvin And The Blue Notes. That's what I heard when I went to homosexual clubs in New York, such as Crisco Disco, Le Jardin, and 12 West. Even though Crisco Disco once refused to let me in, I adored them. Divine, the famed drag queen, was also present. I know what you're thinking: Elton John and Divine being turned away from a homosexual bar. But he was dressed in a kaftan and I was dressed in a brilliantly colored jacket, and they thought we were overdressed: 'Whaddaya think this is? What the hell happened to Halloween?'

You didn't go there to meet guys, or at least I didn't. I went there to dance, and if there was anyone there at the end of the night, that was fantastic. Except for poppers, there are no drugs. You didn't require them. 'Honey Bee' by Gloria Gaynor and 'I'll Always Love My Mama' by The Intruders were enough music. Fantastic CDs, truly motivating and bold music. We recruited Gene Page, who did the strings on all of Barry White's songs, to do the strings on 'Philadelphia Freedom,' and we got the tone and style just right. We must have done something because MFSB covered it and titled an album after it a few months after it came out.

'Philadelphia Freedom' went platinum in America, and Captain Fantastic became the first record in history to debut at number one on the Billboard 200. In 1975, I was everywhere. Not only on the radio, but everywhere. I was at amusement arcades at the time, and Bally produced a Captain Fantastic pinball game. I was on black television as one of the first white performers to be invited to perform on Soul Train. 'Hey, brother, where did you get that suit?' asked Don Cornelius, who was interviewing me.'
But I was still eager to get going. I changed the band's name and let Dee and Nigel go. I called them myself. They took the

news well - Dee was more upset than Nigel, but there was no big fight or bad blood between them. I regret it more now than I did at the time. It had to have been heartbreaking for them; they'd been vital for years, and we were at the pinnacle of our careers. I was always looking ahead at the time, and I had a gut feeling that I needed to overhaul our sound, making it funkier and harder-driving. Caleb Quaye on guitar and Roger Pope on drums, both of whom had previously been on Empty Sky and Tumbleweed Connection, joined me, as did two American studio musicians, James Newton Howard on piano and Kenny Passarelli on bass.

I also tried out another American guitarist, but it didn't work out. For one thing, it didn't work musically, and for another, he freaked out the rest of the band by saying he liked fucking hens up the arse and then cutting their heads off. When you do that, their sphincters clench, forcing you to come. I couldn't tell if he had an extremely horrible sense of humor or an absolutely horrible sex life. There aren't many rules in rock and roll, but there are a few: trust your gut musical instincts, read the fine print before signing anything, and, if at all possible, avoid forming a band with someone who fucks chickens up the arse and decapitates them. Or even mentions it. Whatever it is, having to share a hotel room with them will get on your nerves after a time.

Another issue arose. Bernie's marriage with Maxine had ended, and she'd begun an affair with Kenny Passarelli. So my new bass player was having an affair with the wife of my songwriting partner. It was obviously upsetting for Bernie, but I had enough on my plate without becoming involved in other people's affairs.

I brought the new band to Amsterdam to practice. The practices were amazing - we were a completely shit-hot band - but the days off were chaotic: it turned out that we were also very shit-hot at using drugs. Tony King showed up with Ringo Starr, and we all went on a boat ride through the canals, which quickly devolved into a massive drug party. It had been thoroughly debauched. I'm afraid the Grachtengordel's aesthetic beauty went completely ignored that day. Everyone was too preoccupied with smoking coke and blowing spliff smoke into each other's lips. Ringo became so stoned that he asked to join the band at one point. At least, that's what others told me after he said something I didn't hear. If he did, he presumably forgot about it within ninety seconds after uttering the words.

I was heartbroken, which was one of the reasons I was doing so many drugs. I'd fallen in love with a straight man who didn't love me back. Tony eventually had a gold disc made up and delivered it to me: to Elton John for a million plays of 'I'm Not In Love'.

In truth, my personal life had been a catastrophe since I had broken up with John. I'd constantly fall in love with straight men, chasing after what I couldn't have. This craziness of thinking that today was the day you'd get a phone call from them saying 'oh, by the way, I love you' carried on for months and months, despite the fact that they'd informed you it would never happen.

Or I'd encounter someone I liked the appearance of at a gay bar and fall hopelessly in love before I'd even spoken to them, thinking this was the man I was fated to spend the rest of my life with and mentally drawing out a glorious future. Every time, it was the same type of guy. Blonde, blue eyes, good-looking, and younger than me, so I could smother them with the kind of fatherly love I imagined I'd lost out on as a child. I didn't so much pick them up as take them prisoner. 'Right, you have to give up what you're doing, come on the road, fly around the world with me.' I'd buy them the watches, shirts, and automobiles, but soon these boys had no reason to be there except to be with me, and I was busy, so they'd be left on the sidelines. I didn't realize it at the time, but I was robbing them of their existence. And after three or four months, they'd resent it, I'd get tired with them, and it'd all end in tears. Then I'd hire someone to get rid of them for me and start over. It was horrible behavior: I'd have one departing the airport at the same time as the new one arrived.

It was a decadent age, and many of other pop stars were doing similarly - Rod Stewart occasionally let girls know he was done with them by simply putting a plane ticket on their bed, so he wasn't going to win any chivalry awards either. But something in the back of my mind told me that this couldn't be right.

But I needed some arm candy, someone to talk to. I couldn't handle being alone. There was no time for meditation or seclusion. I needed to be around others. I was quite immature. Underneath it all, I was still the small lad from Pinner Hill Road. The events, gigs, records, and success were all fantastic, but when I was away from them, I was a teenager, not an adult. I was utterly mistaken when I assumed that changing my name meant I'd changed as a person. I wasn't Elton, but rather Reg. Reg remained the same as he had been fifteen years earlier, hiding in his bedroom while his parents fought: nervous, self-conscious, and self-loathing. I didn't want to spend the night with him. If I did, the agony could be overwhelming.

I took an overdose of Valium before going to bed one night while recording with the new band at Caribou studios. There are twelve tablets. I'm not sure what led me to do that, but it was probably some disastrous love affair gone wrong. When I awoke the next morning, I panicked, hurried downstairs, and told Connie Pappas, who worked with John Reid, what I'd done. I blacked out while chatting to her. James Newton Howard heard my breakdown and brought me back to my room upstairs. They summoned a doctor, who prescribed nerve medication for me. With the benefit of hindsight, that seems like an unusual thing to do to someone who has just tried to kill himself with a bunch of nerve pills, but they must have helped, at least in the short term, because the sessions were completed.

On 21 June 1975, the new band played its maiden gig at London's Wembley Stadium. Midsummer Music was more of a one-day celebration than a concert. I'd chosen the lineup myself: Stackridge, a band signed to our label, Rocket, Rufus with Chaka Khan, Joe Walsh, The Eagles, and The Beach Boys. They were all fantastic. They were a hit with the audience. For my headlining show, I played Captain Fantastic and the Brown Dirt Cowboy from beginning to end, all 10 songs. It was the most important show I'd ever done. Everything was perfect, including the sound, support acts, and even the weather. And it was a complete disaster.

Here's something I discovered. If you've chosen to come onstage immediately after The Beach Boys, whose set has included virtually every hit from one of the most incredible and best-loved hit catalogues in pop music history, it's a really, really bad idea to play ten new songs in a row that no one in the audience is particularly familiar with, because the album from which they come was only released a couple of weeks ago. Unfortunately, I discovered this critical lesson about three or four songs into the Wembley concert, when I detected a weariness in the audience, similar to how schoolchildren grow restless following a particularly long assembly. We kept going. We sounded fantastic - as I already stated, we were a shit-hot band. People began to leave. I was scared. I hadn't lost an audience in years. I remembered how I felt onstage in the bars when Long John Baldry insisted on playing 'The Threshing Machine' or doing his Della Reese impersonation.

The natural thing to do is flip it around and begin playing the hits. But I couldn't do it. It was a matter of aesthetic integrity, for one thing. For instance, when we came onstage, I gave a big statement about performing the entire album. I couldn't just start singing 'Crocodile Rock' halfway through. Fuck. I'd have to persevere. Even though I was just a half-hour into the show, I could already predict the reviews. We continued on our journey. The music still sounded fantastic. More individuals departed. I started thinking about the massive post-gig celebration that was planned. It was going to be packed with celebrities who were expected to be blown away by my performance: Billie Jean, Paul McCartney, and Ringo Starr. Great. This is just fantastic. I'm messing up in front of 82,000 people, including half of The Beatles.

We eventually got to the hits, but it was too little, too late, as the critics properly pointed out. We returned to America, having learned both the dangers of artistic honesty and that you're never too successful to fall flat on your face.

I was spending so much time in the States that it made sense to rent a property in Los Angeles. I eventually purchased one at the top of Tower Grove Drive. It was a Spanish Colonial-style mansion built for silent film star John Gilbert. He'd been living there while having an affair with Greta Garbo. There was a cottage in the yard near a waterfall where Garbo reputedly slept when she needed to be alone.

It was a beautiful neighborhood, however a house adjacent burned down not long after I moved in. The fire supposedly started because the owner was freebasing cocaine, something I strongly opposed. Cooking drugs implied you were a druggie, which I had deduced from some remarkably complex internal reasoning that I was not, despite some very overwhelming evidence to the contrary. I'd stay up all night on coke, then quit for six months. So I wasn't a junkie. I was perfectly fine.

It was a lovely home, and I hired a housekeeper named Alice to care after it and nurse me through my hangovers. I filled it with everything I had collected - art nouveau, art deco, Bugatti furniture, Gallé lamps, Lalique, fantastic posters - but I really only lived in three rooms: my bedroom, the TV room, and the snooker room. In reality, I usually exploited the snooker room to entice men. Strip billiards! It generally did the work, especially after a few lines of coke.

Another reason I smoked a lot of coke was that I discovered it was an aphrodisiac, which is surprising considering it absolutely kills the erection side of things for most people. I'm afraid it's never been a problem for me. Quite the contrary. I could stay hard for days if I smoked enough coke. And I liked the fantasy aspect of it: on coke, I did things I would never have had the courage to do or try if I hadn't been. It removes any inhibitions from people. Straight men, too, have their moments. If you offered them a couple of lines, they'd do things they'd never do in a million years. I suppose they'll regret it in the morning - or return back for more on occasion.

But I've never been a big fan of fucking. I was a bystander, a voyeur. I'd set up my perversion by having two or three males do things for me to see. That's where my sexual enjoyment came from: convincing a group of people who wouldn't typically have sex with each other to do it. But I didn't actually take part. I just stood there watching, taking Polaroids, and organizing stuff. The only issue was that I was really house proud, so they'd wind up having sex on the snooker table as I yelled, 'Make sure you don't come on the baize!" It had the effect of puncturing the atmosphere a little. Because I was never interested in having sex, I never caught HIV. I'd very probably be dead if I had been.

Tower Grove Drive was transformed into a large party home, where everyone returned after a night out. In the mid-1970s, Los Angeles was the epicenter of the music industry. In addition, LA featured two fantastic homosexual clubs: After Dark and Studio One. The first was an underground disco, while the second featured cabaret. It was there that I saw Eartha Kitt, who I had admired as a child, but I didn't actually watch her perform. I went backstage before the show to meet her, and her first words to me were, 'Elton John. 'I've never loved anything you've ever done.' Oh, really? Thank you for your candid and honest assessment. I'm going to go home.

We'd go to the roller derby to see the LA Thunderbirds if Dusty Springfield was around. It was all planned, like wrestling, but lesbians liked it because it was basically a bunch of dykes whizzing about on skates and battling each other. We'd also throw excellent lunch and supper gatherings. Franco Zeffirelli stopped by for lunch and disclosed that his close friends referred to him as Irene. One night, Simon and Garfunkel ate dinner and then played charades. At the very least, they attempted to play charades. They were dreadful at it. They were better than Bob Dylan, that's all I have to say about them. He couldn't get the 'how many syllables?' thing out of his head. He couldn't even do sounds like', come to think of it. One of the best lyricists in the world, the greatest man of letters in rock music history, and he can't tell you whether a word has one or two syllables, or what it rhymes with! I started throwing oranges at him because he was so forlorn. So chuckling Tony King informed me the next morning. That's not the kind of phone call you want to get when you're suffering from a hangover. 'Dear, do you recall tossing oranges at Bob Dylan last night?' Oh God.

LA had a peculiar, sinister undercurrent as well. Six years later, the Manson murders hung over the town. They'd left this strange impression that you were never truly safe there, even in a large Beverly Hills mansion. Nobody had security guards or CCTV back then, not even the former Beatles, which is why I awoke one morning to discover a girl sitting on the edge of my bed, staring at me. I couldn't get up because I never slept in anything. All I could do was shout at her to get the fuck out of there. She didn't say anything back, just stared, which was worse than if she'd talked. The housekeeping eventually came down and hauled her out of there. It terrified me since we couldn't figure out how she'd gotten in.

But you didn't need a stalker to warn you about the dark side of Los Angeles. I went to watch the Average White Band perform at the Troubadour one night. They were so good that I joined them onstage and jammed with them, dragging Cher and Martha Reeves on with me. After the show, I took the band to Le Restaurant, which served great food and didn't frown on outré behavior: the management hadn't even blanched at John Reid's birthday party, which was extremely tolerant of them, given that a friend had brought the horse he bought John as a gift into the restaurant and it immediately sat on the floor. We were up until 6 a.m. There was something delightful about spending time with them, a young British band on the cusp of being great, playing a Troubadour residency and dreaming of making it in America: they reminded me of myself five years previously. However, two days later, I received a phone call from John Reid informing me that the Average White Band's drummer, Robbie, had died. They'd gone to another party the next night, up in the Hollywood Hills, and taken heroin from a stranger they thought was cocaine. He died a few hours later in his hotel room.

It might have happened anywhere, but his death seemed to encapsulate LA. It may feel like a location where the weary old phrase about dreams coming true wasn't just a worn old line, but an actuality. It was the city where, more or less, I'd become a celebrity; where I'd had tea with Mae West (to my delight, she swanned in with a lascivious smile and the words, 'Ah, my favorite sight - a room full of men,' which, given that the men present were me, John Reid, and Tony King, suggested she was in for an evening of disappointment). But if you didn't keep your cool - if you took the wrong turn or hung out with the wrong people - LA could just as quickly swallow you up.

Elton John Week was announced by Los Angeles Mayor Tom Watson from October 20 through October 26, 1975. Among other things, I was to be honored with a star on the Hollywood Walk of Fame, just outside Grauman's Chinese Theatre. There were two shows scheduled at Dodger Stadium, each with a 55,000-person capacity. I'd played in front of larger crowds - there were 82,000 people at Wembley Stadium before they decided they'd had enough and started rushing the exits - but the Dodger shows still looked like the pinnacle. I was the first artist to be allowed to perform there since The Beatles in 1966, when the promoter failed to schedule enough security personnel. There had been a mini-riot at the end of The Beatles' set, and the stadium's owners have since prohibited rock concerts. And they had a strange sense of homecoming to them, given that my career had taken off at the Troubadour five years before.

So I leased a Pan Am Boeing 707 plane and flew my mother and Derf, my grandmother, and a slew of my friends here from England, along with the Rocket workers, journalists and reporters, and a TV documentary crew led by chat show presenter Russell Harty. I met them on the runway with Tony King and a fleet of Rolls-Royces and Cadillacs: the kind of welcome I'd been expecting instead of that fucking double-decker bus the first time I arrived in America. I think it was a crazy thing to do, but I wanted my family to see it; I wanted them to have a good time; and I wanted them to be proud of me.

Elton John Week flew over in a flash. My family visited Disneyland and Universal Studios. To commemorate the publication of Rock of the Westies, a party was held on John Reid's boat, Madman. The grand unveiling of the star on the Hollywood Walk of Fame was a flop. I was dressed in a lime-green Bob Mackie suit that was emblazoned with the names of other Walk of Fame stars, as well as a matching bowler hat. I had to ride in a gold-painted golf cart with a huge set of lit spectacles and a bow tie attached to the front. Onstage, I was far from the epitome of timid understatement, but there were constraints. There's a video of it on YouTube, and just from the expression on my face, you can see what a brilliant idea I thought it was. I'm not sure if you've ever been driven very slowly through a mob of shouting fans, in full view of the world's media, on a gold-painted golf cart with a pair of gigantic lit spectacles and a bow tie on the front, but if you haven't, it's a fairly unpleasant experience.

I felt quite awkward and attempted to alleviate the situation by making faces during the speeches and making jokes when it was my turn to speak - 'I now declare this supermarket open!' - but I couldn't wait for it to be over. They later told me that it was the first time in the history of the Walk of Fame that so many people had flocked to an unveiling that Hollywood Boulevard had to be closed altogether.

The next day, I invited my family to Tower Grove Drive for lunch. Rock of the Westies, like Captain Fantastic, debuted at the top of the US album charts. Nobody had ever done it before, not Elvis, not The Beatles, and now I'd done it twice in six months. I was twenty-eight years old and the world's biggest pop artist at the time. I was going to play one of the most important gigs of my career. My family and friends were there to celebrate my triumph. That's when I decided to try to commit suicide once more.

Again, I'm not sure what prompted me to do it, but as my family was dining, I got up from the table by the swimming pool, went upstairs, and downed a load of Valium. Then I returned in my dressing gown, declaring that I'd taken a number of drugs and that I was going to die. And then I jumped in the pool.

I can't remember how many tablets I took, but it was less than the number I'd taken that night at Caribou studios - a clue that, deep down, I had no intention of actually killing myself. This fact was driven home to me when I felt the dressing robe begin to weigh me down. For someone who was supposed to be wanting to end it all - who was obviously convinced that life had nothing more to give him and was filled with a longing for death's compassionate release - I became unexpectedly concerned about drowning. I began swimming frantically to the pool's edge. Someone assisted me in getting out. The most vivid memory I have is hearing my grandmother's voice. 'Oh,' she exclaimed. 'We might as well bleedin' go home, then,' she said, in an obviously irritated tone - unmistakably the voice of an elderly working-class lady from Pinner who's discovered her beautiful holiday in California is now in risk of being cut short.

I couldn't help but laugh. That could have been the exact response I needed. I was expecting 'oh, you poor creature,' but instead got 'why are you acting like such a twain?'

It was an excellent question: why was I acting like such a jerk? I believe I was being dramatic to attract attention. On one level, it seems crazy, given that I was living in a city that had declared Elton John Week, that I was ready to perform in front of 110,000 people, and that an ITV camera crew was filming a documentary about me. How much extra attention does a man require? But I was searching for a different type of attention. I was attempting to convince my family that something was wrong, no matter how well my job was going: it may appear that everything is OK, that my life is ideal, but it is not. I couldn't tell them, 'I think I'm doing too many drugs,' because they'd never understand; they'd never heard of cocaine. I hadn't had the courage to tell them, 'Look, I'm really not feeling well, I need some love,' because I didn't want them to see any flaws in the mask. I was too stubborn - and too terrified of her reaction - to simply pull my mother aside and say, 'Listen, Mum, I really need to talk to you - I'm not doing very well here, I need a little help, what do you think?' Instead, I bottled it up and bottled it up until I went off like Vesuvius and faked this absurd suicide bid. That's who I am: everything or nothing. It wasn't my family's fault; it was all mine. I was too self-confident to accept that my life was not great. It was pitiful.

They summoned a doctor. He gave me this terrible stuff that made me puke because I refused to go to the hospital and have my stomach pumped. And as soon as I vomited, I felt all right: 'OK, I'm better now. So, in any case, I've got these two jobs to do.' It seems ludicrous - and it was - but I recovered swiftly from my deathbed: okay, I attempted to commit suicide, done that, what's next? If anyone else thought something was odd, they kept it to themselves. I was onstage at Dodger Stadium twenty-four hours later.

The performances were a huge success. That's the thing with playing live, at least for me. Even now, whatever agony I am experiencing is simply ignored. When I was onstage, I just felt different than when I was offstage. It was the one time I felt truly in command of what I was doing.

They were major occasions. Cary Grant was backstage and looking stunning. James Cleveland's Southern California Community Choir, gospel singers, performed alongside me. On 'Philadelphia Freedom,' I had Billie Jean King come out and sing background vocals. I had the security personnel outfitted in frilly purple one-piece jumpsuits. Cal Worthington, California's most renowned used-car dealer, came on with a lion for whatever reason, but I suppose that all added to the general merriment. Bernie even made an appearance in front of the audience, which is nearly unheard of.

Bob Mackie designed my sequined Dodgers jersey and headgear. I climbed onto the piano and began swinging a baseball bat about. I pounded the piano keys until my fingers ripped open and bled. We played for three hours and I had a great time. Because of all those years I spent in clubs, backing Major Lance or playing with Bluesology to twenty people, I know how to put on a performance; I've got the experience, so my shows are never really below a certain standard. But occasionally something different happens onstage: you know you can't go wrong from the moment you start performing. It's as if your hands are moving independently of your brain; you don't even need to concentrate; you simply feel as free as a bird, free to do whatever you want. Those are the performances you live for, and Dodger Stadium delivered on both counts. The sound and weather were both amazing. I recall standing onstage and feeling the adrenaline rush through me.

It was a high point, and I was wise enough to realize that it couldn't endure, at least not at that level. Success at that level never lasts; no matter who you are or how amazing you are, your albums will not remain at the top of the charts indefinitely. Someone or something else was certain to appear. I was anticipating that moment, and the prospect did not frighten me in the least. It was almost a relief when Rock of the Westies' second single, 'Grow Some Funk Of Your Own,' failed to chart. For one thing, I was fatigued: exhausted from touring, exhausted from giving interviews, exhausted from my personal life's continual disaster. For another, I'd never intended to have hit singles. I was an album artist who'd done recordings like Tumbleweed Connection and Madman Across the Water, and I'd unwittingly become this massive singles machine, with smash after smash after smash, none of which had been written with the aim of becoming hit singles.

In reality, at the end of 1975, I sat down and tried to compose a hit song for the first time. I was on vacation in Barbados with a large group of pals, including Bernie, Tony King, Kiki Dee, and others. I suggested that we write a duet for Kiki and myself to sing. Bernie and I devised two. 'I don't know who I'm fucking, I don't know who I'm sucking, but I'm always on the bonk,' one of them said. 'Don't Go Breaking My Heart' was the other. I composed the music on the keyboard, came up with the title, and Bernie completed it. He despised the ultimate result, and I can't blame him: Bernie was and still isn't a fan of what he considers shallow pop music. Even he had to acknowledge that it had far more commercial potential than 'I'm Always On The Bonk'.

CHAPTER 7

I only agreed to do the Rolling Stone interview because I was bored out of my mind. The 1976 Elton John global tour was supposed to be free of journalists. I didn't need to conduct any press to advertise it because every date was completely sold out. But I'd been confined in a suite at the Sherry-Netherlands in New York for two weeks - we were performing at Madison Square Garden - and I'd run out of things to do when I wasn't onstage.

It was difficult to leave the motel. It was August, and Manhattan was scorching hot, but there was always a crowd of fans stationed outside the door. If I could get past them, there was anarchy everywhere I went. I'd literally seen little elderly ladies being knocked over and crushed by people wanting to get a good look at me, which is not a scene that makes you feel good about your celebrity. Still, I tried to keep myself busy. I'd seen or been seen by everyone I knew who was in town. I'd been out clubbing at 12 West and listening to WNEW radio. They'd given me champagne, an act of charity they rapidly came to regret when I went on air immediately afterwards and offered listeners my full and open opinion of a rock reviewer called John Rockwell, who'd given me a poor live review: 'I guess he's got smelly feet. I'm sure he has bogeys up his nose.' I went shopping, but I realized I had exhausted the possibilities of retail therapy when I bought a cuckoo clock with a giant wooden penis that popped in and out of it every hour instead of a cuckoo. When I went to see John Lennon, I gave it to him. It seemed like a wonderful present for a man who had everything. When it came to shopping, John and Yoko were just as bad as me. The numerous apartments they owned in the Dakota were so full of beautiful artworks, antiques, and garments that I once sent them a letter rewriting the lyrics to 'Imagine': 'Imagine six apartments, it isn't hard to do, one is full of fur coats, another is full of shoes'. For God's sake, they had herds of prize Holstein cattle. Years later, I inquired as to what had become of them. 'Oh, I got rid of them,' Yoko shrugged. 'All that bleating.'

But, after delivering a penis-themed cuckoo clock to John Lennon, I had nothing else to do, or at least nothing worth seeing a little old lady be hospitalized for. I simply strolled around the hotel. The band was in no mood to hang out with me because I'd fired them all the night before, right before we went onstage.

It had been a strange tour. It had been a big commercial success, and on one level, it had been enjoyable. Kiki Dee had joined us to perform 'Don't Go Breaking My Heart,' which, despite Bernie's reservations, reached Number One on both sides of the Atlantic that summer. We'd driven around Britain, visiting tourist attractions in between gigs, stopping for ice cream and slipping into pubs for lunch. The shows in America had been massive events, with Hollywood stars backstage; a big performance in Massachusetts for the American Bicentennial on 4 July, where I dressed up as the Statue of Liberty; and a guest appearance from Divine, who shimmied around the band despite the fact that one of his high heels broke off the moment he walked onstage.

And I met Elvis Presley backstage at the Capital Centre in Landover, Maryland, a few nights before I performed there. I brought Bernie and my mother with me. It seemed natural: Mum had introduced me to Elvis' music, and now I was going to introduce her to Elvis himself. We were led into a crowded dressing room: I was used to rock stars being mobbed everywhere, but I'd never seen anything like Elvis' entourage. He was surrounded by cousins, old friends from Memphis, and others who appeared to be hired just to offer him beverages and towels. My heart sank as I squeezed through them to shake his hand. There was something seriously wrong with him. He was overweight, grayish, and sweating profusely. Where his eyes should have been, they were expressionless black holes. He moved strangely and sluggishly, like a man recovering from a general anesthetic.

There was a splotch of black hair dye running down his brow. He was absolutely out of it, hardly conscious.

Our conversation was brief and terribly stilted. I was both starstruck and scared, which isn't a recipe for lively discussion. And Elvis... Well, I couldn't tell whether Elvis just didn't know who I was - there was every chance he didn't know who anyone was - or whether he knew quite well and wasn't overjoyed to see me. Everyone knew Elvis didn't like competition - there was a wild rumor that when he visited Richard Nixon in the White House, he literally complained to the US president about The Beatles - and, a couple of years before, I'd been contacted by his ex-wife Priscilla, who said that their daughter Lisa Marie was a huge fan and asked if I'd meet her as a birthday treat. We enjoyed tea at my residence in Los Angeles. Maybe he was upset about it.

When I asked if he was going to play 'Heartbreak Hotel,' he snarled firmly that he wasn't. When I requested for his autograph, I noticed his hands trembling as he picked up the pen. The signature was hardly legible. We then proceeded to see the show. Occasionally, something would flare, a glimmer of the wonderful artist he had been. It would appear for a few lines of a song and then vanish. My biggest memory is of his handing out scarves to the female audience members. He'd previously been known for handing out silk scarves onstage, a magnificent gesture befitting the King of Rock and Roll. But circumstances had plainly changed, and these scarves were cheap nylon items that didn't appear to last long. Elvis, as Mum pointed out, didn't either.

'He'll be dead next year,' she said as we walked away. She was correct.

But I couldn't stop thinking about our meeting for weeks following. It wasn't just that he was in such horrible shape, which was remarkable in and of itself - the last thing I expected to feel when I finally saw Elvis was pity. It was that I could see how he ended up like that, closed off from the outer world, all too effortlessly. Perhaps he'd simply spent too much time stuck in fancy hotels with nothing to do. Maybe he'd seen one too many little elderly ladies stretchered away and concluded the outside world wasn't worth the trouble.

Despite its popularity, the tour felt extremely familiar: the stadiums, the Starship, the celebrities, and even the set we performed. We'd produced a new album, a double called Blue Moves, but it wasn't due out until the autumn, and I'd learnt my lesson the year before about putting new material on an unsuspecting audience at Wembley. Especially if the material was similar to what was on Blue Moves. I'm quite pleased with it, although the music was quite experimental and jazz-influenced, and it was intricate and difficult to play. And the mood was solemn and introspective, with Bernie venting about his divorce from Maxine and me producing music to match. I even penned some lyrics, the first lines of 'Sorry Seems To Be The Hardest Word,' as a result of another terrible affair with a straight guy: 'What can I do to make you love me? 'What can I do to pique your interest?' It's a fantastic album, but it's not the work of two individuals who are cartwheeling down the street, overjoyed with life.

That was the main issue with the tour. The vacation in Barbados had been wonderful, but it seemed like a long time ago. I was in the same emotional state as when I hurled myself into the swimming pool in Los Angeles. My mother and Derf had found me a new place to live named Woodside. It sounded wonderful - a magnificent mock-Georgian mansion in Old Windsor with 37 acres of land - but I couldn't tell you how nice it was because I hadn't been there much since I moved in. I'd had enough time to ask Derf to build some shelves for my record collection and to bring in a small zoo of pets, including a rabbit named Clarence, a cockatoo named Ollie, and Roger, a mynah bird that someone had taught to say 'piss off,' a phrase he later embarrassed himself by using in front of Princess Margaret when I invited her for lunch. But, after Roger arrived and told everyone in the room to piss off, I heeded his advice: there were always recording sessions and tours to go on.

I still enjoyed performing live, but I was physically exhausted. I'd started having seizures, almost like epileptic fits; they weren't often, but they were frequent enough to worry me. I'd had a brain scan, but the neurologist I saw couldn't detect anything wrong with me, despite the fact that I'm sure if I'd told him what was bothering me on a regular basis, he could have made an appropriate diagnosis right away. Bernie didn't appear to be in much better shape than I was. Since his divorce, the only time he wasn't holding a beer was when he was doing a line of coke. I began recommending to him that he try writing with other people in addition to me - not that there was anything wrong with our connection, professionally or personally, but perhaps a change of scenery would be beneficial to both of us.

On the penultimate night of their Madison Square Garden tenure, everything came to a head. I told the band backstage that I couldn't take it any longer. They could receive another year's pay as severance, but there would be no more trips in the near future. I mumbled something non-committal about going away for a bit near the end of the show. I couldn't tell whether I actually meant it or not the moment I uttered it. On the one hand, I knew I couldn't keep schlepping across the world. It was the source of all my issues, I'd told myself. It was the reason I was exhausted, why my relationships failed, and why I was miserable. On the other hand, I still enjoyed performing live. And I'd been traveling since I was eighteen. It was my responsibility. Without it, I didn't truly know what it was like to be an adult. What was I going to do for the rest of the day? Watch Derf erect shelves as a mynah bird tells me to crap off every ten minutes?

So I was in a reflective mood when the Rolling Stone journalist came to my hotel. Cliff Jahr was his name, and he'd been hounding me for an interview for weeks. Cliff was an out-and-proud gay man who'd arrived determined to learn the truth about my sexuality. I don't think he considered it as a political act; at the time, outing people was not seen as a way to protest an oppressive system. I believe he was merely a hungry freelancer looking for a scoop.

Cliff had devised a sophisticated scheme to elicit the information from me. It involved a secret code phrase that he would drop into the dialogue as a signal for the photographer to leave the room, at which point he would use his journalistic skill to persuade me to reveal my darkest secret to him. He didn't get the chance to put his thorough plan into action, bless him. I raised the subject before he did. He inquired if I was in love with anyone, which was a bad question to ask me back then unless you had a few hours to kill and a burning desire to fill them by listening to me moan about the state of my personal life. I began telling him how desperate I was to find love. I lamented aloud that relationships with women would not be as long-lasting as ones with males. He seemed surprised and, to his credit, asked if I wanted him to switch off his tape recorder and speak off the record. No, I said. Screw it. It honestly didn't seem like a huge deal. Years previously, everyone around me had accepted that I was gay. Everyone in the music industry was aware of my relationship with John Reid. And Cliff Jahr couldn't have been surprised, given that I'd already told him about Divine and me getting turned away from Crisco Disco. Let's look at the circumstantial evidence: I'd been trying to get into a homosexual club named after a popular anal lubricant, where the world's most famous drag queen was performing. It couldn't have come as a surprise to learn that I wasn't straight.

He inquired if I was bisexual, and I said that I was. You can see that as avoiding the issue, but to be fair, I'd previously had a connection with a woman, and I afterwards had a relationship with a woman. He inquired if Bernie and I had ever been together, and I told him no. When the name John Reid came up, I lied and stated I'd never had a serious affair with anyone. It was clearly not my place to start outing people in Rolling Stone. I told him that I believed everyone should be able to sleep with whomever they choose. 'But they should stop at goats,' I remarked.

At that point, John Reid poked his head around the door and inquired whether everything was okay. I'm not sure if it was just great timing, or if he'd been listening at the door in a state of increasing terror and couldn't take it any longer when I started making bestiality jokes. Perhaps he also drew the line at goats. I assured John that everything was alright. And I really meant it. I didn't feel relieved, nervous, proud, or anything else that you may expect to feel when you come out publicly. I didn't really feel anything. I'd done all the worrying about my sexuality and what others would think about it years before. I didn't mind.

This was not a sentiment shared by people around me. Nobody ever mentioned anything to me directly. They wouldn't have dared, respecting the amount of money I was making everyone and afraid of inciting our old buddy the Dwight Family Temper to put in one of its show-stopping guest performances. But, around the time the documentary was released, I had the impression that John Reid and my American record label were nervous, waiting to see what devastating influence its discoveries would have on my career.

The dust eventually settled, revealing the full, startling scale of the destruction I had wreaked. There were none. A few nuts wrote to Rolling Stone, pleading with God to spare my warped soul from God's vengeance and eternal damnation. A few radio stations in the United States stated that they would no longer play my albums, but that didn't disturb me in the least: at the risk of appearing arrogant, I was confident that my career would continue without their assistance. People have claimed that the Rolling Stone article caused a drop in my record sales in the United States, although my album sales had begun to fall long before that. Rock of the Westies may have reached number one, but it sold significantly less copies than Captain Fantastic.

Meanwhile, in the United Kingdom, the Sun canceled a competition to win copies of Blue Moves, claiming that the cover - a beautiful Patrick Procktor painting of people sitting in a park that I owned - didn't feature any women, and thus presumably constituted terrifying homosexual propaganda from which the public must be protected. Their argument seemed to be that if a Sun reader saw a painting of several men sitting in a park, they would immediately pull off their wedding ring, dump their wife and children, and race to the next gay bar, screaming 'I Am What I Am' along the way. But that was the extent of the negative replies.

Actually, the British press seemed more interested in what was going on in my thoughts than in what was going on in my sex life. In some ways, I couldn't blame them: I'd been captivated by what was going on up there for the previous year or so. My hair had begun to thin slightly in the early 1970s, but a botched color job in New York had triggered a widespread walkout. I'd been getting my hair colored every hue possible at a salon in London for years, impressed by the way fashion designer Zandra Rhodes seemed to change her hair color to match her outfits. I'm not sure what the New York hairdresser did to it, but it started falling out in chunks not long after. There was almost nothing left on top by the time of the 1976 trip.

I despised the way I looked. Some people are gifted with the type of face that complements a bald head. I am not one of those individuals. Without my hair, I share an unsettling similarity to the animated character Shrek. But help appeared to be on the way. I was recommended to a man in Paris named Pierre Putot, who was allegedly a major pioneer in the art of hair transplants. Hair transplants were so new at the time that any doctor who could be bothered to do them was considered a great pioneer, but I was assured he was the finest. I was promised that if I underwent a simple surgery, I would exit his Paris clinic with a different man, to howls of incredulity! as well as sacre bleu! from admirers who were taken with my new, leonine hairstyle.

That didn't exactly work out. For starters, it wasn't a straightforward procedure. It lasted five hours. I had it done twice, and both times it was excruciatingly painful. The procedure they used was called 'strip harvesting,and it entailed taking strips of hair from the back of my head with a knife and attaching them to the crown. The sound of the hair being pulled out reminded me of a rabbit munching its way through a carrot. I left the clinic in agony after the first procedure, lost my footing trying to get into the back of a waiting car, and slammed the top of my head on the door frame. It was at that point that I realized that however painful a hair transplant was, it was nothing compared to the sensation of banging your head on a car door shortly following a hair transplant. I frantically dabbed my now-bleeding scalp with a tissue, doing the only thing I could think of to keep my mind off the pain. I requested that the driver take me shopping.

To make matters worse, the hair transplant was ineffective. I'm not sure why that didn't work. The doctor was not to blame. Perhaps it was related to the number of medicines I was taking. Perhaps it had something to do with the fact that the one thing they told me not to do in the weeks following the procedure was wear a hat, advice I chose to ignore on the grounds that, without a hat, I now looked like something that appears near the end of a horror film and begins strip-harvesting teenage campers with an ax. Scabs and strange craters covered my skull. I suppose I could have split the difference by wearing something lighter than a hat, like a bandana, but dressing up as a gypsy fortune teller seemed a bit much, even for me.

The press went bananas after hearing about recent happenings at Monsieur Putot's clinic. Nothing I'd done in my job had captivated them in the same way that obtaining a hair transplant had. The paparazzi grew obsessed with photographing me without a hat. You'd think I was hiding the key to endless life and pleasure under there rather than a patch of receding hair. The paparazzi were out of luck; I wore a hat in public almost constantly for the following decade or so. In the late 1980s, shortly before I became sober, I had had enough and colored what was left of my hair platinum blond, as seen on the cover of my album Sleeping with the Past. I had a weave done when I got sober, which is when they take what's left of your hair and put additional hair to it. At the Freddie Mercury Tribute Concert, I debuted my new style. A writer said that I appeared to be wearing a dead squirrel on my head. He was cruel, but I had to admit that he had a point.

I eventually gave up and got a hairpiece created by the same people that produce Hollywood wigs. It's the oddest thing. For years, people were completely preoccupied with my hair, or lack thereof. Then I started wearing wigs, and no one has addressed it since. However, a wig has its own set of disadvantages. I was asleep in my Atlanta apartment a few years ago when I heard voices in the unit. I was convinced that we were being robbed. I put on my dressing gown and crept out to see what was going on. I was almost halfway down the corridor when I realized I hadn't put on my hairpiece. I dashed back to my bedroom, calculating that if I was going to be bludgeoned to death by invaders, at least I wouldn't be bald. I proceeded into the kitchen, wig on, to discover two workmen who had been called up to mend a leak. They apologized profusely for waking me up, but I couldn't help but notice they were staring at me. Perhaps they were starstruck, I reasoned as I returned to bed. Stopping in the washroom, I noticed that the sight of the great Elton John in front of them had not impressed them. They were taken aback when the great Elton John appeared in front of them, his wig on backwards. I looked silly, like Frankie Howerd after a long night in the wind. I removed the item and went back to sleep.

If the general public seemed to accept the news of my sexuality well, I began to question if I could have timed the disclosure a little better. This is one piece of advice I would provide to someone considering coming out publicly. If you want to spend your Saturday afternoons listening to thousands of away fans singing - to the tune of 'My Old Man Said Follow The Van' - 'Don't sit down when Elton's around, or you'll get a penis up your arse,' try not to do it immediately after being appointed chairman of a British football club. I suppose I should give a lecture here condemning the homophobia of football fans in the mid-1970s, but I'll be honest: I thought it was hilarious. It's horrifying, but it's also humorous. It didn't make me feel threatened or scared; it was obviously lighthearted, and you had to take it on the chin. They'd chant it, and all I'd do was smile and wave.

In truth, I had considerably more problems to deal with when it came to Watford FC than anything the opposing fans were singing. Back in 1974, it was a Watford-supporting journalist who came to interview me who first remarked that the club was in difficulty, and not just on the field. I still followed them with zeal, went to watch them whenever I could, and stood on The Bend, the same terrace at Vicarage Road where I'd stood with my father as a child. The fact that they were standing there was not the only thing that brought back childhood memories. Watford were still as hopeless as they had been in the 1950s, languishing at the bottom of the football league. Supporting them reminded me of being a member of Bluesology: I loved them to bits, but I knew we were going nowhere.

I discovered from the journalist that the club was also in financial problems. They didn't have any money because no one wanted to come watch them lose every week. They were anxious for any way to make some. I called them and offered to play a fundraiser concert at the stadium. They agreed, and in exchange, they offered me the opportunity to purchase club stock and become vice-chairman. I dressed up in a bee costume - the closest I could find to the club's mascot, a cartoon hornet named Harry - and brought Rod Stewart along to perform with me. If nothing else, this provided Rod with an afternoon of unending hilarity at the awfulness of Watford's ground - admittedly a crumbling dump with a greyhound track running around the pitch - the team's abysmal results in comparison to his beloved Celtic, and, especially, my new role as vice-chairman.

'Sharon, what the heck do you know about football?'He inquired. 'If you knew anything, you wouldn't back this bunch.'

I told him to go fuck himself. The remainder of the board was quite friendly. They never mentioned having the only vice-chairman in the football league who showed up to meetings with green and orange hair, towering above everyone else due to his platform soles. But my presence didn't appear to make much of a difference at Watford: the team remained dismal, and the club remained bankrupt. A thought kept running through my head. If supporting Watford was as frustrating as being in Bluesology, perhaps it was up to me to do something about it.

So, in the spring of 1976, when the chairman, a local businessman named Jim Bonser, offered to sell me the club outright, I said yes. John Reid was enraged, going on and on about how much of a burden owning a football club would be on my finances. I told him to fuck off as well. This was something I really wanted to do. I've always been competitive, whether it was in squash, table tennis, or Monopoly. Even today, when I play tennis, I don't just want to hit a ball around and get some exercise. I want to play a game and win it. So taking on the chairmanship appealed to that side of my personality. I enjoyed the challenge. Furthermore, I was tired of having my weekends spoiled by Watford's defeat.

I also enjoyed the club. Supporting Watford was a constant in my life, even as everything else had changed beyond recognition. Vicarage Road was around five or six miles from my birthplace. It brought me back to my roots, reminding me that no matter how great, famous, or wealthy I became, I was still a working-class boy from a council house in Pinner.
But there was also something else. I enjoyed being in the club since everything about it was different from the music environment I was used to. There was no glitz, no opulence, no limousines, and no Starship. You took the train to

Grimsby with the players, watched the game, listened to the opposition supporters sing about your allegedly insatiable desire to stick your penis up the arse of anyone nearby, and then you took the train home, carrying a box of local fish given to you as a gift at the end of the game.

There was no nonsense. When you reach a certain degree of success in the music industry, you notice that many people around you have begun telling you what they believe you want to hear rather than what they genuinely believe. No one wants to irritate you or rock the boat. But it wasn't like that at Watford. The staff and players were pleasant and respectful, but they were uninterested in stroking my ego. If they didn't like my new album, they'd joyfully tell me, 'Why don't you perform a song like "Daniel" again? 'I liked that one,' they said, or if they thought the coat I was wearing was silly. The fact that I wasn't getting kid gloves because I was Elton John was driven home very hard whenever I chose to join them in a five-a-side game. I'd get the ball, see a Watford player from the opposing team coming in to tackle me, and the next thing I know, they'd have possession and I'd be flying through the air at tremendous speed, backwards, on my rear.

And there was no negative behavior from me, no diva tantrums. I had to learn to be a decent loser, to shake the directors' hands when we were defeated. I couldn't lose my cool, pout, get drunk, or use drugs because I wasn't there as a huge star whose every desire had to be catered for, but as a representative of Watford Football Club. I once broke the rules. I arrived for a Boxing Day game hungover after a massive coke binge and began helping myself to the boardroom Scotch. The next day, I was given a proper scolding, the kind of reprimand that no one else would dare to give me.

'What on earth do you think you're doing? You're disappointing yourself as much as the club.'
Graham Taylor, the new manager I'd personally persuaded to join Watford in April 1977, delivered the lecture. He was 32

years old when I met him, which was young for a football manager, and he reminded me of Bernie. He, like Bernie, was from Lincolnshire. He, like Bernie, gambled on me. Graham was paid generously for a manager of a team as bad as Watford, but accepting the position was a step back for him. He'd already gotten his previous team, Lincoln City, out of the fourth level and was expected to move on to something far greater, not back down. But, like Bernie, I linked with him right away, and, like Bernie, I didn't interfere with what he did, instead letting him do his job.

And, like Bernie, when things took off for us, they took off in ways we could never have imagined. Graham was an outstanding manager. He surrounded himself with a fantastic back-room team. Bertie Mee, a veteran who'd played in his thirties and knew the game inside out, came from Arsenal to be his assistant. Eddie Plumley was hired as CEO from Coventry. Graham brought in fresh players and nurtured incredible youthful talent. Graham signed John Barnes at the age of sixteen, one of the finest players England has ever seen, for the price of a new football gear. He developed club prospects such as Luther Blissett and Nigel Callaghan into outstanding players. He made them all work harder than they'd ever trained before, and he got them to play exciting football - two large center-forwards, two speedy wingers, a tremendous attack, and plenty of goals, which attracted a lot of attention. He removed the greyhound track and constructed new stands as well as a family enclosure, a space specifically created for parents to bring their children to watch the game safely. Every team now has one, but Watford was the first.

All of this cost money, which meant that John Reid had to whine even more. I didn't mind. I wasn't a businessman, pumping money into the club to make a profit. Watford ran through my veins. I was obsessive to the point of superstition - if we were winning, I wouldn't change my clothing or empty my pockets - and so incredibly passionate that I could actually talk people into being Watford supporters. Muff Winwood, an old friend of mine, was converted from a West

Brom fan to a member of the Watford board. I attended local council meetings in vain, pleading with them to allow us to build a new stadium on the outskirts of town. After games, I'd go to the Supporters' Club, a little building on the main stand, where I'd meet with Watford fans and listen to their opinions. I wanted them to know that I genuinely cared about the club, that we didn't take them for granted, and that Watford would be nothing without them. At Woodside, I arranged enormous celebrations for the players, staff, and their families, complete with five-a-side games and egg and spoon races. I purchased an Aston Martin, had it painted in Watford's colors (yellow with a red and black stripe in the middle), and drove it to away games; I dubbed it the Chairman's Car. I didn't understand how much attention it had gotten until I met Prince Philip. We were conversing politely until he abruptly changed the subject.

'You don't live near Windsor Castle, do you?' he inquired. 'Have you seen the bloody fool who drives around in that dreadful car? It's bright yellow with an absurd stripe. 'Do you know who he is?'

'Your Highness, yes. It's really me.'

'Really?' He didn't seem very surprised by the news. In fact, he looked happy to have identified the moron in question so that he could offer him his counsel. 'What on earth are you thinking? Ridiculous. You come across as a bloody moron. Take it away.'

I'd charter a helicopter if the Chairman's Car couldn't bring me to the game on time. If I couldn't make it because I was abroad, I'd call the club, and they'd plug my call into the local hospital radio broadcast of the game: backstage in America, the band would listen to me in my dressing room, alone, screaming my head off because we'd beaten Southampton in a cup tie. I'd get up in the middle of the night in New Zealand to listen. If it interfered with the start of a gig, I would postpone the start of the gig. I liked it: the excitement of the games, the sense of togetherness, being part of a team where everyone, from the players to the tea ladies, seemed to be striving towards the same goal. I couldn't have paid any money for the personal fulfillment that Watford provided for me.

Besides, I wasn't pouring money down a rabbit hole. I could see the fruits of my labor. Watford began to win and continued to win. We were promoted to the Third Division after only one season. We were in the Second after two. Watford was promoted to the First Division for the first time in their history in 1981. The next year, we were runners-up, the second most successful football team in the United Kingdom. It meant we'd be competing in the UEFA Cup against the best teams in Europe, including Real Madrid, Bayern Munich, and Inter Milan. That's what I'd told Graham I hoped the group would accomplish at our first meeting. He stared at me as if I was insane and began telling me how we'd be lucky to stay in the Fourth Division with the team we had - 'you've got a fucking giraffe for a centre-forward' - before understanding I was dead serious and ready to put my money where my mouth was. We estimated that it would take ten years. Watford had done it in five minutes.

Then, in 1984, we reached the FA Cup Final. The oldest and most famous football competition in the United Kingdom: Wembley Stadium, 100,000 spectators. I was used to Watford doing well at this point - it's remarkable how quickly you become accustomed to success after decades of failure - but just before kickoff, it hit me how far we had gone, from a dismal small club that no one went to watch, that everybody laughed at, to this. The brass band began playing 'Abide With Me,' the traditional FA Cup hymn, and I broke into tears in front of the BBC cameras. That turned out to be the highlight of the day. Everton defeated us by a score of 2-0. It should have been a much closer game - one of their goals should have been disallowed - but they ultimately outplayed us. I was devastated, but we nevertheless celebrated the team's incredible accomplishment.

I felt like I was onstage at Dodger Stadium looking out at the crowd at Wembley before the game started. And, like the Dodger Stadium performances, I guess I knew this was the apex, that it didn't get any better than this. I was correct. Graham resigned a few years later to become manager of Aston Villa. I replaced him with a manager named Dave Bassett, but it didn't work out because the chemistry wasn't right and he didn't gel with the players. I began to wonder if I should have left Watford when Graham did. I still liked the club, but there was something magical about the two of us together that I couldn't recreate without him.

I eventually sold Watford to Jack Petchey, a multimillionaire who built his fortune in the automobile industry. Seven years later, I purchased back a bunch of shares in the club and became chairman again - a businessman rather than someone who cared about the club, I believed Jack was making a dreadful mess of things, and Watford had dropped back into the Second Division. I only decided to do it because Graham agreed to return as manager. The squad performed admirably, but it wasn't the same as the first time; there wasn't the amazing challenge of rising from the ashes. Graham eventually left again, and this time I did as well. In 2002, I stepped down as chairman for good. In an odd sense, our collaboration continued quietly. I called Graham all the time till he died in 2017 to discuss the team: how they were doing, what we thought of the new management. Graham Taylor's heart was always with Watford, no matter what else he accomplished in sport.

I'm quite proud of what we accomplished as a team, but I owe Watford considerably more than Watford owes me. Throughout the worst years of my life, I was chairman: years of addiction and unhappiness, failed marriages, disastrous business dealings, court cases, and never-ending chaos. Throughout it all, Watford were a continual source of joy for me. When I didn't feel loved in my personal life, I knew I was loved by the club and the fans. It offered me something else to focus on, a hobby that could divert my attention away from everything that was going wrong. For obvious reasons, I had no memories of most of the 1980s - I struggled to remember what happened the next day, let alone thirty years later - but every Watford game I saw is forever imprinted in my memory. The night we knocked Manchester United out of the League Cup at Old Trafford, when we were still in the Third Division: two goals by Blissett, both headers, the tabloids that never bothered writing about Watford the next morning dubbed them Elton John's Rocket Men. The night in November 1982 when we were away in the Milk Cup to Nottingham Forest. They thrashed us 7-3, but I felt it was one of the best games I'd ever seen, and Forest's famed manager Brian Clough concurred, before going to Graham and telling him he'd never allow his chairman to sit on the blasted touchline like I did. God only knows what would have happened if I hadn't joined the football club. When I say Watford may have saved my life, I'm not kidding.

CHAPTER 8

In the autumn of 1976, having technically retired from live performing, I began renovating Woodside. There has been a home on the same site in Old Windsor since the eleventh century, originally built for William the Conqueror's physician, but it kept on burning down; the most recent version was built in 1947 for Michael Sobell, who made a fortune manufacturing radios and televisions. It was designed in a mock-Georgian style, but when I decorated it, I chose a style known among interior design experts as Mid-70s Pop Star On Drugs Goes Berserk over Regency or Palladian. Pinball machines, jukeboxes, brass palm trees, and souvenirs adorned the walls. Tiffany lamps stood next to the four-foot-high Doc Marten boots I'd worn when singing 'Pinball Wizard' in The Who's Tommy. Rembrandt etchings competed for place on the walls with gold discs and other items brought to me by enthusiasts. I created a five-a-side football pitch in the grounds and a fully equipped disco immediately off the living room, replete with lighting, mirrorball, DJ booth, and a pair of massive speakers. A duplicate of Tutankhamun's state throne was housed in one room. I had speakers set up outside the home that were connected to the stereo in my bedroom. When I awoke, I'd blast a fanfare through the speakers to alert everyone in the house that I was on my way. This was a camp joke that I felt was hilarious, but guests who weren't expecting it reacted with a pensive expression, as if weighing the possibility that my success had gone to my head.

There was an orangery in the grounds that had been turned into a separate flat with its own garden, which I put my grandmother into. Her second husband, Horace, had died, and I didn't like the idea of her being alone in her seventies. She lived there for the rest of her life, passing away in 1995. That struck me as having a lovely circularity to it. I was born in her house, and she died in mine, despite the fact that her existence there was very self-contained. I didn't want to take away her independence, which she had always had. I knew she was safe since she was behind the gates of Woodside, but she had her own life and friends. I could visit her anytime I wanted, but I could also keep the craziness of my life away from her, shielding her from all the excess and folly. And she appeared to be content there, pottering around in the garden. She was gardening her borders when the Queen Mother came to Woodside for lunch - we'd hit it off well when I met her at Bryan Forbes' house, and she'd invited me to dinner at the Royal Lodge in Windsor. She was a lot of fun. After dinner, she insisted on dancing to her favorite record, which turned out to be an old Irish drinking song called 'Slattery's Mounted Fut,' which Val Doonican recorded.

So, after the odd experience of dancing with the Queen Mum to an Irish drinking song, it seemed pointless to invite her to lunch. She said she was familiar with the family who had lived at Woodside before the war, and I thought she would want to see it again. When she agreed, I thought it would be hilarious not to inform my grandma who was coming. 'Come here, Gran, there's someone who wants to meet you,' I simply said. Unfortunately, my grandmother didn't see the humor in it. When the Queen Mother left, all hell broke loose.

'How could you do such a thing to me? I was talking to the Queen Mother in my bleeding' wellies and gardening gloves! I've never felt so humiliated in my life! Do not do that to me again!'

I hired some help to look after Woodside. Initially, my chauffeur was Bob Halley, and his wife Pearl was the housekeeper: a gorgeous woman but, as it turned out, incompetent in the kitchen. There were two cleaners and a PA named Andy Hill. He was the landlord's son at the Northwood Hills, where I'd played the piano as a youngster, and I'd hired him primarily because I had a crush on him; as that wore off, I recognized he wasn't the perfect fit for the job. There has to be a lesson somewhere in there. I eventually assigned Bob Halley the post of PA.

I asked my mother to come over and handle the house, which turned out to be a terrible error. She was excellent at accounting, but she governed the place with an iron fist. I'd observed a difference in her demeanor. She was still in love with Derf, but she seemed to be reverting to her old self: gloomy, unpleasant, and argumentative, with nothing ever being good enough. I hoped that having her work with me would bring us back together, as we had been at Frome Court when Bernie and I were first starting out. But no. It seemed as if the joy she had felt at my early accomplishment had worn off. She seems to despise everything I did. Her snarky criticism was incessant - about what I dressed, about my friends, about the music I made. And there were numerous financial disagreements. I'm guessing she'd grown up during the war and rationing and had that frugal, waste-not-want-not attitude engrained in her. But, as I believe we've shown, that's not exactly my attitude on spending. I was tired of having my every purchase scrutinized and having to argue with her every time I bought a gift for someone else. There seemed to be no escape from her, no privacy. You wake up after sleeping with someone, and the first person you and your new love encounter is your mother, furiously holding a receipt under your nose and asking, 'Why have you spent this much on a dress for Kiki Dee?'It's just strange. It significantly dampens the ambience of post-coital joy. Worse, she had a history of being completely disrespectful to the rest of the house staff, treating them as if she were the lady of the manor and they were her servants. I was always trying to mend things after she'd lost her cool and yelled at someone. The situation eventually grew too claustrophobic and uncomfortable. She and Derf relocated to the south coast, which was a welcome relief.

One Sunday morning, I was in bed alone at Woodside, half-watching television, when a man with vivid orange hair emerged on the screen and called Rod Stewart a useless old fucker. I hadn't been paying attention, but now I was transfixed: someone slamming Rod was clearly too wonderful to pass up. His name was Johnny Rotten, he was dressed outrageously, and I thought he was funny - a cross between an angry young man and a spiteful old queen, incredibly acidic and witty. A woman named Janet Street-Porter was interviewing him about London's blossoming punk scene. I liked her because she was gobby and daring. To be fair to Rod, Johnny Rotten seemed to despise everything - I was very certain he thought I was a stupid old fucker as well. Nonetheless, I made a mental note to call Rod later to make sure he was aware of the situation. 'Good morning, Phyllis. Did you see the news this morning? There was this new band on called the Sex Pistols, and they said you were a useless old fucker. Rod Stewart is a useless old fucker, they said exactly. Isn't it awful? You're only 32 years old. That's terrible for you.'

I couldn't care less what they thought of me. I was a huge fan of punk. I loved its energy, attitude, and style, and I loved how my old pal Marc Bolan quickly claimed he'd invented it twenty years before; it was the most Marc answer possible. I wasn't surprised by punk - I'd lived through the controversy and social upheaval that rock 'n' roll caused in the 1950s, so I was almost immune to the idea of music producing uproar - but I also wasn't intimidated or rendered obsolete by it. I couldn't see Elton John fans burning their CDs of Captain Fantastic in order to spit at The Lurkers in the Vortex. Even if they did, I couldn't do much about it because it wasn't a musical trend I was interested in following. But I loved The Clash, The Buzzcocks, and Siouxsie And The Banshees. Janet Street-Porter was also wonderful in my opinion. I called her the day after the play and invited her to lunch, and that was the end of it: we've been lifetime friends ever since.

Even if punk had no direct impact on me, it felt like a sign that things were changing. Another indication that things were shifting. There were plenty of them. I'd cut ties with Dick James and DJM. My contract with them expired shortly after the release of Rock of the Westies. They had the right to release a live album called Here and There, which I despised because it was made up of old recordings from 1972 and

1974, and it seemed to exist solely to earn money. That was the end of it. I declined another contract with them and established my own label, Rocket. Dick had been ripping us off for years, John Reid muttered darkly. He thought the contracts Bernie and I signed with Dick in the 1960s were unjust; that the royalty rates we received were too low; and that the manner our international royalties were calculated was suspect. Bernie and I were only collecting fifteen quid out of every £100 we earned after DJM, its administrators, and international companies took their cut. It was simply ordinary business methods in the music industry at the time, but they were incorrect. It all culminated in a court case in the mid-1980s, which we won. I loathed every minute of it because I adored Dick; I never said anything negative about him. Nonetheless, I felt compelled to: the industry needed to reform the way it handled artists. Dick died of a heart attack not long after, and his son Steve blamed me for it. It was horrifying and heartbreaking. That was not how Dick and I's story was supposed to end.

Bernie and I had agreed to take a break from working together in addition to leaving DJM. There was no significant fight or squabble. It simply seemed the appropriate thing to do. We'd been married for eleven years, and it was time to call it quits before our relationship became a rut. I didn't want us to wind up like Bacharach and David, who worked together until they couldn't stand each other's presence. The only thing Bernie had done without me was record a solo CD, on which he read some of his poetry over musical accompaniment provided by Caleb Quaye and Davey Johnstone. Dick James released it, then arranged a very ridiculous meeting in which he insisted on using Bernie as a support act on an upcoming American tour: 'He can read his poems!' It will be well received!'I couldn't see why Dick thought this was a good idea, unless he'd secretly taken out a life insurance policy on Bernie and hoped to earn a quick buck by getting him killed onstage. American rock audiences in the early 1970s were many things, but forty-five minutes of listening to a man read poems about his Lincolnshire boyhood wasn't one among them, no matter how beautiful the poems were. I pointed out that getting Bernie to come onstage and take a bow at the end of a gig was difficult enough, let alone performing an experimental spoken-word support piece, and the idea was fortunately shelved.

Bernie, on the other hand, had gone it alone. He'd collaborated on an album with Alice Cooper, a large concept work concerning Alice's drinking and recent rehab stay. He enlisted the help of our old bassist Dee Murray, as well as Davey Johnstone on guitar. It was an excellent record. I was blown away. So why did I feel strange when I saw Alice Cooper's name next to Bernie's instead of mine in the songwriting credits? There was nothing strange about how I felt. It was quite simple. I was ashamed to say it, but I was envious.

I blocked it out of my thoughts. After all, I'd recently met Gary Osborne, who'd written the English lyrics for 'Amoureuse,' the French song that had finally given Kiki Dee a smash. It was the opposite of working with Bernie - Gary wanted me to compose the music before he started the lyrics - but we came up with some really beautiful tunes together: 'Blue Eyes', 'Little Jeannie', a ballad called 'Chloe'. And we became fast friends. So close that when my then-boyfriend unexpectedly failed to fly up from LA as planned on Christmas Day, I contacted Gary and his wife Jenny in tears. This one had decided he wasn't gay after all and had ran off with an air stewardess who worked on the Starship, a disastrous choice of partner even by my standards. He never told me any of this. He simply vanished. His jet arrived at Heathrow without him, and I never heard from him again. Perhaps I should have expected it, although to be honest, he didn't appear too straight in bed with me. I was in a bad way, sitting at home alone with only a stack of unopened presents and an uncooked turkey for company: expecting a quiet romantic Christmas, I'd given everyone at Woodside the week off. Gary and Jenny altered their plans and drove down from London to spend the night with me. They were a charming couple.

There were certainly additional benefits to not working with Bernie. I was able to experiment with music in ways I had never done before. I flew to Seattle to record a few songs for an EP with producer Thom Bell, the man who had recorded the Philadelphia soul records that had inspired 'Philadelphia Freedom'. He forced me to sing lower than I had previously and wrapped the melodies in opulent strings. One of the tracks we recorded, 'Are You Ready For Love,' went to Number One in the UK 27 years later, demonstrating how timeless Thom Bell's sound is. Following that, I collaborated on several fantastic tunes with new wave singer Tom Robinson. One was called 'Sartorial Eloquence,' a term my US record company decided Americans were too stupid to understand, so they renamed it 'Don't Ya Wanna Play This Game No More,' which didn't have the same poetic quality. Another of Thom's songs, 'Elton's Song,' was a sorrowful portrait of a gay youngster with a crush on one of his buddies, completely different from anything Bernie would have done. I collaborated with Tim Rice, who had spent the 1970s breaking records and winning prizes with musicals he co-wrote with Andrew Lloyd Webber, Jesus Christ Superstar and Evita. We only had one song out at the time, 'Legal Boys,' which appeared on my album Jump Up! in 1982. - but it ended up being one of the most meaningful musical collaborations of my career decades later.

And, every now and then, I write entirely by myself for the first time. One Sunday at Woodside, miserable and hungover, I wrote an instrumental that complimented my mood, and continued chanting one line of lyrics over the top: 'Life isn't everything'. The next morning, I learned that a Rocket employee named Guy Burchett had died in a motorcycle accident around the time I was writing the song, so I titled it "Song For Guy." It was unlike anything I'd ever done before, and my American record label refused to release it as a single, which infuriated me, but it went on to become a massive hit in Europe. Years later, when I met Gianni Versace for the first time, he told me it was his favorite song of mine. He kept expressing how courageous he thought it was. That struck me as a little over-the-top; it was certainly unique, but I wouldn't call it daring. After a while, it became clear that Gianni felt it was really daring because he'd misheard the title and thought I'd called it 'Song For A Gay'.

Some of my experiments, on the other hand, should have stayed in the lab. In early 1978, pop videos were still a novelty, so I decided to get in headfirst. Of course I did: I was going to make the most fantastic, costly, luxurious music video ever for a song called "Ego." We spent a lot of money on it by hiring director Michael Lindsay-Hogg. It was shot in the style of a film. There were dozens of players, stage sets, flaming torches, murder scenes, and sepia-toned memories. I was so dedicated to the endeavor that I volunteered to take my hat off onscreen at one point. We leased a West End theater for a premiere, oblivious to the notion that people who come to see a film premiere expect it to go longer than three and a half minutes. There was some hesitant applause and an unmistakable sense of 'is that it?' when it finished.' permeated the room, as if I'd asked the audience to a black-tie dinner followed by a Twix. So I made them display the entire thing again, which radically changed the atmosphere: 'Is that it?' was immediately replaced by the equally unmistakable air of 'not this again'. Even worse, no one would show the bloody thing - this was before MTV, and there weren't many venues for a video on TV shows - thus the single bombed. If nothing else, this allowed John Reid to go on one of his famous rampages through the office workers, firing people for ineptitude and then having to hire them back shortly thereafter. Since then, I've despised making videos.

Then there was the disco album, which I believe was influenced in part by the amount of time I spent at Studio 54. Every time I visited New York, I went there. It was incredible, unlike any other club I'd ever been to. Steve Rubell, the owner, was gifted with the ability to create a wonderful ambiance, complete with stunning waiters in little shorts and other fascinating personalities. I'm not talking about the celebs, though there were many of them. I'm talking about folks like Disco Sally, who appeared to be in her seventies and always seemed to be having a good time, and Rollerena, a guy who dressed up as Miss Havisham from Great Expectations and skated around the dance floor on roller skates. Even more astonishing, Steve Rubell was able to construct this amazing setting while seemingly perpetually out of his mind on Quaaludes. You got the impression that Studio 54 was a mystical place where anything might and sometimes did happen. Rocket once had a party there, and I overheard Lou Reed and Lou's transgender partner Rachel conversing with, of all people, Cliff Richard. While it was good to see people with, shall we say, varied perspectives on life getting along so well, the mind did boggle a little as to what they were actually talking about.

Downstairs was a basement where celebrities could snort drugs from a pinball game. Going down there was undoubtedly an adventure - one night I was interrupted by a visibly zonked Liza Minnelli, who asked if I would marry her - but what truly drew me to the club was something that no one ever discusses about Studio 54: the music. The music and the waiters, to be sure, but the waiters were a shambles. I'd try to strike up a conversation with them, but they didn't get off work until 7 a.m. Of course, I'd willingly stay till 7 a.m., but by then, the night's excesses had generally taken their toll on me, and nothing would come of it. When your eyes are pointing in various places and it takes three attempts to effectively maneuver your way through the exit, it's difficult to conjure up a sexy vibe.

So the music was the actual draw. I still enjoyed disco as much as I did when I first heard it at gay bars in Los Angeles. That's why I'd had a disco built at Woodside: so I could DJ for visitors and dazzle them with my enormous collection of 12-inch songs. But, I had to agree, the DJs at Studio 54 had a better collection than I had, as well as a sound system that made the speakers I'd brought in from Trident Studios in London sound like a transistor radio with its battery dying.

They could make anyone dance, including Rod Stewart, which was quite an achievement given that Rod used to act as if dancing was against his religion. He was usually a little reluctant to get on the floor, which is where the bottles of amyl nitrate I used to bring with me came in handy. Poppers were popular in homosexual bars in the 1970s: you smelled it and it gave you a brief, legal, ecstatic high. I regret to inform you, Cum, that the brand I had was called, and it seemed to have an especially transformational effect on Rod. I offered him some, and after hours of refusing to leave his seat, he was up and dancing for the remainder of the night. He only paused when he needed another sniff: "Ere, you have any more of that Cum, Sharon?'

Pete Bellotte, who I knew back in the sixties, was one of disco's major producers: Bluesology had performed in Hamburg's Top Ten Club with his band The Sinners. It was great to see him again, and the album we made could have worked if I hadn't decided not to compose any songs for it and instead just sing whatever Pete and his staff writers came up with. This concept was probably prompted by the fact that I only owed my American label, Uni, a couple more albums. I was still enraged by their refusal to release 'Song For Guy,' and had decided that I intended to break out of my contract as soon as possible, with as little effort as possible. Not everything on Victim of Love was bad - if the title track had played at Studio 54, I would have danced to it - but making an album in poor faith is never a good idea. It gets into the music no matter what you do: you can tell it's not coming from an honest place. Furthermore, it was published at the end of 1979, just as a massive disco backlash began in the United States, with special venom intended for rock artists who dared to dabble with the genre. On both sides of the Atlantic, the Victim of Love sank like a stone. Rocket's offices rang once more to the shouts of John Reid firing everyone and then having to employ them all over again.

As I suspected when I announced it onstage at Madison Square Garden, retiring from live performing was not a viable option for me. Or, at the very least, I couldn't. I couldn't decide if it was the smartest or stupidest decision I'd ever taken. My thoughts fluctuated all the time, depending on my mood, with predictable demented outcomes. One day, I'd be perfectly content at home, telling anybody who would listen how fantastic it was to be free of the old cycle of touring, relishing the extra time that enabled me to focus on being chairman of Watford FC. The next thing I knew, I was on the phone with Stiff Records, a small indie label home to Ian Dury and Elvis Costello, volunteering my services as a keyboardist for their upcoming package tour, which they accepted. My newfound desire to perform in front of an audience was fueled by my crush on one of their performers, Wreckless Eric - sadly, he wasn't reckless enough to get engaged with me.

Then I organized a new band of backup musicians based in China, the band Davey Johnstone had formed when I announced my intention to stop touring. We spent three weeks intensively rehearsing for a Wembley fundraising event that I had agreed to attend since I was engaged with the organization behind it, Goaldiggers. During the rehearsals, I began making vague comments about rejoining them on the road. Then, that night, I realized the whole thing was a huge mistake and announced my retirement onstage again, this time without first informing anyone. John Reid was enraged. The candid conversation we had backstage after the show was supposedly heard not only in Wembley but throughout most of north London.

I eventually understood that if I was going to play live again, it had to be something new and challenging. I chose to tour with Ray Cooper, whom I'd known long before I became famous. He'd been in a band called Blue Mink, which was part of the DJM movement - its vocalist, Roger Cook, was also a songwriter contracted to Dick James' publishing business, and almost every member of Blue Mink had ended up helping out on my early recordings. Ray had been my band's percussionist on and off for years, but these gigs would be just me and him, in theaters rather than stadiums.

We'd done a couple of charity concerts at the Rainbow in London before, the first of which had been energized by the presence of the Queen's cousin, Princess Alexandra. She had sat respectfully during the performance, then came backstage, and got the conversation off to a flying start by smiling sweetly and asking, 'How do you have so much energy onstage? 'Do you consume a lot of cocaine?'

It was one of those moments when time seemed to stop while your brain tried to figure out what the hell was going on. Was she very naive, not understanding what she'd just said? Worse yet, did she comprehend what she'd just said? Did she know, Jesus? Had word of my monstrous hunger for coke - already a major issue in the music industry - reached Buckingham Palace? Were they all talking about it over dinner? 'I heard you had lunch with Elton John and met his grandmother, Mother - 'Have you heard he's a total sucker for the old blow?' I gathered myself enough to murmur a wobbly denial.

Despite unexpected inquiries from members of the Royal Family regarding my drug usage, the Rainbow gigs had been thrilling. They were terrifying in the nicest way conceivable - when you're onstage with just you and a percussionist, you can't switch off for a second and let the band take the load. You must concentrate at all times, and your play must be razor-sharp. And it really worked when we went on tour. The shows received rave reviews, and every night, I had the ideal mix of nervousness and exhilaration, exactly as a performer should feel before going onstage. It was liberating, challenging, and gratifying since it was unlike anything I'd ever done before: the songs we performed, the way it was presented, and even the locations we visited. I was eager to visit nations I hadn't visited before, even though I wasn't widely known there: Spain, Switzerland, Ireland, and Israel. And so I found myself flying out of Heathrow, flat on my back with my legs in the air, bound for Moscow.

I was flat on my back with my legs in the air since we were flying Aeroflot, and as soon as we took off, it became clear that the Russian state airline didn't go so far as to bolt the seats to the plane's floor. I couldn't help but notice that there didn't appear to be any oxygen masks in case of an emergency. The plane did have a distinct smell: antiseptic and sharp, it reminded me of the carbolic soap my grandmother used to wash me with when I was a youngster. I never found out what it was, but that was the smell of Russia in 1979 - it was in every hotel.

I'd almost joked with promoter Harvey Goldsmith about playing in Russia. I never imagined that would happen. Western rock music was more or less outlawed under communism - LP tapes were passed around like contraband products - and homosexuality was illegal, so the chances of people accepting to be amused by an openly gay rock star appeared slim. However, Moscow was set to host the Olympic Games in 1980, and I believe they were hoping for some favorable prior publicity. They did not want the Soviet Union to be perceived as a monolithic, drab regime where joy was forbidden. Harvey filed a request through the Foreign Office, and the Russians dispatched a representative from the state music promoter to witness a performance Ray and I gave in Oxford. They approved the tour after determining that we were not the Sex Pistols and posing no significant threat to the morals of communist youth. I went to shoot a documentary with my mother and Derf, a group of British and American journalists, and a film crew led by writers Dick Clement and Ian La Frenais. It was thrilling, a genuine adventure into the unknown, even if it could end abruptly with death by suffocation if the plane lost pressure.

We were greeted at Moscow Airport by a group of dignitaries, two females who would serve as translators, and an ex-army man named Sasha. He was supposed to be my protector. Everyone else in our group suspected he was spying on us for the KGB. I decided he could spy on me all he wanted because he was really attractive, if a little too eager to tell me about his wife and children. We hopped on a sleeper train to Leningrad. It was hot - I'd prepared for winter on the Siberian steppes only to arrive in Moscow during a blazing heatwave - and unpleasant, but it wasn't the Russians' fault. It was because I could clearly hear John Reid in the adjacent sleeper cabin, obviously doing his hardest to attract a Daily Mail reporter, through the thin wall.

The hotel in Leningrad did not appear to be very promising. The cuisine was incredible: 57 different types of beetroot soup and potatoes. What the hell were ordinary people eating if this was what they were served in the nicest hotels? Every floor was patrolled by a stern-faced old lady, a proper Russian babushka on the lookout for any sign of Western immorality. But it turned out to be a great swinging location. The road crew arrived for breakfast the first morning we were there, looking bewildered and delighted. They'd discovered that being from the West and having any link to rock and roll, even if you were only lugging the speakers, made you sexually desirable to the chambermaids. They'd walk into the room, start running a bath to distract the ears of the ever-vigilant babushkas, then strip naked and leap on you. The hotel bar seemed to be a never-ending party, full with individuals who'd traveled from Finland with the express purpose of getting as drunk as possible on cheap Russian vodka. The substance was fatal. Someone approached me and, much to my surprise, handed me a joint. The road crew had found some marijuana in the middle of repressive, communist Russia. They seemed to have all the good fortune. Perhaps it was rubbing off because, not long after, Sasha arrived and suggested we go up to my room. I was so taken aback that I brought up his wife and children without prompting. 'In the army, all the men have sex with each other, because we don't see our wives,' he claimed. So I ended the night stoned, intoxicated, and having sex with a soldier. I'm not sure what I was anticipating from my first forty-eight hours in Russia, but this was not it.

Even if one of its people had not taken me to bed, I would have fallen in love with Russia. The people were unbelievably nice and generous. Strangely, they reminded me of Americans: they radiated instant friendliness and hospitality. We saw the Hermitage and the Summer Palace, as well as Peter the Great's log home and the Kremlin. We visited collections of Impressionist art and Fabergé eggs that were spectacular enough to take your mind off what you were going to eat for lunch. People attempted to offer us gifts everywhere we went: chocolate bars, soft toys, stuff they had to save up for. They'd shove them into your hands on the street or through the windows of your train as it drove away from the station. It made my mother cry: 'These folks have nothing, and they're giving you things.'

The performances were in Leningrad and Moscow, and they were magnificent. I say "turned out" because they were always off to a poor start. All of the best seats were reserved for high-ranking Communist Party leaders, ensuring that the reaction was limited to polite applause. People who wanted to see me were jammed in the back. But they hadn't factored in Ray Cooper. Ray is a fantastic musician who plays the most modest instruments in the most noticeable manner possible. He's the Jimi Hendrix of the tambourine, a natural leader trapped in the body of a percussionist. And in Russia, he played as if every other enormously extravagant performance he'd done had been a warm-up. He'd nudge the audience into clapping along, or jump to the front of the stage and yell at them to get up. It was successful. The children at the rear dashed along the aisles to the front. In between songs, they threw flowers and asked for signatures. I'd been warned not to sing 'Back In The USSR,' so I did. If the KGB had been spying on me, they had clearly not been spying closely enough to discover that telling me not to do something is one of the easiest ways to convince me to do it.

Following the Moscow event, thousands of people gathered outside the venue, screaming my name - far more than could possibly have attended the show. I threw the flowers I'd been given back to them through the dressing room window. My mother observed. 'You'd be better off throwing them a tomato,' she replied, recalling our most recent feast of beetroot soup and potatoes. 'They've most likely never seen one.'

My visit was a waste of time as a public relations exercise for the Soviet Union. Six months later, they invaded Afghanistan, and whatever international goodwill they'd gained by allowing me to sing 'Bennie And The Jets' didn't last long. But that was the start of a lifetime love affair with Russia and Russians for me. Even when people told me I shouldn't, I never stopped going back. If anything, life is worse for homosexual Russians under Vladimir Putin than it was in 1979, but what would I gain by shunning the establishment? In Russia, I am in a highly privileged situation. Despite the fact that they know I'm homosexual, I've always been accepted and welcomed, so I'm not afraid to speak up while I'm there. I can make public statements; I can meet with LGBT people and members of the Health Ministry to promote the work of the Elton John AIDS Foundation in that country. I never saw Sasha again, but I later learnt that he was one of the first individuals in Russia to die of AIDS. It now has one of the world's fastest-growing HIV/AIDS epidemics. That will not change unless we negotiate, unless we get down and discuss. And the discussion must begin somewhere. So I keep returning, and each time I say something onstage about homophobia or gay rights. A few individuals will occasionally walk out, but the great majority will applaud. I owe it to the Russian people to continue doing so. It's something I owe to myself.

If the Ray Cooper shows taught me anything, it was that I belonged onstage. My personal life was still a jumble of different boyfriends and drugs - at one point, I was rushed from Woodside to hospital with what was reported as a heart problem, but had nothing to do with my heart and everything to do with my decision to play tennis against Billie Jean King in the aftermath of yet another coke binge. Aside from Victim of Love, my albums were selling OK - its follow-up, 21 at 33, went gold in America in 1980 - but they weren't selling like they used to, despite the fact that I'd started working with Bernie again, if gingerly, on only a handful of songs each time. The lyrics he gave me felt rather pointed at times. When he sent me a song called 'White Lady White Powder,' a depiction of a hopeless cocaine addict, you didn't have to be a genius to figure out what he was getting at. I had the brass balls to sing it as though it were about another person.

But for a couple of hours onstage, everything else faded away. After the release of 21 at 33, I embarked on a globe tour. I had reformed the original Elton John Band - myself, Dee, and Nigel - and added a couple of excellent session guitarists, Richie Zito and Tim Renwick, as well as James Newton Howard on keyboards. I had dressed down for Ray's gigs, leaving the theatrics to him, but I had decided to go to town again. I contacted my old costumier Bob Mackie and a designer named Bruce Halperin and told them to do their worst: the flares and platforms were obviously gone, in keeping with changing fashions, but Bruce came up with something that looked like a military general's uniform covered in red and yellow thunderflashes and arrows, with lapels that looked like a piano keyboard and a matching peaked cap.

The performances were bigger than ever. In September 1980, I performed in front of 500,000 people in Central Park, the largest gathering I'd ever seen. Bob had created me a Donald Duck outfit for the encore. In principle, it was a brilliant idea, but in practice, it left a lot to be desired. To begin with, I couldn't get the damned thing on properly. I was backstage, one arm through the leg hole and my leg through the arm, laughing as everyone around me begged me to hurry up: 'There's 500,000 people out there and they'll assume there's no encore!' They'll believe the show is done and leave!' When I finally got onstage, it occurred to me that I should have had some sort of dress rehearsal to see how the clothing would look. If I had done that, I might have detected two minor issues. First, I couldn't walk in it since it had enormous duck feet, similar to divers' flippers. Second, I couldn't sit in it because it had an enormous cushioned bum, so the best I could do was perch cautiously on the piano stool. I tried playing 'Your Song,' but I couldn't stop giggling. I had fits of laughter every time I caught Dee's eye, who was wearing a look of tired resignation, the look of a man who had returned after five years to realize that things were still as absurd as ever. Bernie's delicate ballad of burgeoning youthful love was devastated yet again by my choice of stage attire.

But, aside from the duck costume, it was a spectacular show: perfect autumn weather in New York, audience members climbing the trees to get a better view. I performed 'Imagine' and dedicated it to John Lennon. I hadn't seen him in some years. He'd truly gone to ground when Sean was born; the last thing he needed was to be reminded of the inebriated chaos of 1974 and 1975. But after the performance, there was a great party on the Peking, a ship converted into a floating museum on the East River, and he and Yoko showed up entirely unexpectedly. He was as amusing as ever, and ecstatic about producing a new album, but I was too tired to stay long. We agreed to meet up again the following time I was in New York.

The trip continued, covering America before traveling south to Australia. Our plane had barely landed in Melbourne when a stewardess said over the tannoy that the Elton John party would be unable to leave; we would have to remain onboard. My heart plummeted the instant they uttered it; I just knew it meant someone was dead. My first thought was of my granny. Every time I left and walked into the Orangery to say my goodbyes, I wondered if she'd still be there when I returned. John Reid went to the cockpit to find out what was going on and returned in tears, absolutely confused. He informed me that John Lennon had been murdered.

It was impossible for me to believe. It wasn't just the fact that he died; it was the savagery with which he died. Other friends of mine had died at a young age, including Marc Bolan in 1977 and Keith Moon in 1978. But they hadn't perished in the same way that John did. Marc had died in a vehicle accident, and Keith had died from an incurable case of being Keith

Moon. They hadn't been slain by a stranger outside their home for no apparent reason. It was incomprehensible. It was unfathomable.

I had no idea what to do. What could you possibly do? Instead of flowers, I sent Yoko a massive chocolate cake. She had a thing for chocolate. There was no funeral to attend, and we were still in Melbourne when the memorial Yoko had requested was held on the Sunday after his death. As a result, we rented the local cathedral and held our own service at the same time as thousands congregated in Central Park. We sang 'The Lord is My Shepherd,' the 23rd Psalm, with everyone crying: the band, the road crew, everyone. Later, Bernie and I created a song called 'Empty Garden' for him. It was a fantastic lyric. Not romantic or mawkish - Bernie knew John and knew he would have loathed anything like that - just angry, uncomprehending, and heartbroken. It's one of my favorites, but I rarely perform it live. It's too difficult to perform and too emotional. Decades after John's death, we used 'Empty Garden' in one of my Las Vegas presentations, with gorgeous photographs of him provided by Yoko on the screens. I would still cry every time I sang it. I adored John, and I don't think you ever get over their loss when you love someone so deeply.

I received a phone call from Yoko a few years after John died. She said she needed to see me right away and that I needed to come to New York straight away. So I boarded a plane. I had no idea what the conversation was about, but she seemed frantic. When I arrived at the Dakota, she informed me she'd discovered a slew of tapes with unfinished songs that John had been working on soon before his death. She asked if I would finish them so that they could be released. It was incredibly flattering, but I didn't want to do it. I thought it was too soon; the timing was off. Actually, I didn't believe the time would ever come. I was terrified just thinking about it. I wouldn't be so arrogant if I was trying to figure out how to finish songs John Lennon had started writing. And I thought it was a terrible idea to have my voice on the same record as his. Yoko was adamant, but so was I.

As a result, the meeting was quite awkward. I felt awful after I left. Yoko thought she was honoring John's legacy by attempting to fulfill his intentions, but I refused to assist. Even though I knew I was correct, it didn't make it any less depressing. (In the end, she released the songs as is on an album called Milk & Honey.) I went to the movies to watch Monty Python's The Meaning of Life to distract myself. I couldn't stop giggling at Mr Creosote, the horrible man who eats till he explodes. Then I realized how amusing John would have found it. His style of comedy was exactly that: bizarre, caustic, and sardonic. I could almost hear his chuckle, that contagious cackle that used to get under my skin. That's how I'd like to remember him. That is how I remember him.

CHAPTER 9

The sound of someone beating on the door of my hotel suite woke me up. I couldn't remember who it was since I couldn't think of anything. When I opened my eyes, I realized I had the kind of hangover that makes you think it's not a hangover: you can't be this ill from overindulgence - there must be something more severe wrong with you. It wasn't simply my imagination. My entire body hurt. Particularly my hands. When did hangovers start hurting your hands? And, despite my numerous requests, why wouldn't the person at the door just fuck off?

The hammering, however, continued, accompanied by a voice calling my name. Bob Halley was the man. I rolled out of bed. This hangover was incredible. I felt worse than I did after Ringo Starr's New Year's Eve party in 1974, which had begun at 8 p.m. and finished around three thirty the next day. I felt worse than I had in Paris a few years previously, when I'd rented an apartment overlooking the Seine, purportedly to record, then took delivery of some pharmaceutical-grade cocaine and refused to go to the studio at all. John Reid had arrived one morning with the goal of hauling me to a session, only to discover that I was still up from the night before and so inebriated that I was gleefully fantasizing that the kitchen furniture was dancing with me. It could have been on that same vacation to Paris that I chose to shave while absolutely out of my mind and became so excited about the prospect of shaving that I eliminated not just my stubble but also one of my brows. These events tend to blend together.

When I opened the door, Bob gave me a puzzled expression, as if he expected me to say something. When I refused, he continued, 'I think you should come and see this.'

I went into his room after him. He pushed open the door to discover a sight of complete carnage. Except for the bed, every piece of furniture had been destroyed. Everything else was upside down, on its side, or in fragments. A cowboy hat that Bob liked to wear was among the splinters. It was as flat as Yosemite Sam's after Bugs Bunny dropped an anvil on his head.

'Fucking hell,' I exclaimed. 'What occurred?'

A long pause followed. **'Elton,' he finally said. 'You occurred.'**

What exactly did he mean, I happened? What was he on about? I couldn't understand how this was related to me. I was having a fantastic time the last thing I remembered. So why would I destroy anything?

'I was in the bar,' I retorted angrily. **'Along with Duran Duran.'**

Bob gave me another glance, as if he was trying to figure out whether I was serious or not. He then sighed. 'You were,' he confirmed. 'At first,' she says.

Everything had been going so nicely. It was June 1983, and we were in Cannes filming a video for 'I'm Still Standing,' the first single from my upcoming album Too Low for Zero. I'd attempted to keep my involvement in video production to a bare minimum since the 'Ego' catastrophe, but this time I'd chosen to go all in. That was partly due to the fact that the director was Russell Mulcahy, with whom I had previously worked and who I admired. Russell was the guy who took Duran Duran to Antigua and filmed them singing 'Rio' on a yacht in the early 1980s if you wanted your video to look glossy, exotic, and expensive. But I also wanted 'I'm Still Standing' and 'Too Low for Zero' to be commercial triumphs. Bernie and I had returned to full-time writing. We had written some nice songs during our trial separation, but we recognized that in order for the relationship to work, we needed to create an entire album together. I'd enjoyed playing with Dee and Nigel, so I reformed my old band in the studio, with Davey on guitar and Ray Cooper on drums. Skaila Kanga, a friend from the Royal Academy of Music, came and performed harp, much as she had on Elton John and Tumbleweed Connection.

We traveled to George Martin's studio in Montserrat to record, where producer Chris Thomas had together an excellent team of engineers and tape operators, including Bill Price, Peggy McCreary, who had just returned from working with Prince, and a German girl named Renate Blauel. I'd previously recorded some of my previous album, Jump Up!It was 1981, yet this was different. Bernie was present, and it was the first album since Captain Fantastic in 1975 to properly rejoin the original Elton John Band. It was like a well-oiled machine resurrected, but the results didn't sound like the albums we'd done in the 1970s; they sounded completely new. I'd been exploring with synthesizers as well as piano. 'I Guess That's Why They Call It The Blues,' 'Kiss The Bride,' and 'Cold As Christmas' gleamed. And 'I'm Still Standing' seemed to be the album's calling card. The lyric was about one of Bernie's ex-wives, but I also believed it was a message to my new American record company, which was, to put it mildly, a pain in the arse.

Geffen Records was a relatively young label, having been created in 1980, but it established itself by signing the biggest names it could, including not only me, but also Donna Summer, Neil Young, Joni Mitchell, and John Lennon. We were all drawn in by David Geffen's reputation - he had guided The Eagles and Jackson Browne to fame in the 1970s - and the promise of unlimited artistic freedom. But my first album with them, The Fox, had not done well. Get up! had been a sales improvement, but the only one of their big signings who had been a significant hit for them thus far was John, and that was because he was murdered. Before his death, his record with Yoko, Double Fantasy, had gotten negative reviews and had sold poorly. That felt like an unusual way to get a hit. So Geffen panicked and began acting ridiculously. They sacked Donna Summer's producer, Giorgio Moroder, who was responsible for virtually every hit record she had ever released. They put Joni Mitchell in the studio with Thomas Dolby, a synthesizer wizkid, which was about as appropriate for Joni's music as putting her in the studio with an Alpine yodeling choir. They eventually attempted to sue Neil Young for being unpredictable, which, if you understood anything about his career, was tantamount to suing Neil Young for being Neil Young. I didn't like the sound of 'I'm Still Standing,' and thought it sounded like a warning shot across their bows. It was a big, swaggering, self-assured fuck-you song.

A large, swaggering, confident film was required, and Russell delivered with a massive production incorporating aerial shots from helicopters and thousands of dancers dressed in body paint and costumes. My convertible Bentley was delivered to Nice so that I could travel along the Croisette. There was choreography in which I was supposed to participate, at least at first. Arlene Phillips, the choreographer, went pale after seeing my demonstration of the moves I'd honed on the dance floors of Crisco Disco and Studio 54, and abruptly scaled down my involvement in that side of things, until all I really had to do was click my fingers and walk along the seafront in time to the music. Perhaps she was scared I'd outperform the experts, and her later remark about me being the worst dancer she'd ever worked with was a superb double-bluff intended to save their blushes.

Filming began at 4 a.m. and continued all day. As the sun set, the crew called a break, and I returned to my hotel, the Negresco, to freshen up before the night shoot. I happened to run across Simon Le Bon in the lobby. He was in town with Duran Duran, and the two of them were on their way to the pub. Did I want to accompany them? I didn't know him well, but I figured a quick drink would cheer me up. When Simon inquired if I'd ever had a vodka martini, I was undecided about what to order. I didn't. Maybe I should give it a shot.
The details of what transpired afterwards vary. I'm afraid I can't confirm or deny them because I don't remember much beyond thinking Duran Duran were great company and observing how effortlessly the vodka martini went down.

Depending on who you believe, I had six or eight more of them in an hour, along with a couple of lines of coke. I then supposedly returned to the video set, requested that the cameras be switched on, stripped nude and began rolling around on the floor. John Reid was present, acting as an extra in the video as a clown. He remonstrated with me, which I took quite harshly. I felt so awful for him that I punched him in the face. Some witnesses thought I had smashed his nose. That explains why my hands hurt, but I was taken aback. I had never hit someone in my adult life, and I haven't since. I despise physical violence so much that I can't even watch a rugby match. If I was going to break a lifetime habit and hit someone in the face, it might as well be John Reid; he could take it as retaliation for pounding me when we were dating.

John stormed off set, grabbing the Bentley keys and speeding away into the night. The next time anyone heard from him was the next day, when he called Rocket's office and yelled at them to call the AA. He'd driven all night to Calais, taken the ferry to Dover, and quickly broken down. When the breakdown truck arrived, they were understandably alarmed to see a convertible Bentley being driven by a man dressed in a clown suit and make-up and coated in blood.

After John Reid left, someone else managed to get my clothing back on - it took several attempts, I was told - and Bob Halley rushed me upstairs. I smashed up his hotel room to show my displeasure with his involvement. I'd stamped on his cap as a climax, then wandered back to my own room and fell out.

Bob and I were laughing so hard on the bed. There was nothing to do but giggle at the absurdity of it all and then make some regretful phone calls. It was the kind of day that should have made me stop and think about how I was acting. But, and you may be ahead of me here, it didn't work out at all. The primary effect of the events in Nice on my life was that I chose to drink more vodka martinis. From now on, an evening out would begin with four or five vodka martinis, followed by a meal at a restaurant - perhaps L'Orangerie if I were in Los Angeles - a bottle and a half of wine during dinner, and then all back to mine to begin the coke and spliffs. They were my go-to drink partly because they had an extra benefit of making me blank out, so I couldn't remember how heinous I'd been the night before. Occasionally, someone would feel compelled to call and remind me, and I would apologize. I recall one enraged phone conversation from Bernie following a night at Le Dome, a LA restaurant in which I had a financial stake, where I got drunk and delivered what I thought was a humorous speech in which I insulted John Reid's mother. However, there was something reassuring about not knowing firsthand. It meant I could convince myself that it wasn't as horrible as everyone said, or that it was an isolated incidence. After all, because of who I was, no one dared to say anything most of the time. That is the nature of success. It offers you permission to misbehave, permission that will not be removed until your success runs out or you man up and decide to hand it in yourself. And, for the time being, neither of those things were likely to happen to me.

I traveled for the rest of 1983. I went on vacation with Rod Stewart, which had become a regular occurrence. We'd previously visited Rio de Janeiro for the carnival, which was fantastic. We had bought sailor clothes from a fancy dress shop to ensure we could be identified in the crowds. We got them on and exited the hotel, only to discover that a massive navy ship had just docked and that the streets were thronged with sailors in uniform: it was like a Royal Navy conference out there. We went on a safari to Africa this time. We were afraid that everyone would think we were obnoxious, scruffy rock stars, so we insisted on dressing up for dinner every night, despite the blazing weather. Far from being reassured, our other safari-goers, dressed in weather-appropriate attire, were casting concerned glances our way, as if the safari party had been joined by a pair of maniacs.

Then I traveled to China with the Watford team, who were on a post-season tour and the first British football club to be invited. It was weird, but not unattractive, to be in a place where no one knew who I was save the individuals I was with. And China was enthralling. It was prior to the country's formal opening to the West. When I returned there with Watford a few years later, you could see a Western influence creeping in. People were riding their bikes with microwave ovens strapped to their backs, while Madonna albums were being played in pubs. But, for the time being, it felt like I was in another universe. No one was allowed to cheer during football games for reasons known only to the Communist Party of China, therefore the games were played in eerie stillness. We went to Mao's mausoleum and saw him in his crystal coffin, which was an odd experience. I'd seen Lenin's body in Russia, and he appeared to be in good condition, but there was certainly something wrong with Mao, or rather, what had been done to Mao in order to preserve his corpse. He was the same brilliant pink color as those foam-like shrimp delights that kids used to enjoy. I don't want to cast aspersions on the embalmers who worked on him, but Mao seemed suspiciously agitated.

Then, in October, I traveled to South Africa to play Sun City, which was a phenomenally bad idea. The movement against it hadn't really gained traction - that came until when Queen performed there in 1984 - but there was still enough controversy about playing in South Africa to fuel my misgivings. John Reid told me that everything would be alright. Ray Charles, Tina Turner, Dionne Warwick, and even Curtis Mayfield have performed at Sun City. How horrible could it be if the renowned civil rights poet consented to perform there? It wasn't technically in South Africa, but rather in Botswana. There was no racial segregation in the audience.

Of course, it was not fine. The audience might as well have been racially segregated, because the ticket fees meant that even if black South Africans wanted to go, they couldn't. If I had bothered to check into it further, I would have discovered that when Ray Charles performed there, black South Africans were so outraged that they stoned his tour bus, forcing his Soweto concerts to be canceled. However, I did not. I just stumbled into it. It wasn't like traveling to Russia against all odds. People in South Africa who were suffering as a result of apartheid wished for artists to boycott the nation. You couldn't accomplish anything by visiting there. So it's pointless to try to rationalize it. When you mess up, you have to hold your hand up and admit it. Every single one of the black artists I listed later regretted their decision, as did I. When I returned, I signed a public commitment organized by anti-apartheid activists promising never to return.

My father was very ill in England. Backstage after a Manchester show, one of my half-brothers told me he had heart trouble and needed a quadruple bypass procedure. I'd kept my distance over the years, but I called him at home and offered to pay for the surgery privately. He categorically refused. It was a shame, not least for his other children and my stepmother: he loved them and they loved him, and it would have been better for them to attempt to get his health problems resolved as soon as possible. But he refused my assistance. I suggested we meet up in Liverpool during Watford's visit. He wouldn't have to travel very far. He concurred. The only thing we had in common was our love of football. I don't recall him ever coming to watch me perform live or discussing music with me. What I was doing was plainly not his cup of tea.

I brought him to lunch at the Adelphi Hotel before the game. It was all right. We limited ourselves to pleasant small conversation. When the small chat ran out, there was an awkward pause, emphasizing that we didn't actually know each other well. I was still angry at him for how he's treated me, but I didn't say anything about it. I didn't want a big fight since it would have ruined the day and because I was still afraid of him: my life had changed dramatically over the years, but our relationship remained stuck in 1958. We sat in the director's box and watched the game. Watford were thrashed 3-1 - we hadn't been in the First Division long, and the team appeared overwhelmed by playing at a massive stadium like Anfield - but I still think he enjoyed it, though it was difficult to tell. I think that he'd be impressed by the fact that I was now chairman of the club he'd taken me to see as a boy, that Watford fans now sang 'Elton John's Taylor-made army' whenever we scored or advanced on the field. If I couldn't receive a 'well done, son, I'm proud of you' from dad for my music, I hoped I could get one for what we'd accomplished at Watford. But that never came to pass. I've thought about it since, and I'm not sure whether dad had a problem saying things like that to me, or whether he was ashamed by the decisions I'd taken against his preferences. Nonetheless, we parted on good terms. He was never seen again. I didn't see what the point was. There was no genuine friendship to mend. For decades, our lives had been utterly distinct. There were no lovely childhood memories to be chosen over and savored.

We returned to Montserrat in December 1983. Too Low for Zero had been a huge hit, the biggest album I'd made in nearly a decade - platinum in the UK and America, five times platinum in Australia - so we decided to repeat the formula for the follow-up: Bernie writing all the lyrics, the old Elton John Band providing the music, and Chris Thomas producing. Renate Blauel was promoted from tape operator to engineer, which was the only significant change to the team. Everyone liked her, including the other musicians, the crew, and Chris. She was reserved, but fierce and self-assured. Recording studios were a genuine boys' club back then, with few women working there, but she was creating a name for herself simply by being really competent at what she did; she'd stepped up and worked as an engineer for The Human League and The Jam.

I traveled out on Boxing Day and arrived grumpy. My mother and Derf had arrived at Woodside for the holidays, and Mum had quickly reverted to her former job of managing the house and being rude to the servants. She'd gotten into a fight with one of the cleaners, which had escalated into a fight with me, and she and Derf had walked out on Christmas Eve.

But when I arrived, I brightened up. Tony King had arrived the day before me; he'd come out to spend the holidays. He was now in New York, working for RCA alongside Diana Ross and Kenny Rogers. He'd stopped drinking, joined AA, and looked wonderful, despite having some horrific stories about what was going on in the gay scene in Greenwich Village and on Fire Island as a result of a new disease called AIDS. In the studio, I made up characters - an elderly aristocrat named Lady Choc Ice, a lugubrious, Nico-like singer named Gloria Doom - and Tony pretended to interview them. We both liked Steve Jackson, the boy who took Renate's former tape operator job: he was blond and attractive.

Tony left after a few days to return to New York. I called him a few weeks later and told him I had some good news.

'I'm getting married,' I announced.

Tony burst out laughing. 'Oh yes? And with whom are you getting married? That lovely tape operator? 'Will you be Mrs. Jackson?'

'No,' I replied. 'I'm going to marry Renate.'

Tony couldn't stop giggling.

'I'm serious, Tony,' I said. Renate has accepted my marriage proposal. The wedding is in four days. 'Can you book a flight to Sydney?'
The laughter on the other end of the phone abruptly came to a halt.

I'd arrived in Montserrat with my most recent boyfriend, Gary, an Australian I'd met in Melbourne a few years before. It was just another in a long line of young, blond, attractive hostage situations. I'd fallen in love with him, then proceeded to make both of our lives miserable. I had persuaded him to leave Australia and come live with me at Woodside, lavished him with presents, then became bored and urged Bob Halley to send him back. We'd get in touch again, I'd change my mind and invite him back to Woodside, then get bored and instruct Bob to book him a flight back to Brisbane. It was doing nothing except going round and round in circles. Why was it always this way? I knew I was to blame, but I was too dumb to figure out what I was doing wrong. Cocaine is similar to this. It makes you selfish and narcissistic since everything revolves around what you desire. It also causes you to be absolutely unstable, so you have no idea what you want. That's a very bleak mix for life in general, but it's lethal in any form of personal relationship. I can't recommend cocaine highly enough if you want to live in a depressed world of never-ending, delusional nonsense.

Back in Montserrat, though, the tunes poured thick and fast, and there was one more positive aspect of the recording sessions. I began to spend an increasing amount of time with Renate. I had a great time with her. She was intelligent, polite, and quite witty - she had a very British sense of humor. She was stunning, but she didn't seem to notice, always dressed casually in jeans and a T-shirt. She appeared isolated and lonely, a woman in a man's world, and that was precisely how I felt on the inside. We got along so well that I became more interested in chatting to her than in spending time with Gary. I'd make up reasons for us to hang out, inviting her back to the studio after supper under the guise of listening to the day's work, simply so we could talk. I caught myself casually pondering on more than one occasion that she was everything I would have wanted a woman to be if I were straight.

That was obviously a big if. In fact, it was such a massive if that it would have needed a staggering amount of complex, irrational reasoning to see it as anything other than absolutely insurmountable. Fortunately, complicated, irrational thinking was my strong suit back then, and I soon got to work. What if the issue with my relationships wasn't my fault? What if it had something to do with the fact that they were gay relationships? What if a relationship with a woman might make me happy in ways that previous relationships with men had not? What if the fact that I appreciated Renate's presence so much wasn't a kind of affectionate link between two lonely individuals thousands of miles away, but rather a sudden and unexpected stirring of heterosexual desire? What if I'd spent the previous fourteen years sleeping with guys because I hadn't found the proper woman? What if I now had it?

The more I thought about it, the more certain I became that it was real. It was a complicated line of reasoning that didn't stand up to careful scrutiny, or perhaps any scrutiny at all. But, as difficult as it was, it was preferable than confronting the underlying issue.

When I initially mentioned getting married, we were both inebriated in a place called the Chicken Shack. Renate, understandably, brushed it off as a joke. There had been no trace of romance between us up to that moment, not even a kiss. If I had any sense, I would have stopped there. But at this point, I was completely certain that this was the right thing to do. It was just what I wanted; it was going to fix all of my problems at once. In my own way, I was smitten: with the prospect of marriage, with Renate's company. When she wasn't there, I missed her. It felt eerily similar to falling in love.

So, when the entire entourage relocated from Montserrat to Sydney - me and the band to prepare for an Australian tour, Renate and Chris Thomas to mix the album - I took her out to an Indian restaurant for supper and asked her again. I adored her and desired to be with her for the rest of my life. We should tie the knot. Here in Australia, we should do it straight now. It was February 10, 1984, and we could marry on Valentine's Day. This is something I could do. It sounded insane, but it sounded romantic. Renate agreed.

We went back to our hotel, the Sebel Townhouse, gathered everyone in the bar, and shouted the news: 'Hey! 'Can you believe it?' It was met with a sea of shocked expressions, not least Gary's, who'd accompanied us to Australia and now found himself my ex-boyfriend once more. I chose John Reid and Bernie as my best men. The ensuing celebration shattered the record for the most money spent in a single night at the pub. Everyone was definitely in need of a heavy drink to absorb what had just occurred.

The days that followed were a haze. There was a reception to plan, a church to locate, and issues in obtaining a marriage license on short notice to overcome. I called Renate's father and asked for her hand in marriage. He was a businessman from Munich, and he was quite nice, given that he had just learned, out of nowhere, that his daughter was marrying a famously homosexual rock singer in four days. I informed my mother and Derf. They appeared to be as amused as everyone else, though they didn't try to stop me. It was pointless. At that point in my life, everything I said was final, and anyone who dared to dispute me was yelled at and inanimate items were hurled and broken. It's nothing to be proud of, but it's how things were. Instead, some of my pals tried to figure out what I was up to, frequently concluding that I was getting married because I'd decided I wanted children. I let them believe it because, in all honesty, it was a more believable explanation than the reality, but it couldn't have been further from my mind. I was over forty years old and more than capable of acting like a child on my own; the last thing I needed was an actual youngster thrown into the mix. Renate may have changed her mind if she'd had more time to think about it. But I doubt she would have done so.

The wedding was as simple as any wedding can be when one of the groom's best men is his previous girlfriend, to whom he lost his virginity. Renate donned a white lace gown and a gold and diamond pendant I'd given her as a wedding present. She was wearing flowers in her hair. She was stunning. My parents and Renate were not present, but several friends flew in, including Tony King and Janet Street-Porter. Toni, Bernie's new wife, was one of the bridesmaids. Rod Stewart was unable to attend, but his manager Billy Gaff sent a telegram: 'You may still be standing, dear,' it read, 'but the rest of us are on the fucking floor.'

We were besieged by fans and paparazzi on the church steps. People cheered and applauded. Someone fired up their stereo and played 'Kiss The Bride' from Too Low for Zero, which, despite its title, is perhaps the least acceptable song to play at a wedding this side of Tammy Wynette's 'D.I.V.O.R.C.E.'. A voice burst out, delivering congratulations in a very Australian fashion, over the strains of me singing 'Don't say "I do" - say "bye-bye." 'You finally accomplished it!' exclaimed the voice. 'Well done, you old jerk!'

The event was held at the Sebel and was as quiet and subdued as you might expect. White roses had been sent in from our honeymoon destination of New Zealand. There was lobster, quail, and deer loin, as well as vintage Château Margaux and Puligny-Montrachet wines, a five-tier wedding cake, and a string quartet. There were speeches and telegram readings, as was customary. As was customary, John Reid later assaulted someone, this time a Sun reporter whose coverage of the wedding he'd taken issue with.

The group afterwards moved up to my hotel suite, where there was even more booze and drugs. At this point, I should mention that Renate and I decided when we divorced not to disclose the private facts of our marriage in public. And I will respect that. To be honest, I don't have anything negative to say about Renate. Neither does anyone else who has met her. My mother was the only person who was cold to her, and it had nothing to do with Renate or her personality. I think my mother despised the concept of the apron strings being severed, of someone else taking the lead in my life.

It was my fault. I could still shut myself away, alone, with a stash of cocaine whenever I wanted. Everyone at Woodside had grown accustomed to my drug use and accepted it as a way of life. Gladys, one of the cleaners, took me aside one day and quietly said, 'I found your special white medicine on the floor when cleaning your room, so I put it in your bedside drawer,' and there it was, still on the mirror where I'd been slicing out lines. I suppose I assumed that being in a committed relationship would put an end to that kind of behavior. But it didn't work that way. That was not the case at all.

CHAPTER 10

It's important to note that Renate did not simply marry a gay drug addict. That alone would have been disastrous. But she married a gay drug addict whose life was about to go wild in ways he never imagined. I had a number of years that were rather typical by my standards. Watford lost the FA Cup final, which I witnessed. Ice on Fire is another CD I created. It was the first time Gus Dudgeon and I had worked together since the mid-1970s. In the United Kingdom, the huge hit was 'Nikita,' a love ballad to a Russian named Bernie, whether by mistake or malice. I built up a backstage area with fake grass and a BBQ for other performers to visit during Live Aid. Freddie Mercury came, still buzzing after Queen's show-stealing performance, and gave me a very Freddie-esque assessment of the headgear I'd selected to perform in: 'Darling! What the fuck did you have on your head? You resembled the Queen Mother!'I visited Wham!'s farewell show at Wembley Stadium in the summer of 1986, where I marked George Michael's monumental choice to abandon the frivolity of pop music and declare himself a mature singer-songwriter by arriving in a Reliant Robin dressed as Ronald McDonald. George wanted to sing 'Candle In The Wind' to demonstrate his newfound seriousness, but I surprised him with a pub piano version of 'When I'm Sixty-Four' instead.

Later that year, however, things began to go severely off-piste for me. It all started when I discovered something was wrong with my voice while on tour in America. It was strange. I was performing at Madison Square Garden, and while I could sing well, I couldn't talk louder than a whisper offstage. I determined that the best line of action would be to rest my voice in between gigs and make a joke about it. I obtained a Harpo Marx wig and a raincoat and began wearing them backstage while blasting a horn instead of speaking.

But when we arrived in Australia, my voice deteriorated. My new album was released just as we arrived. It was called

Leather Jackets, and it was as near to a complete failure as anything I'd ever released. I had always tried to be strict about avoiding using drugs in the studio, but that rule was utterly broken this time. The coke had exactly the expected effect on my creative judgment. I slapped whatever I wanted on leather jackets. 'Heartache All Over The World' was supposed to be the major single, a tune so light you could raise it up with your little finger. There were old outtakes, songs that weren't good enough for previous albums but that, after a couple of lines, I recognized as forgotten gems that the audience wanted to hear right away. I co-wrote a dreadful song with Cher called 'Don't Trust That Woman,' the words of which were unbelievable: 'you can rear-end her, oooh, it'll send her'. You could tell how I felt about it by the fact that I refused to put my name to it, instead crediting Cher and my old made-up studio character Lady Choc Ice. Of course, if you despise a song so much that you refuse to admit you composed it, it's generally a bad idea to record and release it, but I was so drunk that rationality was entirely lost on me.

It wasn't all bad: 'Hoop Of Fire' was very classy, especially in comparison to the company it was keeping, and a ballad called 'I Fall Apart' was another example of Bernie's incredible ability to put words in my mouth that were so perfectly represented my personal predicament that I thought I wrote them myself. However, there was no getting past the reality that Leather Jackets had four legs, a tail, and barked whenever a postman arrived at the door.

So I wanted the following tour to be something unique, something so big and fantastic that it would erase the memory of the album that came before it. I told Bob Mackie to go as crazy as he liked on the costume front, which is how I ended up onstage in Australia variously wearing a giant pink Mohican wig with leopard skin sides, another wig based on the explosive hairstyle made famous by Tina Turner in the eighties, and an outfit that made me look like Mozart had joined a glam rock band - a white sequined suit teamed with an eighteenth-century powdered wig, white make-up and a fake beauty spot. The Mozart costume was meant to be a witty reference to the second half of the event, in which I was performing with the Melbourne Symphony Orchestra. If somebody thought I was being arrogant, a rock star acting like a great classical composer, it was because I had established the connection first.

Nobody had ever tried going on tour with an orchestra and playing rock and roll before. It meant that, for the first time, I could perform the songs from my early albums live in their entirety, replete with Paul Buckmaster's lovely arrangements. Gus Dudgeon flew in to supervise the sound. We individually mic'd up every instrument in the orchestra, which no one had ever done before, and the impact was breathtaking: when the violins came in on 'Madman Across The Water,' it took the top of your head off. They produced a lot of noise - with the bass cellos and double basses in full flight, I could feel the stage trembling beneath me - which was fortunate because the main attraction was struggling to make any noise at all.

It was a strange and disconcerting sensation for a singer: everytime I opened my mouth onstage, I had no idea what was going to happen. I used to sound fine at times. Other times, I'd rasp and croak and wheeze my way through the notes. For some reason, it appeared to affect me more when I spoke rather than sang. I'd try to introduce a song, and nothing would come out at all. It was as if someone had answered a long-held critic's cry by discovering a means to turn me off.

Something was obviously incorrect. For a while, I relied on the old sore throat cure that Leon Russell had given me backstage at the Troubadour in 1970: gargling with honey, cider vinegar, and hot water. It made no difference at all. After a show in Sydney in which I was racked by coughing fits and spat up gunk in a variety of colors so lurid that Bob Mackie's costumes looked sober in comparison, sanity prevailed and I agreed to see an ear, nose, and throat specialist named Dr John Tonkin.

He inspected my larynx and informed me that I had vocal cord cysts. He didn't know whether they were malignant or benign at this point. If they were cancerous, my larynx would have to be removed, and I would never be able to speak or sing again. He wouldn't know for sure unless he did a biopsy. Then he grimaced and glanced at me. 'You do smoke marijuana, don't you?' he explained.

I went completely still. I'd only started smoking spliffs to dull the effects of all the cocaine I was using, but I quickly learned that I liked them on their own. It was a different kind of drug than coke and liquor, and I thought it made me more friendly, despite mounting evidence that they were making my behavior as antisocial as it could be.

However, marijuana did not make me want to go out and party or stay up all night. It simply made me chuckle while also making music sound wonderful. I used to get stoned and listen to Kraftwerk because their music was so simple, repetitive, and hypnotic. Of course, being me, I couldn't just smoke a joint and listen to Trans-Europe Express or The Man Machine every now and again. I got as enthusiastic about marijuana as I was about everything else. By the time of the Australian tour, one member of the road crew was almost entirely dedicated to rolling joints. He accompanied us everywhere we went, carrying a shoebox full of the items.

When Dr Tonkin asked if I smoked marijuana, I chose to ignore the finer points of the spliff-roller on staff. 'A little,' I mumbled. Dr Tonkin rolled his eyes, stating firmly, "I believe you mean "a lot," and urged me to stop. It could have caused the cysts directly, and even if it didn't, it wasn't helping. I never smoked another one after that. At the time, I wasn't exactly a master of self-control when it came to alcohol and drugs. I lost count of the number of times I told myself 'never again' while suffering from a bad hangover, only to forget I'd said it after the hangover passed. I would sometimes stick to my decision for months, but I always ended up turning back.

There's nothing like being absolutely afraid to help you quit something, and nothing like the term 'cancer' to make you absolutely terrified. Dr Tonkin also advised me to cancel the rest of my Australian tour, but I declined because there was still a week of gigs in Sydney left. For one thing, canceling would have been prohibitively expensive - there were over a hundred musicians participating, and we were meant to be filming and recording the gigs for a live CD. But, more significantly, if I was never going to sing again, I wanted to postpone the day I stopped for as long as possible.

When I told the band and crew what had transpired, I resolved to maintain the same stoic, show-must-go-on demeanor. Instead, I walked into the Sebel Townhouse's bar - yeah, there again - and croaked, 'They think I've got throat cancer,' before breaking down in tears. I couldn't help myself. I was terrified. Even if the operation was successful and the biopsy proved negative, I might be done as a singer - Julie Andrews had come out of a procedure to remove a cyst on her vocal cords with her voice entirely damaged.

We completed the tour. Sick and afraid, I stormed out of the final event at the Sydney Entertainment Centre, which was being broadcast live on television, just minutes before it began. As I rushed out of the venue, I could hear the orchestra playing the overture. I passed Phil Collins as he was walking in: he was grabbing his seat at the last minute to avoid being disturbed by people. He was taken aback to find the star attraction walking in the opposite direction.

'Oh, hey, Elton... where are you going?'

'Home!' I yelled, not pausing.

I had a history of storming out of venues when I was supposed to be onstage. I had stormed out of a Christmas show at the Hammersmith Odeon a few years before, between the end of the set and the encore. My automobile went as far as the Hogarth Roundabout before I decided to return: it's approximately ten minutes away from the event, but as we turned the car around, we learned the journey back would take much longer because it entailed navigating around a one-way system. Surprisingly, the audience was still present when I returned.

I didn't even make it to the car this time before I changed my mind. It ended up being the best show of all time. I got through it because I was afraid I'd never be able to sing again. 'Don't Let The Sun Go Down On Me' was a standout. My voice was scratchy and raspy, but I don't think I've ever done that song better: it was usually quite show-stopping with the orchestra roaring away, but every lyric seemed to have a new meaning, a different focus that night.

After the tour, I traveled to an Australian hospital and underwent the operation. Everything went perfectly. There was no cancer present. The cysts were extracted. After I recovered, I discovered that it had permanently altered my voice, but I liked how it sounded. I couldn't sing falsetto anymore, but there was something about the tone that I enjoyed. It felt more mature and powerful; it had a new type of strength. I couldn't believe my good fortune. I thought 1987 had gotten off to a horrible start, but now there was only one way to go: up. I couldn't have been more mistaken.

The first headline appeared in the Sun in February 1987: ELTON IN VICE BOYS SCANDAL. But, in retrospect, it was only a matter of time before the Sun came for me: I was homosexual, successful, and opinionated, which made me fair meat for a vendetta in the Sun's eyes. Its editor at the time was Kelvin MacKenzie, a man so toxic that the Environmental Agency should have quarantined him. The Sun wasn't so much a newspaper under his supervision as it was a vigorous daily endeavor to see how much racism, misogyny, xenophobia, and, especially, homophobia could be squeezed into sixty-four tabloid pages. It's difficult to convey the ugliness of the Sun in the 1980s to anyone who doesn't remember it. It treated everyone equally, whether they were famous or not. It discovered a legal gap that allowed it to identify rape victims even though no one had been arrested for the act. When a TV actor named Jeremy Brett was dying of heart disease, the Sun sent journalists to confront him in hospital and ask him if he had AIDS, a disease it also told its readers they couldn't contract through straight sex.

I read the narrative about me with my mouth agape. The irony was that there were dozens of men all over the world who could have potentially sold a sex and drugs exposé on me: ex-boyfriends, irritated one-night stands. The Sun, on the other hand, had managed to uncover someone I'd never met, who'd sold them a tale about an orgy somewhere I'd never visited - the home of Rod Stewart's manager Billy Gaff.

To be fair, they couldn't have gotten a narrative like this if they had discovered someone who had truly slept with me. It wasn't so much that it was entirely contrived as it was. It was that it appeared to be wholly made up by a raging maniac. I had supposedly prepared for the orgy by wearing a pair of "skimpy leather shorts." Shorts made of leather? I've dressed in some absurd old gear, but I've never, ever prepared for a night of passion by squeezing into a pair of leather shorts - you know, I'm trying to convince someone to sleep with me, not take one look and go screaming in the opposite direction. In addition, I was allegedly 'twirling a sex aid' between my fingers and 'looked like Cleopatra'. Cleopatra, of course: last monarch of the Ptolemaic kingdom, lover of Julius Caesar and Mark Antony, and history's most famed dildo-twirler and leather shorts wearer.

On one level, it was hilarious, but on another, it wasn't. It implied that the rent boys engaged were underage. People believe a falsehood is true if it is repeated frequently enough, especially if it is printed. What if people truly believed it? What on earth was I expected to do? My mother and Derf were planning to read it, as well as my grandma. Oh, Auntie Win: she worked in a newsstand. I imagined her, scared, accepting delivery of that morning's Sun and selling copies to people who knew who her nephew was and were laughing at her.

My first thought was to lock myself away in Woodside and drink vodka martinis. Then I received a call from Mick Jagger. He'd heard the story and wanted to share his thoughts. He advised me not to sue them under any circumstances. When he filed a writ against the News of the World after they falsely claimed he bragged to an undercover reporter about his drug use in the 1960s, they reacted by spying on him and then setting up the famous drug bust at Redlands: he and Keith Richards were imprisoned before their sentences were overturned due to public outrage. Surprisingly, the conversation had the opposite effect that Mick planned. As I explained to Mick, I didn't care what the press thought about me. I'd occasionally get upset about a negative review or a harsh remark, but that's what happens when you put yourself out there. You just have to put up with it and move on. But why should I allow them to get away with lying about me?

I could demonstrate that what they were claiming was false. I had been in New York, eating lunch with Tony King and debating the finer points of my Tina Turner wig with Bob Mackie on the date I was meant to be at Billy Gaff's house, dressed up like an extra in a Village People film and swinging a dildo around like a majorette. Hotel bills, restaurant receipts, and aircraft tickets proved it. I had the financial means to take them to court. They're fucked. I planned to sue.

After I issued the first writ, the Sun continued to print stories that were packed with more and more lies; each time one emerged, I issued another libel writ against them. Some of the lies were very revolting - they claimed I'd paid rent boys to pee on them - while others were simply odd. The only problem with this story was that I didn't own any Rottweiler dogs, only two German shepherds, both of whom nearly deafened the RSPCA when they came down to check on their wellbeing when they came down to check on their welfare.

Even when it became clear that the public did not want to know, The Sun persisted. What they were doing clearly had no effect on my popularity - the stories were widely publicized - but the live album we'd recorded on the Australian tour was a huge hit, going platinum in America, and the version of 'Candle In The Wind' released as a single unexpectedly went Top Ten on both sides of the Atlantic. They were having an effect on the Sun itself. The newspaper's sales dropped every time they ran an article about me on the main page. I'm not sure if people recognized it was all false, if they viewed it as a vendetta against me and thought it was unfair, or if they were just tired of hearing about it.

Knowing they were in big trouble, the Sun became increasingly desperate to get something on me, anything that would genuinely stick. Everywhere I went, I was being followed. The penthouse apartment of the Century Plaza in Los Angeles was bugged when I slept there. Our solicitors had informed us that it might be - it was the suite where President Reagan often stayed - so we had the place swept by the FBI. Someone was trying to scare me into calling the lawyers off. They promised £500 to any rent boy who claimed to have slept with me. Not unexpectedly, they were swamped with applicants, but they were all so plainly made up that even the Sun was hesitant to use them.

It's worth emphasizing that Renate didn't just marry a gay drug addict. That would have been terrible on its own. But she married a gay drug addict whose life was set to take unexpected turns. By my standards, I experienced a lot of years that were fairly typical. Watford were defeated in the FA Cup final, which I witnessed. Another CD I made called Ice on Fire. It was Gus Dudgeon and I's first collaboration since the mid-1970s. 'Nikita,' a love ballad to a Russian named Bernie, was a great hit in the United Kingdom, whether by accident or on purpose. During Live Aid, I set up a backstage area with fake grass and a BBQ for other performers to visit. Freddie Mercury arrived, still buzzing from Queen's show-stealing performance, and offered me a very Freddie-esque evaluation of the headwear I'd chosen to perform in: 'Darling! What in the world were you thinking? You reminded me of the Queen Mother!'I went to Wham!'s farewell concert at Wembley Stadium in the summer of 1986, where I arrived in a Reliant Robin dressed as Ronald McDonald to commemorate George Michael's significant decision to renounce the frivolity of pop music and declare himself a mature singer-songwriter. George had planned to sing 'Candle In The Wind' to show off his newfound seriousness, but I surprised him with a bar piano rendition of 'When I'm Sixty-Four' instead.

However, after that year, things began to go seriously off-piste for me. It all began when I found a problem with my voice while on tour in America. It was peculiar. I was onstage at Madison Square Garden, and while I could sing beautifully, I couldn't speak louder than a whisper. I decided that resting my voice in between concerts and making a joke about it would be the best course of action. I got a Harpo Marx wig and a raincoat and started wearing them backstage while blasting horns instead of speaking.

My voice weakened after we came to Australia. My new album was just released when we arrived. It was called Leather Jackets, and it was as close to a flop as anything I'd ever put out. I had always attempted to avoid using drugs in the studio, but that rule was completely shattered this time. The coke had the desired effect on my creative thinking. On leather coats, I slapped whatever I wanted. The major hit was going to be 'Heartache All Over The World,' a tune so light you could raise it with your little finger. There were old outtakes, songs that weren't good enough for earlier albums but that I recognized as forgotten jewels that the audience wanted to hear straight immediately after a few lines. I co-wrote a terrible song with Cher called 'Don't Trust That Woman,' the lyrics of which were incredible: 'you can rear-end her, oooh, it'll send her'. The fact that I refused to put my name to it, instead crediting Cher and my old made-up studio character Lady Choc Ice, said a lot about how I felt about it. Of course, recording and releasing a song that you dislike so much that you refuse to admit you wrote it is normally a horrible idea, but I was so inebriated that logic was completely lost on me.

'Hoop Of Fire' was very classy, especially in comparison to the company it was keeping, and a ballad called 'I Fall Apart' was another example of Bernie's incredible ability to put words in my mouth that so perfectly represented my personal predicament that I thought I wrote them myself. However, it was impossible to ignore the fact that Leather Jackets had four legs, a tail, and barked whenever a postman knocked on the door.

So I wanted the next tour to be something special, something so large and spectacular that it would erase the memory of the previous record. I told Bob Mackie to go as crazy as he liked on the costume front, which is how I ended up onstage in Australia variously wearing a giant pink Mohican wig with leopard skin sides, another wig based on the explosive hairstyle made famous by Tina Turner in the eighties, and an outfit that made me look like Mozart had joined a glam rock band - a white sequined suit teamed with an eighteenth-century powdered wig, white make-up and a fake beauty spot. The Mozart costume was intended to be a satirical reference to the event's second half, in which I performed with the Melbourne Symphony Orchestra. If someone thought I was being arrogant, like a rock star impersonating a famous classical composer, it was because I had made the connection first.

Nobody had ever attempted to go on tour with an orchestra and play rock & roll. It meant that I could finally perform the songs from my early albums live, complete with Paul Buckmaster's exquisite arrangements, for the first time. Gus Dudgeon flew in to monitor the sound. We mic'd up every instrument in the orchestra individually, which had never been done before, and the result was breathtaking: when the violins came in on 'Madman Across The Water,' it took the top of your head off. They made a lot of noise - with the bass cellos and double basses flying about, I could feel the stage quivering beneath me - which was fortunate because the main attraction struggled to make any noise at all.

It was a bizarre and unsettling sensation for a singer: I had no idea what would happen when I opened my mouth onstage. I used to sound rather good at times. Occasionally, I'd rasp, croak, and wheeze my way through the notes. For some reason, it seemed to have a greater impact on me when I spoke rather than sang. I'd try to start a song, but nothing would come out. It felt as if someone had discovered a way to switch me off in response to a long-held critic's cry.

Something was clearly wrong. For a time, I relied on an old sore throat remedy recommended by Leon Russell backstage at the Troubadour in 1970: gargling with honey, cider vinegar, and hot water. It didn't make any difference. After a performance in Sydney when I was plagued by coughing fits and spat up mucus in a rainbow of hues that made Bob Mackie's costumes look somber in comparison, logic triumphed and I consented to see an ear, nose, and throat specialist named Dr John Tonkin.

He examined my larynx and discovered that I had vocal cord cysts. At this stage, he had no idea whether they were cancerous or benign. My larynx would have to be removed if they were malignant, and I would never be able to speak or sing again. He wouldn't know for certain unless he performed a biopsy. 'You do smoke marijuana, don't you?' he asked, grimacing.' He elaborated.

I came to a complete halt. I'd only started smoking spliffs to counteract the effects of all the cocaine I was taking, but I quickly discovered that I like them on their own. It was a different kind of drug than coke and whiskey, and I believed it made me more friendly, despite accumulating evidence that it was making my behavior as antisocial as possible.

Marijuana, on the other hand, did not make me want to go out and party or stay up all night. It simply made me laugh while simultaneously making music sound fantastic. I used to get high and listen to Kraftwerk's music because it was so basic, repetitive, and hypnotic. Of course, I couldn't just smoke a joint and listen to Trans-Europe Express or The Man Machine now and then. I became as passionate about marijuana as I was about everything else. One member of the road crew was nearly totally committed to rolling joints by the time of the Australian tour. He went everywhere with us, carrying a shoebox full of the goods.

I chose to disregard the finer nuances of the spliff-roller on staff when Dr Tonkin asked if I smoked marijuana. 'A little,' I admitted. Dr Tonkin rolled his eyes, stating firmly, "I believe you mean "a lot," and urged me to stop. It could have caused the cysts directly, and even if it didn't, it wasn't helping. I never smoked another one after that. At the time, I wasn't exactly a master of self-control when it came to alcohol and drugs. I lost count of the number of times I told myself 'never again' while suffering from a bad hangover, only to forget I'd said it after the hangover passed. I would sometimes stick to my decision for months, but I always ended up turning back. There's nothing like being absolutely afraid to help you quit something, and nothing like the term 'cancer' to make you absolutely terrified. Dr Tonkin also advised me to cancel the rest of my Australian tour, but I declined because there was still a week of gigs in Sydney left. For one thing, canceling would have been prohibitively expensive - there were over a hundred musicians participating, and we were meant to be filming and recording the gigs for a live CD. But, more significantly, if I was never going to sing again, I wanted to postpone the day I stopped for as long as possible.

I resolved to maintain the same stoic, show-must-go-on demeanor when I told the band and crew what had happened, but instead I walked into the Sebel Townhouse's bar - yeah, there again - and croaked, 'They think I've got throat cancer,' before breaking down in tears. I couldn't help myself. I was terrified. Even if the operation was successful and the biopsy proved negative, I might be done as a singer

I stormed out of the final event at the Sydney Entertainment Centre, which was being broadcast live on television, just minutes before it began, sick and afraid. As I rushed out of the venue, I could hear the orchestra playing the overture. I passed Phil Collins as he was walking in: he was grabbing his seat at the last minute to avoid being disturbed by people, and he was taken aback to find the star attraction walking in the opposite direction.

'Oh, Elton, where are you going?'

I yelled, 'Home!' without pausing.

I had a history of storming out of venues when I was supposed to be onstage; I stormed out of a Christmas show at the Hammersmith Odeon a few years before, between the end of the set and the encore. My car got as far as the Hogarth Roundabout before I decided to return: it's about ten minutes away from the event, but as we turned the car around, we discovered the journey back would take much longer because it involved navigating around a one-way system.
My voice was scratchy and raspy, but I don't think I've ever done that song better: it was usually quite show-stopping with the orchestra roaring away, but every lyric seemed to have a new meaning, a different focus that night.

After the tour, I traveled to an Australian hospital for the operation, which went flawlessly. There was no cancer present, and the cysts were extracted. When I recovered, I discovered that it had permanently altered my voice, but I liked how it sounded. I couldn't sing falsetto anymore, but there was something about the tone that I liked. It felt more mature and powerful; it had a new type of strength.

The first headline appeared in the Sun in February 1987: ELTON IN VICE BOYS SCANDAL. But, in retrospect, it was only a matter of time before the Sun came for me: I was homosexual, successful, and opinionated, which made me fair meat for a vendetta in the Sun's eyes. Its editor at the time was Kelvin MacKenzie, a man so toxic that the Environmental Agency should have quarantined him. The Sun wasn't so much a newspaper under his supervision as it was a vigorous daily endeavor to see how much racism, misogyny, xenophobia, and, especially, homophobia could be squeezed into sixty-four tabloid pages. It's difficult to convey the ugliness of the Sun in the 1980s to anyone who doesn't remember it. It treated everyone equally, whether they were famous or not. It discovered a legal gap that allowed it to identify rape victims even though no one had been arrested for the act. When a TV actor named Jeremy Brett was dying of heart disease, the Sun sent journalists to confront him in hospital and ask him if he had AIDS, a disease it also told its readers they couldn't contract through straight sex.

The irony was that there were dozens of men all over the world who could have potentially sold a sex and drugs exposé on me: ex-boyfriends, irritated one-night stands. The Sun, on the other hand, had managed to uncover someone I'd never met, who'd sold them a story about an orgy somewhere I'd never visited - Rod Stewart's manager Billy Gaff's home.

To be fair, they couldn't have gotten a narrative like this if they had discovered someone who had truly slept with me. It wasn't so much that it was entirely contrived as it appeared to be wholly made up by a raging maniac. I had allegedly prepared for the orgy by wearing a pair of "skimpy leather shorts." Shorts made of leather? I've dressed in some absurd old gear, but I've never, ever prepared for.

On one level, it was hilarious, but on another, it wasn't. It implied that the rent boys engaged were underage. People believe a falsehood is true if it is repeated frequently enough, especially if it is printed. What was I supposed to do? My mother and Derf, as well as my grandma, were planning to read it. Oh, Auntie Win: she worked in a newsstand. I imagined her, scared, accepting delivery of that morning's Sun and selling copi

My first thought was to lock myself away in Woodside and drink vodka martinis, but then I got a call from Mick Jagger, who said he'd heard the story and wanted to share his thoughts, and he advised me not to sue them under any circumstances. When he filed a writ against the News of the World after they falsely claimed he bragged to an undercover reporter about his drug use in the 1960s, they reacted by spying on him and then setting

I had been in New York, eating lunch with Tony King and debating the finer points of my Tina Turner wig with Bob Mackie on the date I was supposed to be at Billy Gaff's house, dressed up like an extra in a Village People film and swinging a dildo around like a majorette. Hotel bills, restaurant receipts, and aircraft tickets proved it. I had the financial means to take them to court.

After I issued the first writ, the Sun continued to print stories that were packed with more and more lies; each time one emerged, I issued another libel writ against them. Some of the lies were very revolting - they claimed I'd paid rent boys to pee on them - while others were simply odd. The only problem with this story was that I didn't own any Rottweiler dogs, only two German shepherds, both of whom nearly deafened the RSPCA when they came down to check on their wellbeing when they came down to check on their welfare. Even when it became clear that the public did not want to know, The Sun persisted. What they were doing clearly had no effect on my popularity - the stories were widely publicized - but the live album we'd recorded on the Australian tour was a huge hit, going platinum in America, and the version of 'Candle In The Wind' released as a single unexpectedly went Top Ten on both sides of the Atlantic. They were having an effect on the Sun itself. The newspaper's sales dropped every time they ran an article about me on the main page. I'm not sure if people recognized it was all false, if they viewed it as a vendetta against me and thought it was unfair, or if they were just tired of hearing about it.

Knowing they were in big trouble, the Sun became increasingly desperate to get something on me, anything that would genuinely stick. Everywhere I went, I was being followed. The Century Plaza penthouse apartment in Los Angeles was bugged when I slept there. Our solicitors had informed us that it might be - it was the suite where President Reagan frequently stayed - so we had the place swept by the FBI.

The most they could do was get their hands on some stolen Polaroids from my house. They were maybe ten years old. One of them showed me doing a blow job on a guy. They were humiliatingly printed in the paper. I tried to console myself by remembering that I was the first artist in history to debut at the top of the US charts with two consecutive albums; the first artist in history to have seven consecutive American Number Ones; and the first artist in history to appear in a national newspaper giving someone a blow job. Furthermore, it appeared to be a sign of desperation on the part of the Sun. It's not exactly a Pulitzer Prize-winning story, gay man sucking penis. Furthermore, it was written in a way that I couldn't help but think revealed more about the journalist than it did about myself. Everything was 'disgusting' and 'secret perversion'. How boring does your sex life have to be for a blow job to be the pinnacle of unfathomable depravity?

It carried on for months and months, until I'd served seventeen libel writs on them. I'd want to tell you that I never wavered in my will to defeat them, but that wasn't the case. Some days I'd be fine, righteously enraged and ready to take them on. Other days, I'd be in tears, completely despondent, even humiliated. I hadn't done any of the things they claimed I had, but I knew I'd set myself up for something like this to happen. My drug use was a well-kept secret. I'd never been with anyone under the age of 18, but I'd also never been particularly picky about who I slept with. Someone I slept with a few years ago had helped themselves to a sapphire and diamond ring, a watch, and some cash before leaving. I was concerned about the court case, about having my private life scrutinized in public, and about what the Sun might do to malign me.

The thought of it prompted me to do what I'd always done when things became too much for me. I'd close myself away in my room, just like I used to when my parents fought, and try to ignore what was going on. The only difference was that I would now isolate myself with an abundance of liquor and drugs. I'd go three days without eating, then wake up hungry and stuff myself. I used to be afraid of gaining weight and would make myself sick by hopping up and down until I puked. I had developed bulimia, though I had no idea what it was at the time. What I did know was that certain foods made me vomit more quickly than others. Anything stodgy, like bread, was a challenge; you'd wind up hunched over the toilet, retching and retching. I understood you had to stick to soft foods, therefore my diet became strange. My notion of supper when I was binging was two jars of Sainsbury's cocktails and a pint of Häagen-Dazs peanut butter ice cream. I'd shovel it in and then bring it back up, sneaking away to make myself ill, hoping no one would see. Obviously, they did - you return smelling of puke and appearing as if you've been sobbing, because vomiting causes your eyes to water - but no one would dare to question me about it for fear of the consequences. Everything about it, from what I ate to how I behaved, seems terrible now, but it was second nature to me back then; it was simply how I was.

Even so, when things were really awful, I'd finally pull myself out of it, consoled by two thoughts. One was that, as far as the Sun was concerned, I was completely correct - if even one word of what they had stated had been accurate, I would never have dared to sue them. And the other was that, no matter how bad things felt, I knew of others in far worse situations than mine, people who'd found the strength to deal with issues that made mine seem minor. In a doctor's waiting room a few years previously, I read a Newsweek magazine piece about an American adolescent named Ryan White. His narrative scared and impressed me at the same time. He was an Indiana hemophiliac who had contracted AIDS from a blood transfusion, and AIDS was a condition that had been on my mind a lot. Neil Carter, John Reid's PA, was the first person I knew who died of it: he was diagnosed, then died three weeks later. Following that, the floodgates appeared to open. Whenever I spoke with Tony King in America, where the disease was more advanced, he'd tell me about a sick old buddy or a friend of a friend. Julie Leggatt, John Reid's secretary, was the first woman in the United Kingdom to be diagnosed with AIDS. Tim Lowe, my ex-boyfriend, had tested positive. Vance Buck, a nice blond guy from Virginia who liked Iggy Pop and whose portrait was on the inside cover of my record Jump Up!, directly below the lyrics to 'Blue Eyes,' the song Gary Osborne and I had written with him in mind, was another ex. It was horrific, but ask every homosexual man who grew up in the 1970s and 1980s, and they'll tell you a similar story: everyone lost someone, and everyone remembers the fearful atmosphere.

But it wasn't simply Ryan White's AIDS diagnosis. It was what had occurred to him as a result of catching the sickness. In his hometown of Kokomo, he had been shunned. The superintendent of his school district refused to allow him to attend classes for fear of infecting his classmates. He and his mother, Jeanne, became embroiled in a lengthy legal struggle. When the Indiana Department of Education ruled in his favor, a group of parents sought an injunction to prevent his return, and they were granted permission to organize an auction in the school gymnasium to gather funds to keep him out. When that failed, parents established an alternative school to keep their children away from him. He was insulted on the street, his school locker was spray-painted with the word FAG, and his belongings were stolen. His mother's car's tires were slashed, and a gunshot was fired through the family's front window. When the local newspaper backed him up, they received death threats. Even their Methodist church turned its back on them: no one in the congregation would shake Ryan's hand and say 'peace be with you' during the Easter service.

Ryan and his mother, Jeanne, acted with incredible decency, bravery, and compassion throughout. Christians who sincerely adhered to Christ's teachings forgiven those who made their already difficult lives even more difficult. They never condemned, only attempted to teach. Ryan rose to prominence as a bright, empathetic, and vocal advocate for individuals living with AIDS at a time when the disease was still portrayed as God's retribution on gays and drug addicts. When I found out he enjoyed my music and wanted to meet me, I contacted his mother and invited them to a show in Oakland, followed by a trip to Disneyland the next day. They were my absolute favorite. Jeanne reminded me of the women in my family, particularly my grandmother: she was working-class, straight-talking, hard-working, and friendly, but she had an indestructible core of steel. And Ryan appeared to be extraordinary. He was so sick that I had to push him in a wheelchair around Disneyland, but he was never furious, resentful, or cracked. He didn't want compassion or pity. Speaking with him, I got the impression that he didn't want to waste his time feeling sorry for himself or angry at others since he realized he didn't have much time left to enjoy - life was literally too short. He was just a sweet child trying to live as normal a life as he could. They were a wonderful family.

We stayed in touch after that. I'd call, send flowers, and inquire if there was anything I could do to assist. I saw Ryan whenever I could see him. When they couldn't take it any longer in Kokomo, I borrowed Jeanne the money she needed to relocate her family to Cicero, a little town outside of Indianapolis. I tried just giving her the money, but she insisted on it being a loan - she even drafted a contract and forced me to sign it. I remembered them every time I felt despondent about my condition. That was true bravery in the face of something absolutely horrifying. Stop wallowing in self-pity. Just get started.

Nonetheless, I maintained a modest public presence until Michael Parkinson became involved. I'd appeared on his chat show in the 1970s, when I ended up playing a pub piano as Michael Caine sang 'Maybe It's Because I'm A Londoner,' and we'd become friends. When the Sun's stories initially emerged, he contacted me and informed me he had a new chat show on ITV called One to One, with each episode devoted to a single guest. Why didn't I go to Leeds and be on it? I told him I wasn't sure, but he persisted.

'I'm not doing this for me,' he added, 'I'm doing this for you. I know you, and I know how the Sun is. You aren't saying anything publicly, and you should. People would presume you have something to hide if you don't say anything.'

So I ended up doing the show. You can see the effect these events were having on me if you look at the clips on YouTube. I was unshaven, dressed casually, and appeared haggard and pale. But everything went swimmingly. The majority of the audience was plainly on my side. I informed Michael about the Sun and how they had tried to pay the receptionist at my doctor's office to pass over my medical records.

'I believe they want to look at my sperm,' I explained. 'Which is odd, since if the stories they've been printing are true, they must have seen bucket loads of stuff.'

Not long after, the rent boy who made the first charges in the Sun told another tabloid that he'd made everything up and had never met me. 'I even don't like his music,' he added. The Sun absolutely folded on the morning of the first libel case, which was scheduled to go to court. They proposed a settlement of £1 million. It was the largest libel compensation in British history, but it was a good bargain for them because if the case had gone to court, they would have had to pay me millions. Rather than preparing to testify, I went to see Barry Humphries at the Theatre Royal, Drury Lane, and laughed myself silly at Dame Edna Everage. Following that, we waited in the West End for the first edition of the next morning's newspaper to appear at the newsstands. When the Sun was forced to apologize for making things up, it was known for publishing the correction as little as possible and burying it here. But I thought their apology had to be as big as the initial charges - a front-page banner headline: SORRY ELTON.

People afterwards said it was a watershed moment that revolutionized British newspapers, but I'm not convinced it changed the Sun all that much. Two years later, they published the most infamous set of lies in their history, about the behavior of Liverpool fans during the Hillsborough disaster, so it's not like double-checking their facts became a great priority overnight. What did alter was how the media treated me because they recognized I would sue them if they made up stories. I did it again a few years later, when the Daily Mirror reported that I'd been seen at a Hollywood party telling guests I'd discovered a fantastic new diet, then chewing food and spitting it out instead of swallowing it: ELTON'S DIET OF DEATH. I hadn't even been to America yet. I received £850,000 and donated it to charity. The money was secondary. The goal was to make one thing abundantly obvious. You are free to say whatever you want about me. If you think I'm a talentless, bald old poof, you're welcome to say so. I might think you're a jerk for saying it, but if it were illegal to express strong feelings about individuals, I'd be in jail right now. But you cannot lie about me. Otherwise, I'll see you in court.

Renate and I divorced in the spring of 1988. Our marriage had lasted four years. It was the correct thing to do, but it felt terrible. I'd crushed someone's heart that I adored and who loved me unreservedly, someone I couldn't fault in any way. She could have taken me to the cleaners and I wouldn't have blamed her: everything that had gone wrong had been all my fault. Renate, on the other hand, was too stately and decent for that. Despite all of the suffering, there was no animosity. For years after that, whenever something bad occurred to me, the press would show up at her house, expecting her to spill the beans, and she never, ever did: she simply told them to leave her alone.

After we divorced, I saw her once. She'd left Woodside for a lovely cottage in a little community. Despite everything that had happened, there was still a genuine affection there. I invited her to Woodside when I had children because I wanted her to meet them; I wanted to see her; I wanted her to be a part of our life and us to be a part of hers in some manner. But she refused, and I didn't press the subject. I have to respect her feelings.

CHAPTER 11

It was the state of the squash court that made me realize my collecting habit had gotten a little out of hand. When I initially moved in, one of the things I liked about Woodside was the squash court. Anyone who came over would be challenged to a game. But no one had played squash at Woodside in a long time since no one could get inside the court. The place was crammed with packing cases, and the packing cases were crammed with items I'd bought on tour, on vacation, at auctions, and so on. I hadn't been able to unpack anything because there was practically no more room in the house for anything else. Paintings, posters, gold and platinum discs, and framed prizes occupied every inch of wall space. My record collection was strewn throughout the place. I had a maze-like room for it, with corridor after corridor of floor-to-ceiling shelving housing everything I'd bought since I was a kid: I still had the 78s I'd spent my pocket money on in Siever's in Pinner, with 'Reg Dwight' written in ink on the labels and photos of the artists Sellotaped to the sleeves. But I'd outgrown the space by purchasing someone else's record collection as well. Bernie Andrews, a BBC radio producer who had worked on Saturday Club and with John Peel, owned every single released in the United Kingdom between 1958 and 1975, thousands and thousands of them. Of course, a lot of them were terrible: even in pop's most spectacular years, the good overwhelmed the bad. However, it appealed to my compulsive collector's attitude. Having every single released in the United Kingdom! It seemed like a crazy childhood wish had come true.

I might have been able to cope if I had only collected records, but I didn't. I am a collector of everything: art, antiques, clothing, chairs, jewelry, and glassware. Beautiful art deco vases and Gallé and Tiffany table lamps stood on the floor since there was no place on any tables - an astonishing situation given how much furniture I'd managed to stuff into every room. Walking around the house felt like I was taking part in the most costly obstacle course in the world. You could shatter something worth thousands of pounds if you put your foot wrong or turn around too quickly, which I can assure you is quite easy to do if you spend a big portion of your time drunk and on drugs. It didn't create a really relaxing living atmosphere. I'd have folks over and spent half of my time warning them to be careful or monitor what they were doing. I'd periodically poke my head around the squash court door - there was just about enough room if you breathed in - and feel strangely despondent. Owning stuff had always made me happy since I was a child, but now it just made me feel overwhelmed. What was I going to do with everything?

I devised a radical solution a few months after Renate and I divorced. I intended to sell it. It's all there. Every artwork, every memento, every piece of furniture, every object d'art. All the clothes, jewelry, spectacles, and other presents that fans had sent me. Except for the albums, everything in the house is new. I contacted Sotheby's, who had recently organized a massive posthumous sale of Andy Warhol's belongings, and told them I wanted to auction the entire collection. They dispatched experts to Woodside to investigate. The experts looked faint as they walked away. I couldn't tell whether they were taken aback by the sheer volume of items I was selling - one of them told me, quietly, that I had the world's greatest private collection of Carlo Bugatti furniture - or by the sheer hideousness of some of it. I liked to think I had a decent eye for art and furnishings, but I also had a high tolerance for flashy kitsch. Things in my house made my previous stage clothes look like the epitome of subtle good taste. A admirer had brought me a model of a bonobo gorilla dressed in an Edwardian gown, along with a note explaining that it was a sculpture illustrating the futility of war. The volume and tuning controls were situated on her tits, and the radio was shaped like a doll wearing a see-through negligee. A pair of brass bath taps were affixed to big Perspex testicles.

I decided to keep some original Goon Show scripts that I'd bought at an auction, as well as four paintings: two Magrittes, one Francis Bacon portrait of his lover George Dyer that people had told me I was crazy to spend £30,000 on back in 1973, and The Guardian Readers, the Patrick Procktor painting that had appeared on the cover of Blue Moves. Everything else is up for grabs.

Before you get the incorrect impression, I should clarify that I had no intention of living a more simple and meaningful life, free of the shackles of consumerism and burdened by material possessions. If anyone thought so, they were quickly disabused when I went to Sotheby's for a meeting regarding the next auction and instead ended up buying two paintings by Russian avant-garde painters Igor and Svetlana Kopystiansky. It was more that I desired a fresh start. I wanted to extensively repaint and remodel Woodside. I didn't want to live in a lunatic pop star's mansion any longer; I needed somewhere to call home.

Sotheby's spent three days merely transporting everything from Woodside to their London warehouse. There was so much to sell that four different auctions were required. One was for stage costumes and memorabilia, another for jewelry, another for art deco and art nouveau, and another for 'various collections,' which contained everything from Warhol silkscreens to luggage to sporrans - I looked to have bought two of those.

I used a shot of some of the lots for the cover of my new album, Reg Strikes Back: it seemed appropriate following the events of 1987. Before the auction, Sotheby's staged an exhibition. They only displayed a fifth of the items for sale, but the Victoria and Albert Museum was packed. Surprisingly, former Prime Minister Edward Heath came to look at it: perhaps he was looking for a pair of bath taps with Perspex testicles attached. The auctions were a resounding success. To deal with the masses, they had to put up crash barriers outside. Paintings sold for twice the expected price.

Things I expected fans to buy just a few pounds went for thousands. Everything was gone, including the bonobo gorilla symbolizing the folly of war, the sporrans, and the doll-in-a-negligee radio. They even auctioned the banners that were displayed outside Sotheby's to promote the auction.

I did not attend. The day the removal vans arrived, I left Woodside. I didn't return to the residence for another two years. I didn't realize it at the time, but by the time I returned, my life would have changed much more than my home.

While the house was being evacuated, I decided to go to London. I initially slept in a hotel, the Inn On The Park, which was the setting for the famous story of me calling the Rocket office and demanding that they do something about the wind outside that was keeping me awake. This is obviously the ideal time to clarify unequivocally that this story is a complete urban legend, that I was never insane enough to request that my record business do something about the weather, that I was merely disturbed by the wind and wanted to change rooms to somewhere quieter. I'm afraid I can't tell you since the story is entirely accurate. I was insane and delusional enough to call Rocket's international manager, Robert Key, and ask him to do something about the wind outside my hotel room. I was determined not to move rooms. It was 11 a.m., I'd been awake all night, and there were drugs all over the place: the last thing I wanted was the hotel personnel rushing in to assist me in moving to a different level. I rarely described the scenario to Robert. To his credit, he gave my plea very little consideration. I could hear Robert on the other end of the phone, with his hand over the receiver, telling the others of the office, 'Oh God, she's finally lost it.' Then he talked to me again. 'Are you fucking insane, Elton? Now put the phone down and go back to bed.'

I began renting a property in west London, although I spent the majority of my time on tour or in America. I'd fallen in love with an Atlanta resident named Hugh Williams. But I also ended up in Indianapolis. Ryan White had been happier since relocating to Cicero, but nothing could stop his condition from progressing. His mother Jeanne called me in the spring of 1990 to tell me that he had been transported to Riley Hospital for Children with a severe respiratory infection. He was on artificial life support. I took off right away. I attempted to be useful around the hospital for the next week while Ryan went in and out of consciousness. I didn't know what else I could do to assist. I cleaned up the space. I went to get sandwiches and ice cream. I decorated vases with flowers and purchased stuffed animals for the other children on the unit. I pretended to be Jeanne's secretary, answering phones and completing the work that I had engaged Bob Halley to do for me. Ryan had become a celebrity after becoming a visible champion for AIDS patients. When word came out that he was dying, Jeanne was inundated with individuals wanting to offer their support, which was too much for her to handle. When Michael Jackson called, I held the phone up to Ryan's ear. Ryan had no choice but to listen. He was too feeble to respond.

I would think of Jeanne and her daughter Andrea when I returned to my hotel. They were seeing Ryan's slow and agonizing death. They had asked for a miracle, but it never arrived. They had every right to be irritated and bitter. But they didn't think so. They were stoic, forgiving, patient, and compassionate. Even when things were bad, I like being around them, but they made me feel ashamed of myself in ways I'd never felt before. I wasted half my life being angry and resentful over little matters. I was the type of guy who would call people and yell at them because the weather outside my Park Lane hotel didn't suit me. Whatever else was wrong with my childhood, I hadn't been raised to act that way. What the fuck had happened to me? I'd always been able to rationalize my behavior to myself or make a joke about it, but now I couldn't: real life had infiltrated my famous bubble.

Because they heard I was in town, they asked me to perform at the Hoosier Dome for Farm Aid, a nonprofit founded by

Neil Young, Willie Nelson, and John Mellencamp. Everyone from Lou Reed to Carl Perkins to Guns N' Roses performed at the massive event. I had been excited to be involved, but now I didn't want to leave Jeanne by Ryan's bedside; I knew he didn't have much time left. I dashed over there, literally running onstage in the same clothes I had worn to the hospital. I performed without a backup band, rushed through 'Daniel' and 'I'm Still Standing,' dedicated 'Candle In The Wind' to Ryan, and then exited the stage. I was back at the hospital in an hour, and I was there when Ryan died the next morning, at 7.11 a.m., on April 8. He was eighteen years old. It was a month before his senior year in high school.

Jeanne had requested me to be one of the pallbearers and perform at his funeral. I performed 'Skyline Pigeon' while holding a photo of Ryan on top of my keyboard. It was a song from my first album, Empty Sky, one of the first really beautiful things Bernie and I had written, and it seemed to match the occasion: 'dreaming of the open, longing for the day that he can spread his wings and fly away again'. The funeral was a tremendous occasion. CNN broadcasted it live. Michael Jackson and Barbara Bush, the First Lady, were both present. There were hundreds of people standing outside in the rain and hundreds of press photographers around. Some of the mourners were those who had made the Whites' lives miserable in Kokomo; they came to apologize and begged Jeanne to forgive them, which she did.

Ryan was buried in an open casket. Following the service, relatives and close friends filed towards his body to say their final goodbyes. He was dressed in his faded denim jacket and mirrored sunglasses, his choice of clothing for burial. I placed my hands on his cheeks and told him I adored him.

In an odd mood, I returned to my hotel. There was something more seething behind the grief: I was angry with myself. I kept thinking about Ryan and how much he had done in such a short period of time to help individuals with AIDS. He was a poor boy who had transformed public perceptions. Ronald

Reagan, who had done his utmost to ignore AIDS while president, had written an article that was published that morning in the Washington Post, praising Ryan and decrying the 'fear and ignorance' that surrounded the disease. I was the world's most famous gay rock star. I'd spent the 1980s seeing friends, coworkers, and ex-lovers die horribly; years later, I had all of their names engraved on plaques and hung them on the wall of Woodside's chapel. But what exactly had I done? Almost nothing. I made it a point to be tested for HIV every year, and by some miracle, I came back negative every time. I'd done a couple of benefit shows and worked on a charity single, a cover of Burt Bacharach's 'That's What Friends Are For,' with Dionne Warwick, Stevie Wonder, and Gladys Knight. It was a phenomenal success; it was the best-selling single in America that year, and it raised $3 million. Because I'd known Elizabeth Taylor for years, I'd attended several of her charity events. She had a great image, but she wasn't at all like that in real life. She was really polite and friendly, and she was amusing - she had a filthy English sense of humor - yet you had to be careful with your jewelry around her. She was fixated. If she saw you wearing something she liked, she'd just seduce you into giving it to her; you'd walk into her dressing room wearing a Cartier watch and leave without it, never quite knowing how she'd gotten it off you. I'm sure she utilized the same technique when it came to fundraising. Despite everyone advising her that getting engaged with AIDS would harm her career, she had the courage to stand up and do something, helping to found the American Foundation for AIDS Research and pushing Hollywood to pay attention.

I should have done the same. I should have been fighting on the front lines. I should have done what Liz Taylor did and put my head on the chopping block. Everything I'd done so far - charity singles, celebrity fundraisers - seemed frivolous and showbizzy, and I should have been marching with Larry Kramer and ACT UP. I should have used my celebrity to seek attention and make a difference. I was feeling ill.

I switched on the television and saw the funeral coverage, which just made matters worse. It was a lovely service, and my performance was appropriate. But I was terrified every time the camera focused on me. I looked terrible for reasons that had nothing to do with Ryan's death and everything to do with the way I was living my life. I was puffy and grayish. My hair was completely white. I appeared tired, fatigued, and unwell. I was 43 years old and looked around seventy. God, my condition. Something had to give.

But not just yet. When I left Indianapolis, my life returned to what I considered normal. I had finished a new album before Ryan became seriously ill, and now I had to promote it, which I had failed to do while Ryan was dying. Sleeping with the Past was recorded in Puk Studios in rural Denmark. I guess the objective was to escape the press, which was crawling all over the place because of my divorce from Renate, and to avoid the kind of behavior that had occurred during the production of Leather Jackets. In some ways, it worked. Even I couldn't even figure out where to find narcotics in the Danish countryside. It was the dead of winter, bitterly cold and desolate: you'd have had better luck locating a cocaine dealer on the moon. But every night, we'd go to the neighboring town, Randers, and drink in the bars, marveling at how Danes drank. Lovely individuals, extremely welcoming, always willing to appeal to my competitive side by challenging us to a game of darts, but when you see them with alcohol, their old Viking background becomes quite clear. I shouldn't have tried to keep up with them, but my competitive drive won out again. The natives drank a fatal schnapps known as North Sea Oil. I'd become accustomed to waking up on the floor of someone else's room, my tongue glued to the roof of my mouth, gripped by the certainty that this specific case of alcohol poisoning would be fatal. Other members of the team fared considerably worse than me: on producer Chris Thomas's birthday, I hired a brass band to knock on his door first thing in the morning and blast into 'Happy Birthday To You'. You can imagine how fantastic that sounded to a man suffering from a severe hangover.

It's important to note that I'm discussing the working week here, with the schnapps, pubs, and hangovers. On weekends, I let my hair down. I'd jet to Paris and party there. Boy, a gay club on the rue de Caumartin, was a favorite of mine. In truth, I was beginning to think I was getting too old for clubbing, but the music at Boy kept me coming back. Laurent Garnier and David Guetta DJed there; it was the beginning of house and techno taking over Paris's clubs, and it felt as fresh, exhilarating, and daring as disco had in the 1970s. When I hear 'Good Life' by Inner City, I remember the dance floor in Boy going crazy.

Sleeping with the Past turned out extremely good, despite my visits to Paris and the amount of North Sea Oil consumed throughout its production. The plan was to create an album influenced by old soul music, similar to what I used to play in nightclubs in the 1960s, hence the title. Songs like 'Amazes Me' and 'I Never Knew Her Name' are prime examples. The one music I wasn't convinced about was 'Sacrifice,' a ballad. I didn't want it on the album, demonstrating the same immaculate business instincts that prompted me to threaten Gus Dudgeon with strangulation if 'Don't Let The Sun Go Down On Me' was ever published. I was talked into it, but then the record label wanted to release it as a single, which seemed ridiculous - it was a five-minute lament, no one would play it. Initially, it was released as the B-side to a song called 'Healing Hands,' which I believed was much more marketable. The track didn't chart until nearly a year later, in June 1990, when DJ Steve Wright began ignoring the label and playing the flip side on his Radio One show. Then it took off: I got my first British solo Number One in three weeks.

Remembering how I felt about my response to the AIDS problem following Ryan's funeral, I chose to donate all proceeds to four British AIDS charities, and I promised to do the same with every single one I released in the future. I donated to Stonewall, a new organization that was advocating for LGBT rights in the aftermath of Section 28, a recent law that prohibited local governments and schools in the United Kingdom from 'promoting' homosexuality. When I performed at the International Rock Awards, a televised event, I confronted the host, a homophobic comedian named Sam Kinison who specialized in AIDS jokes. He'd appeared on Howard Stern's radio show a week after Ryan's funeral, sniggering about it. I stated that I was simply there to oppose Kinison and that the awards event should never have hired him. His reaction was tremendous. He began to complain that I owed him an apology and that what I'd said was "way out of line." A man who went around laughing at 'faggots' dying, whose entire act was intended to be creating offence and shouting the unsayable, was suddenly supposedly profoundly offended by being called a name. He could dish it out but not receive it. He could fucking whistle for his apology.

And I performed at the opening of Donald Trump's new casino in Atlantic City to raise funds for Ryan's charity. Jeanne White was my guest, although the gigs weren't very good. I was bolstering myself with booze and drugs while making errors onstage. It wasn't anything major - the occasional lost phrase and a fluffed piano line. Nobody in the audience seemed to notice, and no one in the band mentioned it. I've never been a fan of post-gig inquests, where everyone sits around and discusses where things went wrong: tell people when they've played fantastic, don't stay around nitpicking over minor mistakes for hours, just let it go. But I knew deep down that I'd broken one of my unwritten rules. I'd undoubtedly sprinted offstage at the conclusion of previous shows, pathetically eager to have a line, but I'd made a point of never doing drugs before going on stage: it seemed like letting an audience down.

Hugh had some good news for me back in Atlanta. He was fed up with drinking and using drugs. He realized he couldn't stop without assistance. So he was heading to rehab. He'd enrolled in a residential treatment program at Sierra Tucson, the same rehab center where Ringo Starr had been treated for alcoholism a few years before. That day, he was leaving.

You'd think that after what occurred in Indianapolis - the guilt I'd felt in the presence of Ryan's mother and sister, the anguish of seeing myself at the burial - this would have been pleasant news. I should have asked to accompany him. Instead, I went berserk. I was enraged. Hugh was my most recent accomplice: if he admitted he had a problem, it meant I had a problem. He was, by implication, accusing me of being a drug addict.

He wasn't the first person to urge me to get assistance. My valet, Mike Hewitson, had written me a really rational, level-headed letter after he'd quit working for me, 'you've really got to stop this nonsense, stop shoving that bloody crap up your nose,' and I'd answered by refusing to talk to him for a year and a half. Tony King had attempted to speak with me. He had come to see me with Freddie Mercury, and Freddie had warned him that I appeared to be in difficulty and that Tony should intervene: 'You need to watch after your friend.' That judgment should have held a lot more weight coming from Freddie, who was no saint when it came to booze and drugs himself. Instead, I dismissed Tony's words as sanctimonious preaching from a recovering alcoholic. And George Harrison had tried to talk to me a few years before at an outrageous party I'd thrown at a property I was renting in Los Angeles. I'd put lights in the garden, asked Bob Halley to fire up the grill, and invited everyone I knew who was in town. I was completely out of my mind by the middle of the evening when a scruffy-looking guy I didn't recognize strolled into the party. What the hell was his name? It must be a member of the staff, perhaps a gardener. I demanded loudly to know what the gardener was doing while sipping a drink. A stunned hush was shattered by the sound of Bob Halley's voice: 'Elton, that's not the fucking gardener. 'This is Bob Dylan.'

I went over to grab him and start steering him towards the home, buzzed out of my head and eager to make amends.

'Bob! Bob! Bob!' We can't have you dressed like that, sweetheart. Come upstairs, and I'll outfit you with some of mine right away. Come on, darling!'

Bob looked at me in horror. His expression suggested he was struggling to think of something he wanted to do less than dress up like Elton John and coming up empty-handed. It was the late 1980s, and one of my recent outfits included a pink suit and a straw boater with a scale model of the Eiffel Tower on top, so you couldn't really blame him. But I wasn't deterred because I was full of cocky confidence. As I proceeded to shove him out of the garden, I heard George's mordant, Scouse-accented voice crying out to me.

'Elton,' he explained. 'I believe you should go steady on the old marching powder.'

Bob managed to argue his way out of wearing my clothes, but it didn't erase the fact that one of The Beatles was publicly telling me to stop doing cocaine. I simply laughed it off.

But this time I didn't laugh it off. The Dwight Family Temper was unleashed in full force. Maybe it touched home harder this time because, after Indianapolis, I knew Hugh was correct. The resulting brawl was a disaster. I yelled and screamed. I shouted the most terrible, painful things I could think of to Hugh, the type of stuff that literally comes back to haunt you years later, absolutely out of the blue, and you still clench your teeth and grimace. Nothing made a difference. Hugh had made up his mind. That afternoon, he went to Arizona.

Hugh later invited me to visit him at the treatment center, which was incredible given how we parted. That was a huge oversight. I arrived and left in twenty minutes, which was long enough for me to make a big fuss. I blew up again - this facility was a shithole, the therapists were a bunch of creeps, he was being indoctrinated, he had to leave right away. When he refused, I rushed out and boarded an aircraft back to London.

When I arrived, I walked straight to my leased property and shut the door. I spent two weeks alone in my bedroom, sniffing cocaine and drinking whisky. When I ate on rare occasions, I became ill immediately thereafter. I was awake for days on end, watching porn and doing drugs. I refused to answer the phone. I'm not going to answer the door. If someone knocked, I'd stay in perfect silence for hours afterwards, rigid with anxiety and fear, afraid to move in case they were still outside, spying on me.

I occasionally listened to music. I played Peter Gabriel and Kate Bush's 'Don't Give Up' over and over, crying at the lyrics: 'no fight left or so it seems, I am a guy whose dreams have all deserted'. I'd spend entire days making meaningless lists of music I had, songs I'd written, people I'd like to work with, football teams I'd seen: anything to occupy the time, give me a reason to take more drugs, keep myself from falling asleep. I was meant to attend a Watford board meeting, but I called and informed them that I was ill. I didn't wash, and I didn't dress. I sat around wanking in a puke-covered dressing robe. It was heinous. Awful.

I didn't always want to see Hugh again. I was desperate to talk to him at times, but I couldn't reach him. He'd moved into a halfway home, and no one would tell me where he was after the mess I'd created at the treatment center. I eventually became so ill that I realized this was it. I couldn't stand it any longer. If I kept going for a few more days, I'd be dead: I'd either overdose or have a heart attack. Was that truly what I desired? I had a feeling it wasn't. I didn't want to self-destruct, despite my destructive behavior. I had no idea what I was doing, but I didn't want to die. I'd found Hugh's ex-boyfriend, Barron Segar, who informed me he was in a halfway home in Prescott, four hours north of Tucson. I dialed Hugh's number. He sounded tense. He stated we could meet if certain conditions were met. I needed to meet with his counselor first. He wanted to visit me because he had things he wanted to say to me, but he wouldn't say them until I was also present with a counselor. He didn't say anything specific, but I had a feeling an intervention was in the works. I paused for a time, but I was past telling myself that, even though things were horrible, I was intelligent, successful, and wealthy enough to deal with them on my own. I was too depressed and embarrassed of myself to even try. As a result, I agreed to do whatever it required.

Robert Key accompanied me, and Connie Pappas met us at LAX. I called Hugh's therapist. He said the encounter had to be part of Hugh's therapy. We'd both write a list of things we didn't like about one other and read it out to each other. I was afraid, but I went ahead with it.

The next day, I found myself in a small motel room in Prescott, facing Hugh. We sat so close together that our knees touched, holding our lists. I was the first to go. I mentioned that I didn't enjoy how untidy Hugh was. He strewn his clothing all over the place. He never put CDs back in their cases after playing them. He neglected to switch off the lights after leaving the room at night. Stupid, niggly little irritations, the kind of things that irritate you about your partner on a daily basis.

Hugh's time came next. I realized he was trembling. He was even more afraid than I was. 'You're a drug addict,' he pointed out. 'You're an alcoholic,' I say. You're a bulimic with a food addiction. You have a sex problem. You are codependent.'

That was the end of it. A long pause followed. Hugh was still trembling. He was unable to look at me. He expected me to erupt again and storm out.

'Yes,' I replied. 'I am,' she says.

Hugh and his counselor both looked at me. 'Well, do you want help?' his counselor inquired. 'Do you wish to improve?'

I began to cry. 'Yes,' I replied. 'I require assistance. 'I want to improve.'

CHAPTER 12

Lutheran Hospital,
Park Ridge,
Illinois
10 August 1990

We've lived together, you and I, for sixteen years, and boy, have we had some great times. But now it's time for me to sit down and tell you how I really feel about you. I loved you so much. At first, we were inseparable – we seemed to meet so often, either at my house, or at other people's. In the end, we were so fond of each other that I decided I couldn't be without you. I wanted us to be a great couple and to hell with what other people thought.

When I first met you, you seemed to bring out everything that had been suppressed before. I could talk about anything I wanted for the first time in my life. There was something in your make-up that brought all my walls and barriers crashing down. You made me feel free. I was never jealous if other people shared with you. In fact, I liked turning other people on to your charms. I realize how stupid I must have been, because you never really cared for me. It was all one-sided. You only care about how many people you can trap on your web.

My body and brain have suffered greatly because of my love for you – you have left me with permanent physical and mental scars. Remember that romantic saying, 'I would die for you'? Well, I nearly did. Still, you're a hard lady to get rid of. We've split so many times before but I always went back to you. Even though I knew it was a mistake, I still did. When there was no one else to comfort me, you were only a phone call away at any hour of the day or night. You never cease to amaze me – I've sent cars to pick you up and I even sent planes so that you and I could spend some hours or days together. And when you finally arrived, I was ecstatic to embrace you once more.

We had great parties with people. We had great, intense talks about how we were going to change the world. Of course, we never did, but boy, could we talk! We had sex with people we barely knew and who we really didn't give a damn about. I didn't care who they were as long as they slept with me. But, in the morning, they were gone, and I was alone again. You had gone too. Sometimes I wanted you so insatiably, but you had vanished. With you by my side, I was all-conquering, but with you gone I was just a sad little child again.
My family never liked you at all. In fact, they hated the spell you had me under. You managed to push me away from them and lots of my friends. I wanted them to understand how I felt about you, but they never listened, and I would feel anger, and hurt. I felt ashamed because I cared more about you than I did about my own flesh and blood. All I cared about was myself and you. So I kept you to myself. In the end, I didn't want to share with you anymore. I just wanted us to be alone. I became more miserable, because you ruled my life – you were my Svengali.

I guess I'll try and come to the point of this letter. It's taken me sixteen years to realize that you've taken me nowhere. Whenever I tried to have a relationship with someone else, I always brought you along at some point. So I have no doubts that it was me who was the user. But I found no compassion and love – what love I had for anyone was always superficial.

I had grown tired and hateful towards myself, but recently, I met someone again – someone I loved and trusted, and that person was adamant that this was going to be a two-way love affair, not a three-way one. He made me realize how self-centered I had become, and he made me think about my life and my sense of values. My life has ground to a halt. I now have the opportunity to change my way of living and thinking. I am prepared to accept humility, and therefore have to say goodbye to you for the final time.

You have been my whore. You have kept me from any sort of spirituality and you have kept me from finding out who I really am. I don't want you and I to share the same grave. I want to die a natural death when I go, at peace with myself. I want to live the rest of my life being honest and facing the consequences rather than hiding behind my celebrity status. I feel as though, after sixteen years with you, I was dead anyway.

Once more, white lady – goodbye. If I run into you somewhere – and, let's face it, you're such a woman about town – I'll ignore you and leave immediately. You've seen me enough over the years and I'm sick of you. You've won the fight – I surrender.

Thanks but no thanks,

Elton

I sensed a shift in my mood the instant I said the words "I need help." It felt as if something inside me had been turned back on, like a pilot light that had gone out. I had a feeling I was going to get well. But it wasn't quite as simple as that. First and foremost, they couldn't find a clinic in America that would accept me. Almost all of them only treated one addiction at a time, whereas I had three: cocaine, alcohol, and food. I didn't want them to be treated consecutively, which would have required traveling from one clinic to another for four months. I wanted them all to be treated at the same time.

They eventually found a place. I almost refused to go in when I saw it. Hugh's treatment center, which I had previously deemed to be a terrible shithole, was really luxurious. It was set in the countryside just outside Tucson, with breathtaking views of the Santa Catalina Mountains. It featured a large swimming pool and yoga courses were held around it. Mine was just a regular general hospital: the Lutheran, in Park Ridge, a Chicago suburb. It was a massive grey monolithic structure with mirrored glass windows. It didn't appear to be a facility that offered yoga by the pool. The only thing it could see was a shopping center parking lot. But Robert Key remained with me, and I was too embarrassed to flee. In any case, there was nowhere else to go. He dropped me off at reception, hugged me, and then flew back to England. On July 29, 1990, I checked in under the name George King. They told me I had to share a room, which didn't sit right with me until I met my roommate. Greg was his name, and he was gay and quite gorgeous. At the very least, there was something beautiful to gaze at around here.

Six days later, I checked out once more. It wasn't simply that it was difficult there, though it certainly was. I couldn't sleep: I'd lie awake all night, waiting for the 6.30 a.m. alarm. I experienced panic attacks. I had mood swings, not from high to low, but from low to even lower, a cloud of melancholy and worry that built and thinned but never lifted. I was constantly sick. I was exhausted. I was feeling lonely. You were not permitted to make phone calls or communicate with anyone outside. They let me break that rule once, when it was announced on TV that guitarist Stevie Ray Vaughan had died in a helicopter crash. He was on tour with Eric Clapton at the time, and his chopper was part of a convoy of musicians and crews that had taken off. Ray Cooper was a member of Eric Clapton's band. The news was unclear - at one point, they wrongly stated that Eric had also perished - and I had no idea if Ray was in the chopper that had crashed. They finally let me know, after much persuading, that Ray was fine.

Most importantly, I was embarrassed. Not because of my addictions, but because we were expected to do things for ourselves - clean our rooms, make our beds - which I was utterly unfamiliar with. I'd let myself get to the point where I shaved and wiped my arse while paying others to do everything else. I had no idea how a washing machine worked. I had to ask another patient, Peggy, to show me around. She was friendly and helpful after she realized I wasn't joking, but that didn't change the fact that I was a forty-three-year-old man who didn't know how to clean his own clothes. I realized I had no idea how much items cost when it came time to spend my $10 weekly budget on stationery or chewing gum. I hadn't done any shopping in years that didn't include an auction house or a high-end designer boutique. It was heinous: the absolutely unneeded bubble that celebrity and fortune allow you to construct around yourself if you're stupid enough to allow it. I see that all the time now, especially with rappers: they appear everywhere with massive, meaningless entourages — larger than the one I observed surrounding Elvis, which startled me at the time. They often do it in the name of charity - offering a job to pals from back home when back home is somewhere no one wants to be - but it's a risky thing to do. You believe that by surrounding yourself with people, you are making your life easier. But in truth, you're just separating yourself from the actual world, and the more separated you are from reality - the more detached you go from the person you're naturally destined to be - the tougher your life becomes and the less happy you become. You end up with something akin to a medieval court, with you as the queen and everyone else jockeying for position, afraid of losing their place in the pecking order, and fighting to see who can be closest to you, who can have the most influence over you. It's a terrible, soul-destroying place to live. And you made it yourself.

The underlying issue was that the treatment was based on the Alcoholics Anonymous 12-step method, and as soon as my therapist mentioned God, I flipped out. I didn't want to know about religion because it was dogma, intolerance, the Moral Majority, and people like Jerry Falwell who claimed that AIDS was God's punishment for homosexuals. It is a stumbling hurdle for many people. Years later, when I tried to persuade George Michael to enter rehab, he dismissed it out of hand, saying, 'I don't want to know about God, I don't want to join some cult.' I tried to explain that I had thought the same thing, but that only made things worse: he thought I was being patronizing and smug. But I had been there as well. I stormed out of the meeting that afternoon in Chicago, returned to my hotel, packed my belongings, and departed.

I made it all the way outside to the pavement. I sat down on a seat with my suitcase and sobbed. I could easily make some phone calls and leave, but where was I going? Return to London? To what end? All day in a puke-covered dressing robe, snorting coke and watching porn? It wasn't a really appetizing prospect. I dragged my bag back inside the hospital, embarrassed. I almost walked out again a few days later. My therapist warned that I wasn't taking recovery seriously enough: 'You're not working hard enough, you're just here for the ride,' I snapped. I informed him that if I hadn't been serious about recovery, I would have left a long time ago. I said he was targeting me because I was famous. He ignored my arguments, as if he wasn't paying attention. As a result, I dubbed him a cunt. That seemed to pique his interest. I was dragged in front of a disciplinary committee and admonished about my language and behavior.

But it was also agreed that I would be assigned a different counselor, Debbie, who appeared less concerned with making an example of me because of who I was, and I began to make progress. I enjoyed the routine. I preferred to do things for myself. I came to terms with the concept of a greater power, if not God. It all made sense. Everything from Ray Williams putting me in touch with Bernie almost as an afterthought, to picking up that magazine with Ryan White's story in it in the doctor's waiting room, to the decision to clear out the contents of Woodside, was starting to look less and less like a rash impulse and more and more like a premonition that my life was about to change, was starting to look less and less like a rash impulse and more and more like a premonition that my life was about to change. I began to enjoy going to AA meetings. After a while, I was allowed to have visitors, including Billie Jean King and her partner Ilana Kloss, as well as Bernie and my friends Johnny and Eddi Barbis. I had to write all the time, including a farewell letter to cocaine, which Bernie saw and broke down in tears when he came, and a list of the repercussions of my drug and alcohol misuse. It was difficult at first, but once I started, I couldn't stop. When I arrived at the hospital, a consultant asked how I was feeling, and I told him the truth: I didn't know. I wasn't sure whether I'd had any true feelings in years, or if everything was the consequence of the incessant ups and downs caused by drugs and alcohol. But now it all came spilling out. The list of implications was three pages long. Self-hatred. Depression is severe. Going on stage when high on drugs.

It was cathartic, but the group meetings brought my concerns to the forefront. There were survivors of the most heinous crimes present. We were told to tell our worst, dirtiest secret at one point. I spoke briefly about my previous relationships, about my uncanny ability to take over other people's lives for selfish, delusory motives. Then it was the turn of a girl from someplace in America's Deep South, who was looking for help with food addiction. It took her 45 minutes to tell her story, first because she was sobbing so hard she couldn't get the words out, and then because she was straining to be heard over the sound of everyone else crying. Her father had molested her as a child. She had gotten pregnant when she was a teenager. She was too afraid to inform anyone, so she ate more and more to gain weight and conceal her pregnancy. She eventually delivered the baby herself, terrified and alone.

So the meetings were not for the faint of heart, but I learned to enjoy them. After years of misleading others and myself, they forced me to be honest. If someone else has the courage to stand there and tell you about being abused by their own father, it pushes you to step up and tell the truth about yourself - anything less is an insult to their fortitude. While you're an addict, it's all about lying, hiding your tracks, convincing yourself that you don't have a problem, and convincing others that you can't do anything because you're sick, while in reality you're just intoxicated or hungover. Being truthful was difficult, but it was liberating. You were free of the baggage that came with lying: embarrassment and shame.

When people had tried to help me in the past, my normal response was to declare that they didn't understand; they weren't Elton John, so how could they possibly know what it was like to be me? However, it soon became clear that the other addicts at the meetings did understand. They were only too aware. Everyone was instructed to write down what they liked and disliked about me during one meeting. On a board, they made two lists: my positive points and my bad points. I began talking about what had been stated, going over it again and again, gently accepting the comments. I felt I was doing okay until someone interrupted me and pointed out that I had gone on and on about the bad remarks but had never addressed any of the positive ones. That, they argued, was an indication of low self-esteem. They were correct, I realized. Maybe that's why I like performing so much. Because you find it difficult to accept personal compliments, your life becomes focused on finding a more impersonal alternative: chart placements, crowds of nameless faces applauding. No wonder I always claimed that my difficulties vanished onstage. It's no surprise that my life offstage had devolved into a shambles. I returned to my room and wrote in the blue folder where I kept my writing. I AM WORTHY, I AM A GOOD PERSON. It was the beginning.

I was ready to go after six weeks. I flew back to London and informed the Rocket headquarters that I would be taking some time off. There will be no shows, new songs, or recording sessions for at least a year, possibly eighteen months. That was unprecedented - I hadn't taken more than a few weeks off a year since 1965 - but it was readily accepted. The only thing I'd do was honor an unbreakable commitment to a little private charity show with Ray Cooper at the Grosvenor House hotel, which was terrifying but we made it through. I saw the artwork for a career-spanning box set I had planned before going into treatment and asked for it to be changed while I was there. To Be Continued... felt bright and hopeful, even prophetic, given that I'd picked it before cleaning up. But I wanted it to showcase a contemporary photo rather than a compilation of vintage shots from the 1970s and 1980s, so that the title seemed to comment on my life now rather than my past. And it was the only work I did for the following year, unless you include abruptly appearing onstage in drag at one of Rod Stewart's Wembley Arena shows and sitting on his lap while he tried to sing "You're In My Heart." And I don't: spoiling Rod has never felt like work, but rather like a thoroughly pleasant hobby.

Hugh and I spent some time together in Atlanta, but our relationship began to deteriorate. Both of our therapists had warned us against staying together, saying that it wouldn't work and that the dynamic of the relationship would shift irreversibly now that we were sober. We both laughed at that: half of my writing in recovery had been about how much I loved Hugh and missed him. So we rented an apartment and moved in together, only to realize, much to our surprise, that the dynamic of our relationship had irreversibly changed now that we were sober, and it wasn't working well. We weren't fighting, and we weren't screaming at each other, but it was sad. We'd been through a lot together, but it was finally time for both of us to move on.

So I spent the majority of the next eighteen months in London, where I settled into a calm routine. I bought the property I'd been renting and where I'd spent my final binge. I lived by myself. I didn't bother hiring help because I preferred to do things myself. I received a Mini and a dog from Battersea Dogs Home, a small mutt named Thomas. I would get up at 6.30 a.m. every day. and go for a walk with Thomas. It was fantastic. It's a recovering addict's cliché to say that you notice things about your surroundings that you didn't notice before - oh, the beauty of the flowers, the glories of nature, all that nonsense - but it's only a cliché because it's true. That's probably one of the reasons I started collecting pictures once I became sober. I'd spent much of my career surrounded by brilliant photographers - Terry O'Neill, Annie Leibovitz, Richard Avedon, Norman Parkinson - but I never considered it an art form until I quit drinking and taking drugs. I took a vacation to the south of France and paid a visit to a friend of mine, Alain Perrin, who resided outside Cahors. He was perusing black and white fashion images with the intention of purchasing some. I was transfixed as I idly peered over his shoulder. Irving Penn, Horst, and Herb Ritts created them. I knew Herb Ritts - he'd photographed the cover of Sleeping with the Past - but it felt like I was seeing his art for the first time. Everything about the photographs Alain was gazing at appeared fantastic to me: the lighting, the shapes it had produced and contorted. I ended up buying twelve of them, and that was the beginning of a never-ending obsession: photography is the love of my life in terms of visual art.

But I first noticed a shift in how I perceived things when wandering around London. A scorching summer had given way to a cool fall. It was wonderful to get up early in the chilly weather and walk Thomas around Holland Park or the grounds of St James's Church, watching the leaves transform. Previously, I had only ever gotten up at that hour if I was still up from the night before.

I'd jump in my Mini after walking the dog and drive to see a psychiatrist. I'd never been to one before, and it proved to be a steep learning curve. Some of the psychiatrists I've visited throughout the years have been fantastic, and they've really helped me understand myself. And some of them turned into nightmares, more interested in my celebrity and what being associated with me could accomplish for them. One of them was even fired for abusing his patients - female patients, mind you, lest anyone imagine I was one of his victims.

I spent most of my time in meetings. My sponsor had given me explicit orders to attend an AA meeting as soon as I crossed customs in London. After missing football for several weeks while in America, I opted to witness a Watford game instead. My sponsor's phone rang that night. He yelled at me when I informed him what I'd done. He could really yell as a driver for the city of Chicago's sanitation service, where he spent most of his life conversing with his coworkers above the roar of his garbage truck. That night, he sounded as if he was attempting to communicate with someone on the other side of the Atlantic without the use of a telephone. I was taken aback, but also abashed, because I was more used to shouting at people than being shouted at. He was a lovely man - I became his son's godfather - but he was genuinely angry, and his anger was motivated by concern for me.

So I took his counsel. I got quite serious about going to meetings for Alcoholics Anonymous, Cocaine Anonymous, Anorexics and Bulimics Anonymous, and others. Meetings were held at Pimlico, Shaftesbury Avenue, Marylebone, and Portobello Road. I used to attend three or four meetings a day. In a month, I went from zero to one hundred. Some of my friends began to suspect that I was now addicted to attending addiction groups. They were undoubtedly correct, but it was a vast improvement over what I had previously become addicted to. Maybe there was a meeting I could go to to deal with it.

At the very first meeting I attended, a photographer jumped out and snapped a photo of me departing. Someone must have recognized me and alerted them, which was clearly against the regulations. The following day, it was on the main page of the Sun: ELTON IN ALCOHOLICS ANONYMOUS. I let it go because they didn't propose I wear leather shorts or twirl a dildo this time. It didn't matter to me who knew. I was making a good decision. I continued to attend the sessions because I enjoyed them. The people I met were pleasant. I always volunteered to make the tea, and I developed long-lasting friendships with individuals I'm still in contact with today: ordinary folks who viewed me as a recovering addict first and Elton John second. In a strange way, the meetings reminded me of my time at Watford FC - there was no special treatment for me, and there was that similar sense of everyone pulling together for the same goal. You've heard some incredible things. Women in Anorexia and Bulimia support groups would talk about taking a single pea, chopping it into four pieces, and eating a quarter for lunch and a quarter for dinner. 'That's absurd,' I'd think, but then I remembered how I'd been a few months before - unwashed and furious out of my mind at 10 a.m., practically doing a line of coke every five minutes - and realized they must have thought the same about me.

Not everything that transpired in the months following my sobriety was positive. My father died at the end of 1991, never fully recovered from the heart bypass surgery eight years earlier. I did not attend his funeral. It would have appeared hypocritical, and the journalists would have flocked in droves, turning the event into a circus. My father did not share in my popularity, so why should the consequences befall him in the end? Besides, I'd already done enough mourning for my connection with my father, and I'd achieved a sort of peace with it: I wanted things to be different, but they were what they were. You have to sometimes look at the hand you've been dealt and toss in the cards.

There was also Freddie Mercury. He hadn't told me he was sick; I'd only learned about it through mutual friends. I visited him frequently when he was dying, but I could never stay for more than an hour. It was too sad for me to watch him like that. Someone so vital and necessary, who would have merely gotten better with age and grown stronger and stronger, dying in such a horrific, arbitrary way. They may have kept him alive with antiretroviral medications a year later. Instead, they were powerless to help him. He was too feeble to get out of bed, he was losing his sight, and his body was covered in Kaposi's sarcoma sores, but he was still Freddie, gossiping and being utterly outrageous: 'Did you hear Mrs. Bowie's new album, dear? 'What on earth does she think she's doing?' He lay there, surrounded by Japanese furniture and art catalogs, interrupting the conversation to call auction houses to bid on objects he loved the look of: 'Darling, I've just bought this, isn't it wonderful?' I couldn't tell if he didn't realize how near to death he was, or if he did but was determined not to let what was happening to him stop him from being himself. In any case, I thought it was fantastic.

He eventually decided to stop taking any medication other than pain relievers and died at the end of November 1991. Tony arrived at my front door on Christmas Day, carrying something in a pillowcase. When I opened it, it was a watercolor by Henry Scott Tuke, an Impressionist who portrayed male nudists and whose work I had collected. There was a message with it: 'Darling Sharon – thought you'd love this. 'With love, Melina.' He'd seen it in one of his auction catalogs and bought it for me while he was lying there. He was thinking about Christmas gifts for a Christmas he must have known in his heart he wouldn't see; he was thinking about other people when he should have been thinking about himself. As I have stated, Freddie was great.

Some people have a difficult time transitioning from addiction to sobriety, but I was the polar opposite. I was overjoyed. I never wanted to use it again; all I wanted was to wake up every morning without feeling like trash. Surprisingly, I would constantly fantasize about cocaine. I still do it virtually every week, despite the fact that it's been twenty-eight years since I last did a line. It's the same dream every time: I'm snorting coke when I hear someone enter the room, usually my mother. Then I try to cover what I'm doing, but I spill it and it all over the floor and all over me. But it never made me crave cocaine. Quite the contrary. When I wake up, I can almost feel the numbing sensation of the cocaine slipping down the back of my throat - always the part of doing it that I loathed - and I just think 'thank God that's gone'. I occasionally wish I could have a glass of wine with my meal or a beer with some friends, but I know I can't. I don't mind if others are drinking around me: it's my problem, not theirs. But I never feel like having a line, and I can't stand being near those who do. I know the moment I step into a room. I have a feeling folks are on it. The way they're speaking - slightly louder than necessary, not really listening - and how they're behaving. I simply leave. I don't want to do cocaine, and I don't want to be around others who are, since it's a drug that makes people act like jerks. I wish I'd realized that 45 years ago.

Every time I traveled to a foreign nation to play live, I looked out the location of the AA or NA meeting and went there as soon as I arrived. I attended meetings in Argentina, France, and Spain. I traveled to Los Angeles and New York for meetings. I also attended meetings in Atlanta. Despite my breakup with Hugh, I was still in love with the city. Hugh had introduced me to some wonderful people from outside the music industry, whose company I thoroughly loved. It was a terrific music town, with a thriving soul and hip-hop scene, but it was weirdly easygoing; I could go to the movies or the shopping center on Peachtree Road without being bothered.

I was spending so much time there that I decided to purchase an apartment, a 36th-floor duplex. I couldn't help but notice how lovely the views were, as was the real-estate agent who sold it to me. He was known as John Scott. I asked him out, and we ended up dating.

I eventually quit attending meetings. I'd gone almost every day for three years - something like 1,400 meetings - but I'd ultimately determined that they'd done everything they could for me. I came to the point where I didn't want to talk about booze, cocaine, or bulimia on a daily basis. I believe because I was a high-profile addict who publicly changed his life, I became someone to whom my peers turned if they had a problem. It's become a running gag - Elton always rushing into action anytime a pop celebrity has a problem with alcohol or drugs - but I don't mind. If someone is in distress and requires assistance, I call them or leave my phone number with their manager, simply stating, 'Listen, I've been there, I know what it's like.' They can contact me if they need to. Some of those folks are well-known. I got Rufus Wainwright into treatment - he was taking so much crystal meth that he went briefly blind at one point - and I'm Eminem's AA sponsor. Whenever I call to check on him, he always says, 'Hello, you cunt,' which I think is very Eminem.

And some of them no one knows about, and I'm not going to tell you about them now: they chose to keep their difficulties private, which is OK. It's quite satisfying in either case. It's a fantastic thing to help individuals get sober.

But you can't help everyone. It's an awful sensation. You end up just watching from the sidelines, knowing what's going to happen and knowing that their story can only end one way. Whitney Houston's aunt, Dionne Warwick, requested me to call her, but either the messages I left didn't get through or she didn't want to know. And George Michael had no desire to know. I nagged him because I was concerned and because common acquaintances kept contacting me to see if I could help. He penned an open letter to Heat magazine, the majority of which was spent urging me to fuck off and mind my own business. I regret our disagreement. But, more importantly, I wish he were still alive. George was my favorite. He was a wonderfully talented man who had been through a lot, yet he was the sweetest, kindest, most generous man I'd ever met. I really miss him.

After I became clean, George was one of the first individuals I performed with. As much as I enjoyed my time off, I knew it couldn't go forever, and I didn't want it to - I needed to come back to work, even if it seemed intimidating. I'd started thinking about playing live again, so I agreed to perform onstage at one of George's shows to test the waters. He was performing a series of gigs at Wembley Arena. This time, I didn't dress up as Ronald McDonald or drive a Reliant Robin. I wore a baseball cap and we sang 'Don't Let The Sun Go Down On Me,' as we had done at Live Aid six years before, in 1985. It felt fantastic. When my name was called, the audience went berserk, and when the duet was released as a single, it went to Number One on both sides of the Atlantic. I reserved a studio in Paris and tentatively proposed creating a new album, which became known as The One.

I only stayed for twenty minutes the first day before fleeing in a panic. I can't remember what the issue was. I guess I thought I couldn't make an album without alcohol or drugs, which made no sense. It just took one listen to Leather Jackets to understand the reverse was true: it was pretty persuasive evidence that I couldn't compose an album while on drugs. I returned the next day and eventually got used to everything. The only serious issue was a song named "The Last Song." Bernie's lyrics were about an AIDS patient reconciling with his estranged father, who had excommunicated him when he discovered he was gay. They were lovely, but I couldn't bring myself to sing them. It was shortly after Freddie died. Vance Buck was also dying somewhere in Virginia, and I knew it. I started bawling every time I tried to record the vocals. I eventually got it, and 'The Last Song' was later used as the end of And the Band Played On, a docudrama about the discovery of, and fight against, HIV. It was played over a collage of photographs of famous AIDS victims. Half of them were individuals I knew: Ryan, Freddie, and Steve Rubell, proprietor of Studio 54.

By that time, I had established the Elton John AIDS Foundation. I continued to volunteer, but the more I did, the more I realized I needed to do. The most moving experience for me was volunteering for a charity called Operation Open Hand, which distributed meals to AIDS patients throughout Atlanta. I did it with my new lover, John. When we knocked on the door of some houses, the person inside would only open a crack. They were covered in lesions and didn't want to be seen because of the stigma associated with AIDS. Sometimes they wouldn't even open the door. You'd leave the dinner on the step, and as you went away, you'd hear the door open, the food stolen, and the door slam shut again. These people were dying horrifically, but it appeared like they were dying in shame, alone, cut off from the rest of the world. It was horrifying, like something you'd read about in the Middle Ages - sick people being thrown out of society due to fear and ignorance - but it was occurring in America in the 1990s.

It would not leave my mind. Eventually, I asked John if he would help me start our own charity, focusing on HIV prevention and the basic necessities that people with HIV required to live a better, more dignified life: food, lodging, transportation, and access to doctors and counselors. John ran it from his Atlanta kitchen table for two years. Virginia Banks, who worked on my team in Los Angeles, was appointed secretary. There were four of us on the staff, including myself. We had no experience and knew nothing about infrastructure, but I knew we needed to keep overheads low. I'd seen far too many charity foundations, particularly famous ones, squander money. When you arrived at a charity event, everyone had been flown in and escorted about at the charity's expense. Even now, some thirty years later, our costs are low. We put on some glamorous events, but they're all paid for. They receive no compensation from the charity.

I threw myself wholeheartedly into the AIDS Foundation. My counselor had asked me in treatment what I planned to do with the extra time and energy I would now have. I was sober, saving time and energy that had previously been spent on drugs or recovering from them. They referred to it as the hole in the doughnut and inquired as to how I intended to fill it. I boasted about my lofty goals, including learning to speak Italian and cook. Of course, neither of these events occurred. I believe the AIDS Foundation filled the hole in the doughnut by providing me with a new feeling of purpose outside of music. I was so certain that it would work that I auctioned off my record collection to acquire funds to get it started. There were 46,000 singles, 20,000 albums, and even 78s with 'Reg Dwight' proudly inscribed in biro on the sleeves. It was sold in a single lot for $270,000 to an unknown bidder. I persuaded anyone who I believed could help to get involved: businessmen who could show us how to manage things as efficiently as possible; individuals from my record company; Robert Key from Rocket; and Howard Rose, the agent who'd guided my live career since the day I arrived in America.

I solicited suggestions from friends. Smash Hits, an annual fundraising tennis tournament founded by Billie Jean King and Ilana Kloss, has been running since 1993: tennis luminaries were eager to participate following the death of Arthur Ashe. As competitive as ever, I frequently participated, albeit the most famous thing I've done on a tennis court is fall flat on my arse while attempting to sit in a director's chair courtside at the Royal Albert Hall. The Academy Awards Viewing Party was another game changer. Patrick Lippert, a political activist who formed Rock the Vote, effectively gave it to us. He always organized an Oscars fundraiser for one of his causes, but after being diagnosed with HIV, he decided to change the event into an AIDS foundation benefit and asked if we wanted to be a part of it. The first party was hosted in 1993 at Maple Drive, Dudley Moore's restaurant. We had 140 people there - the whole capacity of the restaurant - and raised $350,000, which felt like a lot of money at the time. The following year, we did it again, and even more celebrities showed up, including Tom Hanks, Bruce Springsteen and his wife Patti, Emma Thompson, and Prince. But Patrick was not present. Three months after the first party, he died of AIDS at the age of thirty-five. He, like Freddie Mercury, simply did not receive antiretroviral medications that could have saved his life.

The Elton John AIDS Foundation has raised over $450 million since then, and we've organized some fantastic events. Aretha Franklin last performed live at our 25th anniversary gala at New York's Cathedral of St John the Divine. She was slated to play the prior year but had to cancel due to illness. She was dying of cancer and had retired, but she made an exception for us. When she came, I was taken aback by how pale, weak, and ill she appeared. I found myself asking her if she wanted to sing backstage. I guess I was actually wondering if she was well enough to sing. She simply smiled and nodded, saying, 'I would never let you down again.' I believe she was aware that this was her final performance, and she appreciated the fact that it was for a good cause and that the gala was held in a church, where her singing career had begun. She tore the roof off while singing 'I Say A Little Prayer' and 'Bridge Over Troubled Water'. Her voice had not been harmed by her illness, and she sounded fantastic. I cried my eyes out as I stood at the front of the stage, seeing the greatest vocalist in the world sing for the final time.

The AIDS Foundation has provided me with opportunities and taken me to places I would not have visited otherwise. I've had to testify in front of Congress multiple times, asking the US government to increase AIDS funding, which was curiously less nerve-racking than I thought. It was a piece of cake compared to trying to persuade Watford Borough Council's planning committee to allow us to build a new football stadium. I expected a nasty reception from the more right-wing, religiously devout Republicans, but they were, once again, the absolute example of open-mindedness, flexibility, and sweet reason when compared to some members of Watford Borough Council's planning committee.

And, unexpectedly, working with the AIDS Foundation would indirectly lead to the most profound and significant transformation in my life. We'll get to that later.

CHAPTER 13

I don't want to seem mystical - or worse, smug - but it was difficult to shake the impression that life was congratulating me on becoming sober. Since 1975, The One has been my best-selling album globally. Woodside's renovations were completed two years later, and I moved back in. It was fantastic. It finally appeared to be a place where a normal person could live, rather than a coked-up rock star's ridiculous country lot. Tim Rice called me out of the blue, ten years after we'd last created a song together, and asked if I wanted to work with him again. Disney was apparently developing their first animated feature based on an original story rather than an existing work, and Tim wanted me to be a part of it. I was piqued. I'd previously produced a movie soundtrack for Friends, a 1971 picture that received some rather scathing reviews - I recall Roger Ebert calling it a "sickening piece of corrupt slop," but not many critics agreed. I'd avoided soundtracks ever since, but this was plainly something different. The songs required to be narrative in nature. The idea was to create pop songs that kids would enjoy rather than the typical Broadway-style Disney score.

It was an odd procedure. Tim followed Bernie's lead and penned lyrics first, which was fine. In fact, composing a musical was similar to writing the Captain Fantastic record in that there was a storyline: there was a precise sequence that you had to follow; you always knew which order the songs had to go in ahead of time. But I'd be lying if I said I never had reservations about the project or, more specifically, my role in it. I have many weaknesses, but you could never accuse me of being an artist who takes himself too seriously. Even still, there were days when I'd find myself sitting at the piano, contemplating the direction my career seemed to be headed. I wrote a song called "Someone Saved My Life Tonight." I came up with the phrase 'Sorry Seems To Be The Hardest Word'. 'I Guess That's Why They Call It The Blues,' I wrote. And there was no avoiding the reality that I was now creating a song about a farting warthog. To be honest, I thought it was a very nice song about a warthog who farted a lot: at the risk of sounding arrogant, I'm pretty confident mine would be towards the top of a list of the finest songs ever written about warthogs who fart a lot. Still, it was a far way from The Band storming backstage and asking to hear my new album, or Bob Dylan stopping us on the stairs and complementing Bernie on "My Father's Gun." But I determined that something about the absurdity of the circumstance attracted me and continued.

It was the correct choice. I think the end product was just wonderful. I'm not the type of artist who invites people over to play my new album, but I was so taken with The Lion King that I booked a few private screenings for friends to see it. I was ecstatic about the whole event; I knew we were on to something spectacular. Even yet, I had no idea it would become one of the highest-grossing pictures of all time. It exposed my music to an entirely new audience. 'Can You Feel It Tonight?' won an Oscar for Best Original Song, with three of the five nominees coming from The Lion King, including 'Hakuna Matata,' the song about the farting warthog. Except for my first Greatest Hits compilation, the soundtrack sold eighteen million copies, which is more than any album I've ever produced. As an extra bonus, it blocked The Rolling Stones' Voodoo Lounge from reaching number one in America for the entire summer of 1994. I tried not to be overjoyed when I heard Keith Richards was enraged, complaining about being 'beaten by some fuckin' cartoon'.

Then it was announced that it will be turned into a stage musical, for which Tim and I were invited to write new songs. I kept telling people that translating an animated film into a stage musical was both impossible and doomed to failure, demonstrating my incredible ability to foresee exactly what isn't going to happen - I couldn't see it at all.

But Julie Taymor, the director, did an outstanding job. It opened to excellent reviews, was nominated for eleven Tony

Awards, won six, and went on to become the most successful Broadway show in history. The whole performance looked incredible, and the sheer inventiveness with which they staged it was astounding, but I found the sensation of actually sitting through it oddly unpleasant. It had absolutely nothing to do with the show itself. It was only that I was used to making records where I had the final say or having complete control over my live shows. This was something I'd helped build, but once it got onstage, it was completely out of my hands. The arrangements and vocals were different from how I had recorded the tunes. Every syllable in musical theater must be well enunciated; it's a whole different technique of singing than anything a rock or pop musician performs. It was an entirely new sensation for me, both amazing and a little unsettling. I was utterly out of my comfort zone, which, it gradually dawned on me, was an excellent place for a forty-year-old artist to find himself.

Disney was so pleased with The Lion King's popularity that they approached me with a proposal. It was for an absurd sum of money. They wanted me to make additional films, do TV shows, and write books; there was even discussion of opening a theme park, which threw me for a loop. There was only one issue. I'd committed to do another film with Jeffrey Katzenberg, who was the chairman of Disney at the time of The Lion King's production but left a few months later to form DreamWorks with Steven Spielberg and David Geffen. But he didn't just leave: his departure sparked one of the great Hollywood fights amongst studio executives, so epic that books have been written about it. The Disney agreement was exclusive: it excluded anything involving Jeffrey, who was now suing them for breach of contract and $250 million, which he eventually received. There was nothing in writing with Jeffrey, but I'd given him my word - he was one of the people who had gotten me involved with The Lion King in the first place. As a result, I had to decline Disney's offer. At the very least, the world avoided an Elton John theme park.

But, while my world looked to be full of fresh ideas and chances, abstinence had done little to improve my love life. My connection with John Scott had ended some time ago, and nothing had happened since then. I tried not to think about how long it had been since I'd had sex, in case the sound of me howling in agony scared the Woodside staff.

I realized I didn't know any gay men who were accessible. When I got sober, I stopped going to locations where I may meet them. I didn't believe I'd be enticed by a vodka martini if I went to a club or a bar, but there seemed little use in putting this idea to the test. And, furthermore, I'd started to believe I was getting a little old for that kind of behavior even before I went into rehab. I'm sure the music at Boy would have sounded just as great as it always does, but there comes a point when you start to feel like the dowager duchess at the debutantes' ball, peeking down your pince-nez at the latest arrivals.

It all came to a head one Saturday afternoon when I was moping around the house, feeling completely sorry for myself. I had one eye on the football, where Watford were attempting to worsen my melancholy by losing 4-1 away at West Brom. I was planning another exciting evening in front of the TV when I had an idea. I called a pal in London and described my situation. I asked him if he could round up some folks and invite them to supper that evening. I'd send a car to London for them despite the short notice. I realized as I was saying it that it sounded a little sad, but I was desperate to meet some homosexual men who weren't in Alcoholics Anonymous. I wasn't looking for sex; I was simply lonely.

Around seven o'clock, my pal and four people he'd enlisted arrived. They explained that they had to leave early to attend a Halloween party in London, but I didn't mind. Everyone who had come seemed to be quite pleasant. They were amusing and talkative. We ate spaghetti bolognese and laughed a lot - I'd nearly forgotten what it was like to have a conversation that wasn't about my job or my sobriety. The only person who didn't seem thrilled to be there was David, a Canadian in a tartan Armani waistcoat. He was obviously shy and didn't say much, which I felt was a shame because he was quite attractive. I later discovered that he'd heard a lot of gossip on the London gay scene about the inadvisability of having anything whatsoever to do with Elton John, unless you had a burning desire to be showered with gifts, forced to put your life on hold in order to be whisked away on tour, then summarily dumped - usually by his personal assistant - when he met someone else, or lost his temper with you during a post-cocaine comedown, or announced he was getting married to a woman. I should have been upset, but given my history, the gossips of the London gay scene had a point.

He eventually revealed that he was interested in cinema and photography, which sparked the conversation. I offered to walk him around the house and show him my photo collection. I liked him more the more I chatted to him. He was quiet but confident. He was obviously quite intelligent. He claimed to be from Toronto but had recently relocated to London. He lived in Clapham and worked for the advertising firm Ogilvy & Mather in Canary Wharf, where he was one of their youngest board directors at thirty-one. Something resonating between us, a flash of chemistry, I thought I sensed. But I tried to forget about it. Elton John, the new, improved, sober Elton John, wasn't going to fall madly in love with someone within minutes of meeting them.

Still, when it was time for them to leave, I asked for his phone number in what I thought was a casual manner, implying nothing more than future stimulating conversations about our shared interest in photography down the road. He wrote down his entire name, David Furnish, handed it over, and they were off.

The next morning I found myself pacing around the house, trying to figure out when you could contact someone who'd been out the night before at a Halloween party without appearing like the type of person they'd have to seek a restraining order against. I decided that eleven thirty was a reasonable time. David answered the phone. He sounded exhausted but unsurprised to hear from me. It turned out that my casual request for his phone number had not been as casual as I had anticipated. I might as well have dropped to my knees, emotionally grasped his ankles, and refused to let go until he handed it over, based on the reaction of his buddies, who'd spent the entire ride back to London relentlessly tormenting him and shouting the chorus of 'Daniel' at him. I asked if he wanted to get together again, and he agreed. I inquired as to what he was doing that evening, when I happened to be in London. I pretended as if this was a miraculous coincidence, but if David had been in Botswana that evening, I suppose I would have been there as well: 'The Kalahari Desert? What a lucky break! I have a meeting there early tomorrow morning!'I invited him to my Holland Park home, where I would order a Chinese takeout.

I hung up the phone and told my driver that my plans for the day had altered and that we needed to get to London right away. I called the most famous Chinese restaurant in Knightsbridge, Mr Chow, and inquired if they performed delivery. Then I realized I had no idea what kind of food he liked, so I played it safe and ordered from the extensive menu.

When the Chinese takeaway arrived, or rather didn't stop arriving - by the time they'd finished delivering all the boxes, the space looked like the squash court at Woodside before I had the auction - David seemed a little surprised, but other than that, our first date went extremely well. No, I wasn't hallucinating; there was something vibrating between us. It wasn't just a physical appeal; our personalities complement one another. We didn't stop talking once we started.

But David had some reservations about our involvement. For one thing, he didn't want to be known as Elton John's Latest Boyfriend, with all the attention it would entail. He had a life and a career, and he didn't appreciate having his independence flipped upside down because of who he was dating. For another thing, he was only halfway out of the closet. His London pals knew he was gay, but his family and coworkers didn't, and he didn't want them to find out through a paparazzi shot in a tabloid.

So, for the first few months, our relationship was very modest and discreet: we were courting, to use an old-fashioned term. We primarily stayed at the house in Holland Park. Every weekday morning, David would leave for work in Canary Wharf, while I would go to the studio or conduct promotion for the duets CD I'd just published. I made a video for the version of 'Don't Go Breaking My Heart' I'd recorded with RuPaul: for once, I appeared joyful while filming. I was overjoyed. I couldn't quite put my finger on what was wrong with the relationship. Then it dawned on me what it was. I was in a perfectly regular relationship for the first time in my life, one that felt equal and had nothing to do with my work or the fact that I was Elton John.

Every Saturday, we'd give each other a card to remember the fact that we'd met on a Saturday, and - if you've recently eaten, you might want to skip to the following sentence in case you get sick - listen to Tony! Toni! Toné!'s 'It's Our Anniversary. There were many secluded dinners and weekends away. When I phoned him at work, I had to use a fictitious identity - George King, the alias I'd used when I checked into treatment. It struck me as incredibly romantic. A hidden love! I'd only ever had the kind of covert love that you have to keep hidden because the other person clearly isn't interested in you.

But, as much as I enjoyed the concept of a hidden romance, I was horrible at putting it into action. After twenty-five years of making a profession by being as flamboyant and OTT as possible, my idea of keeping things low-key was wildly at variance with everyone else's. If you're trying not to bring attention to your relationship, it might not be the best idea to give your partner two dozen long-stemmed yellow roses at work on a daily basis, especially if he works in an open-plan office. With the benefit of hindsight, the Cartier watch was also most likely a mistake. David had to wear it all the time because it was so expensive. He couldn't leave it at home in case his apartment was broken into because he didn't have insurance. When asked where it came from - and if it had anything to do with the fact that his desk had suddenly turned into a stand at the Chelsea Flower Show - he invented a beloved grandmother back in Canada who had recently died and left him some money in her will, then spent an awkward afternoon fending off a succession of sad smiles, supportive hugs, and expressions of condolence. When we planned a weekend in Paris and I went to meet him at Charles de Gaulle Airport, I was properly schooled on the importance of being unseen by any photographers or admirers who happened to be present. I became aware of some shoving and pointing going on around me while waiting in the arrivals lounge. I was in a state of anxiousness by the time David appeared.

'Get in the car as soon as possible,' I hissed. 'I believe I've been identified.'

David laughed. 'Really? I'm curious why.'He directed his eyes to my clothes,' he claimed. I had determined that a pair of harlequin-check leggings and an oversized top adorned in brightly colored rococo designs, coupled with a large jeweled crucifix around my neck, would allow me to walk through the airport unnoticed. I could maybe have drawn more attention to myself, but only if I'd turned there with a piano and began playing 'Crocodile Rock'.

Gianni Versace, my favorite designer, designed the leggings and the big short. I was always dressed in his clothes. I'd discovered his modest boutique in Milan at the end of the 1980s and became enamored with it. I felt I'd found a genius, the best male designer since Yves Saint Laurent. He used the best fabrics, but his designs were not stuffy or formal: he designed men's garments that were enjoyable to wear. When I met the man behind them, my already high opinion increased.

Meeting Gianni was almost as strange as discovering I had a long-lost identical brother in northern Italy. We were nearly identical: same sense of humor, same love of gossip, same collecting interest, same restless thinking. He couldn't stop thinking, always coming up with some new way to do what he did, which was everything. He could design children's garments, glassware, dinner sets, and album covers - I asked him to design The One's sleeve, which he accomplished beautifully. He had impeccable taste. He'd always know of a small Italian church down a side street with the most magnificent mosaic work in the nave, or a tiny business producing the most fantastic porcelain. And he was the only person I'd ever met who could shop as well as I could. He'd go out to purchase a watch and return with twenty.

He was actually worse than I was. Gianni was so expensive that I appeared to be the epitome of austere life and self-sacrifice in comparison. He mistook Miuccia Prada for a communist since she designed a nylon purse rather than crocodile or snakeskin or whatever ridiculously rich material he was working with that season. He would try to get me to buy the most extravagantly priced items.
'I've found you the most beautiful tablecloth; you must purchase it for Christmas dinner. It's made by nuns and takes them thirty years to complete; look at it, it's fantastic. A million bucks is required.'

That made even me cringe. I mentioned that I thought a million dollars was a tad extravagant for something that would be entirely destroyed the moment someone spilt a little gravy on it. Gianni's face was frightened, as if he was pondering the prospect that I, too, was a communist.

'But Elton,' he said, 'it's lovely... the craftsmanship.'

I did not purchase the tablecloth, but this had no effect on our friendship. Gianni quickly became my best buddy. I used to adore picking up the phone and hearing his voice say, "Allo, bitch.' I introduced him to David, and they hit it off like a house on fire. Of course they did; there wasn't much not to appreciate about Gianni, unless you designed nylon purses. He had a large heart and was amusing. 'When I die, I want to be reincarnated even more gay,' he would cry hysterically. I want to be extremely gay!' David and I would exchange bewildered looks, wondering how that was even possible. There were leather bars on Fire Island that weren't as openly gay as Gianni.

Being in a normal relationship occasionally made me realize how odd my own life was. I planned a little lunch gathering for David to meet my mother and Derf. Our relationship was no longer a secret by that point. Someone from David's office had seen us getting out of a car outside Planet Hollywood in Piccadilly. He'd been summoned to his boss's office, told him everything, and then made preparations to return to Toronto for Christmas and spend time with his family. I was terrified because David had mentioned that his father was pretty conservative, and I knew how terrifying coming out might be if your family wasn't supportive. I'd had an affair in Atlanta with a guy named Rob, whose parents were deeply religious and anti-gay. He was a darling, but you could tell the conflict between his sexuality, religion, and his parents' beliefs was gnawing at him. We remained friends, and after we split up, he paid me a visit on my birthday and sent me flowers. He walked onto the freeway the next day and hurled himself in front of a lorry.

David's family couldn't have taken the news any better - I think, more than anything, they were relieved he wasn't harboring secrets from them any more - but I had still avoided introducing him to my mother for as long as I could. She had acquired a pattern of... not precisely seeing off my lovers, but being chilly towards them, making their life and mine more difficult, as if she despised the presence of anyone who detract attention from her.

The issue with the lunch party, however, was not my mother. One of the other visitors, a psychiatrist, notified me at the last minute that his client Michael Jackson was in England and asked if he might accompany him. This didn't sound like the best plan I'd ever heard, but I couldn't say no. I'd known Michael since he was thirteen or fourteen, when Elizabeth Taylor showed up on the Starship with him in tow after a gig I'd played in Philadelphia. He was the cutest kid you could ever imagine. But, in the intervening years, he began to isolate himself from the world and from reality, just like Elvis Presley did. God only knows what was going on in his head, and God only knows what prescription pills he was being pumped full of, but every time I saw him in his later years, I thought the poor guy had completely lost his marbles. That is not meant in a lighthearted manner. He was a disturbing person to be around since he was actually mentally ill. It was heartbreaking, but you couldn't stop him: he was gone, off in his own world, surrounded by people who only told him what he wanted to hear.

And now he was on his way to lunch where my boyfriend was to meet my mother for the first time. Fantastic. I figured the best course of action would be to call David and casually drop this knowledge into the conversation. Perhaps if I pretended there was no problem here, he'd take it in stride. Or maybe not - I hadn't even finished casually mentioning the change in lunch arrangements when I was interrupted by an angry cry of "Are you fucking KIDDING me?"I tried to soothe him by lying through my teeth, stating that the stories he'd heard about Michael's oddities were highly exaggerated. Given that some of the allegations of Michael's peculiarities had come directly from me, this probably wasn't very convincing. But, I insisted, it wouldn't be as bizarre as he might think.

In that regard, I was completely correct. The lunch was not as odd as I had anticipated. It was stranger than I had anticipated. Because of Michael's vitiligo, we had to sit inside with the blinds drawn on a sunny day. The poor man appeared to be fragile and unwell. He was covered in make-up that looked like it had been applied by a madman. His nose was taped to his face with a sticking plaster to keep what was left of it in place. He sat there, not saying much, simply emitting waves of unease the way other people emit an air of assurance. I got the idea he hadn't eaten in front of other people in a long time. He certainly wouldn't eat anything we served him. He brought his own chef, but he didn't eat anything he prepared. He eventually got up from the table and left without saying anything. Two hours later, we located him in a cottage on the grounds of Woodside where my housekeeper lived: she was sitting there, silently watching Michael Jackson play video games with her eleven-year-old son. For whatever reason, he couldn't seem to handle adult company. While all of this was going on, I could see David through the gloom, sitting at the other end of the table, valiantly trying to make bright conversation with my mother, who was contributing to the tense atmosphere by spending the majority of the meal telling him that psychiatry was a waste of time and money in a voice loud enough for Michael Jackson's psychiatrist to hear. When she took a breather, I noticed David looking around, as if looking for someone who could tell him what the hell he'd gotten himself into.

It didn't take an unexpected visit from Michael Jackson to make David's reality look entirely strange. I could make it appear that way without the assistance of the self-proclaimed King of Pop. Most of my greatest excesses had been curtailed by rehab, but not all of them: the Dwight Family Temper appeared particularly resistant to any form of treatment or medical intervention. When I felt like it, I was still fully capable of throwing terrible tantrums. I believe David first saw one up close on the night I was to be inducted into the Rock and Roll Hall of Fame in New York in January 1994. I didn't want to go because I don't understand the Rock and Roll Hall of Fame. I loved the original concept of it - honoring the true pioneers of rock and roll, the artists who paved the way in the 1950s for the rest of us, especially those who got ripped off financially - but it quickly devolved into something entirely different, a big televised ceremony with tickets costing tens of thousands of dollars. It's simply a matter of getting enough big personalities interested each year to fill seats.

The prudent thing to do would have been to deny the invitation, but I felt obligated. Axl Rose, whom I admired, was inducting me. I contacted him while he was being ripped apart in the news because I know how lonely it can be when the papers are tearing you apart, and I simply wanted to offer some comfort. We hit it off right away and ended up singing 'Bohemian Rhapsody' together at a Freddie Mercury Tribute concert. I was chastised for it since a Guns N' Roses song named 'One In A Million' contained homophobic lyrics. I wouldn't have touched him if I thought it mirrored his personal views. But I didn't since I thought the song was clearly written from the perspective of someone other than Axl Rose. The Gay and Lesbian Alliance Against Defamation gave me a hard time when I performed with him at the Grammys, but it was evident that his lyrics were about creating a persona - an intentionally repulsive persona at that. I didn't believe any of them were homophobes any more than I believed Sting was having an affair with a prostitute named Roxanne or Johnny Cash shot a man in Reno wanting to see him die.

As a result, I went to the Rock and Roll Hall of Fame. As soon as I arrived, I realized I'd made a mistake and turned around, shouting about how the place was a fucking tomb. I pulled David back to the motel, where I felt terrible for blowing them out. So we returned. The Grateful Dead were performing with a cardboard cut-out of Jerry Garcia because Garcia wasn't there: he thought the Rock and Roll Hall of Fame was a bunch of nonsense and refused to attend. I decided Jerry had a point, turned around, and departed with David in tow. I had just changed out of my suit and into my hotel dressing gown when I felt another sense of remorse. So I changed back into my suit and we headed back to the awards ceremony. Then I became enraged at myself for feeling bad and stormed out again, enlivening the drive back to the hotel with a lengthy oration, given at great volume, about what a waste of time the entire evening had been.

David's sympathetic nods and murmurs of agreement were beginning to sound strained at this point, but I assured myself that he was rolling his eyes at the Rock and Roll Hall of Fame rather than at me. This made it easy to determine, ten minutes later, that, all things considered, we should return to the ceremony. The other customers seemed shocked to see us, but you couldn't blame them: we'd gone back and forth to our table more than the wait staff.

I'd like to say it ended there, but I'm afraid there was another change of heart and frantic return to the hotel before I got onstage and claimed the medal. Axl Rose gave a great speech, I brought Bernie up onstage and presented him with the trophy, and then we went. David eventually broke the silence as we drove back to the motel.

'Well,' he replied calmly, 'that was quite a spectacular evening.' He then hesitated. 'Is your life usually like this, Elton?' he inquired plaintively.'

Even though it was my idea to begin with, I believe nights like that piqued David's interest in Tantrums and Tiaras. A film studio wanted to do a documentary about me, but I believed it would be more intriguing if it was made by someone close to me, who would have access to me that I would never offer to anybody else. I didn't want sanitized nonsense; I wanted people to know what it was like to be me: the humorous and absurd portions. And I got the impression David wanted the rest of the world to know what he had to put up with. It was a way for him to make sense of this bizarre life he'd become a part of, that had become his life as well. So he set up a little office in the tram I'd purchased in Australia - you see, I knew it'd come in handy one day - and began recording.

I wasn't concerned about people seeing my horrible, irrational side. I'm fully aware of how ludicrous my life is, and fully aware of what a jerk I am when I lose my cool over nothing - I go from naught to nuclear in seconds, and then calm down just as quickly. My temper was certainly acquired from my parents, but I honestly believe that every creative person, whether a painter, a theater director, an actor, or a musician, has the propensity to behave in an entirely ridiculous manner. It's the shadow side of being creative. Certainly, almost every other artist I'd met seemed to share that component of their personality. Dusty Springfield, Marc Bolan, and John Lennon all did it. They were wonderful people who I adored, but everyone knows they all had their flaws. Dusty had so many that she told me she'd figured out the secret to having a successful tantrum: if you got to the point where you started hurling inanimate objects across the room, make sure you didn't hurl anything expensive or difficult to replace. I'm just more forthright than a lot of folks, especially these days. Today, record firms provide pop singers with media training; they literally educate them on how to cover up any weaknesses in their character and never say anything inappropriate.

You don't have to be an expert on my career to recognize that I come from a different age, when pop stars were advised what they should and shouldn't say to the media. I'm overjoyed, despite the fact that I've said things that have sparked outrage and kept the media running headlines like THE BITCH IS BACK for decades. Keith Richards looked like a monkey with arthritis, which was maybe a bit unfair, but he'd been very filthy about me: he got as good as he gave. The only time I got in trouble was when I told Parade, an American Sunday newspaper magazine, that Jesus may have been a very educated, super-compassionate gay man. I simply meant that no one knows anything about Jesus' personal life, and that you may draw all kinds of ideas about forgiveness and empathy from his teachings. But the religious nuts didn't see it that way: the main notion they seemed to have inferred from Jesus' teachings was that you should go around inciting people to kill anyone who says something you don't agree with. Officers from the Atlanta police department ended up sleeping in my guest room for a week. Protesters were carrying signs outside the apartment complex, one of which screamed ELTON JOHN MUST DIE - not exactly what you want to see when you get home in the evening. The person in possession of it made a video on YouTube threatening to kill me. He was eventually jailed, and the protests went down.

Nonetheless, I believe that a world in which artists are instructed not to say anything that would offend anyone and are presented as ideal figures is dull. Furthermore, it is untrue. Artists are not without flaws. Nobody is flawless. That's why I despise whitewashed rock star documentaries in which everyone tells you what a fantastic person they were. Most rock stars can be awful at times. Tantrums and Tiaras intended to illustrate that they can be fabulous and charming as well as outrageous and dumb.

It was not universally regarded as a good concept. George Michael was terrified when he viewed some of the footage, not because of what he saw - he already knew what I was like - but because I was intending to release it. He saw it as a terrible error. John Reid indicated he was on board with the proposal, but then went around discreetly sabotaging the entire endeavor. He went behind my mother's back and advised her not to get involved because it was all about sex and drugs after she agreed to be interviewed for it.

I was enraged, but I didn't care what other people thought. I normally can't stomach watching myself in anything, but Tantrums and Tiaras were great because they were authentic. David and producer Polly Steele simply followed me around on my 1995 world tour with little Hi-8 camcorders, and I forgot I was being shot much of the time. It's hilarious to hear me make these utterly ludicrous threats, like saying I'll never return to France because a fan waved at me while I was trying to play tennis, or that I'll never make another video because someone unintentionally left my clothing in the back of a car. It was cathartic to see, and I believe the shock of seeing myself changed the way I behaved - that, and a lot of treatment. I still have a temper - you can't change your DNA - but I'm much more aware of how much energy it is, and how totally ridiculous I feel once I've cooled down, so I try to keep it in check: perhaps with varied degrees of success, but at least I'm trying.

The only thing I regret about Tantrums and Tiaras is how popular it became. It truly produced the whole genre of reality TV where you peek into the lives of a celebrity, or worse, someone who has become famous as a result of being on reality TV. It's not exactly uplifting to have Being Bobby Brown and The Anna Nicole Show on your conscience. There's a chance that Keeping Up with the Kardashians is ultimately my responsibility, for which I can only apologize to the human race and seek forgiveness.

Tantrums and Tiaras was ultimately released in 1997, and David was returning from a press appearance in Pasadena for its American debut when I learned of Gianni Versace's murder. I'd bought a house in Nice, and Gianni was supposed to fly out to France the following week for a holiday with David and me - the tickets were booked - when a serial killer shot him outside his Miami mansion: he'd already murdered men in Minnesota, Chicago, and New Jersey, and was supposed to have become obsessed with Gianni after meeting him briefly at a nightclub years before, though I don't think anyone knows whether he actually met him or not.

When John Reid called to tell me what had happened, I immediately broke down. I switched on the TV in my bedroom and sat there, weeping, watching the broadcast. Gianni had gone about his morning routine. He received every international newspaper and magazine every day. There were constantly stacks of them lying about his house, covered with Post-it notes: ideas that had piqued his interest, things he believed he could work with, and things he found inspiring. He was no longer alive. It was like John Lennon's death: there was no explanation, nothing that made it any easier to grasp, no way to rationalize it even somewhat in your thoughts. Another arbitrary murder.

His family invited me to sing at his memorial service at Milan's Duomo. They wanted me to sing the 23rd Psalm with Sting again, the same song I'd done in Sydney's cathedral after John died. The service was chaotic. There were paparazzi, film crews, and photographers everywhere, including the chapel. It was claustrophobic, but in a strange sense, it was just what Gianni would have wanted. He was obsessed with notoriety to the point where it was the one thing that drove me insane. You'd travel on vacation with him to Sardinia, and every single location you went, Gianni's PR guys would have called ahead of time and alerted the press. I'd tell him I hated it, but he didn't understand: 'Oh, Elton, but they love you, they want to take your picture, isn't it beautiful? 'They adore you.' At the cathedral, two officials - monsignors or cardinals or whatever they were - summoned me and Sting and began questioning us about our performance: I believe they didn't want us to sing because we weren't Catholics. It felt like being taken out in front of the school by the headmaster at assembly, except it was in the middle of a memorial ceremony in a cathedral crowded with TV cameras and flashes going off.

We were eventually allowed to sing, and the show went over without a hitch. I couldn't help but cry. I don't think I've ever seen a person so overcome with sadness as Allegra, Gianni's little niece. He died when she was eleven, and he adored her, leaving her his half of the firm in his will. She blamed herself for his death since she used to go to the newspaper with him every morning, but the day he died, she was in Rome with her mother. She believed that if she had been present, her uncle would not have been slain. She had a serious eating disorder after his death. She'd go missing, and they'd find her hiding in the house's wardrobes, clutching his old garments, items that still smelled like him. It was dreadful. It's really terrible.

In fact, after Gianni's death, the entire Versace family disintegrated. Donatella had always struggled with a cocaine addiction. Except for Gianni, everyone was aware. He was really ignorant when it came to drugs. He didn't even drink:

he'd have a glass of red wine with Sprite and ice cubes in it, which I'm sure tastes horrible enough to put you off looking into alcohol any further. He would go to bed early at Versace events, and then the party would truly begin, with Donatella leading the charge. He could see there was something wrong with her, but he couldn't figure out what it was. I recall strolling about Woodside's garden with him and hearing him say, 'I don't understand my sister - one day she's good, one day she's nasty, she has moods, I don't get it.' I told him she was a cocaine addict and that I'd done coke with her several times before becoming clean. He couldn't believe it - he had no idea what her life was like when he wasn't there.

But following his murder, Donatella's cocaine habit spiraled out of hand. I didn't see much of her - she avoided me because she knew I didn't approve - but then, one night, she showed up backstage at a gig I was doing in Reggio Calabria, completely out of her mind, high. She was sobbing at the side of the stage as I was performing. Throughout the show, she never stopped crying. Either she despised my performance or she was seeking assistance.

As a result, we decided to organize an intervention. It was arranged by David and her publicist Jason Weisenfeld at Allegra's eighteenth birthday party in Gianni's old apartment on Via Gesù. I was waiting in this small sitting room with David and Jason, as well as our friends Ingrid Sischy and her partner Sandy. Donatella and Allegra entered, dressed to the nines in Atelier Versace gowns, and sat on a divan as everyone spoke in turn. There was a deafening hush. You never know how an intervention will work out: if the individual being targeted is unwilling to recognize they have a problem, it will be a disaster. Donatella abruptly spoke up. 'My life is like your candle in the wind!' she exclaimed. 'I'm ready to die!'

We got her on the phone with The Meadows, a recovery facility in Scottsdale, Arizona. We could only hear her side of the conversation, and it was incredible. sure, sure... cocaine...

also pills... well, a handful of this pill, a handful of that pill, and if that doesn't work, I take all the pills and mix them together... yes... OK, I come now, but one condition: NO OILY FOOD,' she says.

She left, still in her gown, having presumably been informed that oily food was not on the menu. The following day, we received a phone call from Jason Weisenfeld, who informed us that she had been admitted. The facility's restriction that residential patients couldn't wear make-up had apparently gone down quite badly, and there had been a bit of a commotion when Donatella realized she'd forgotten to take deodorant, but she was fine: she went on to complete the program and get clean. We complimented Jason for completing the task.

'Yeah,' he said glumly. 'All I have to do now is walk around Scottsdale looking for a fucking Chanel deodorant,' she says.

We invited Gianni's partner Antonio to stay with us in Nice after the burial. He was upset, and he never got along with the rest of Gianni's family. It was a dark, gloomy summer, sitting in the house we'd just bought, which we'd designed in a manner influenced by Gianni's taste, and which we'd been eager to show off to him and receive his feedback on. David told me one night that it was past time for me to consider employing professional protection. I'd never thought about it before, not even after John was murdered. In the 1970s, I hired a bodyguard named Jim Morris, although it was more of a camp act than anything more. He was a bodybuilder who'd been crowned Mr America, and he was out gay - no small feat for a black macho guy back then - and he spent more time on stage carrying me on his shoulders than anything else. We appeared to be in desperate need of security now. Things had shifted.

And our summer was about to get wilder. We were awakened by the sound of the fax machine going off one Sunday morning near the end of August. David went to look at it and returned with a sheet of paper containing a handwritten letter from a friend in London: "so sorry to hear about this awful news." We had no idea what it meant. It couldn't be referring to Gianni, who had been dead for six weeks. I turned on the television, feeling increasingly uneasy. That's how I learned Princess Diana had died.

CHAPTER 14

I first met Diana in 1981, soon before she married Prince Charles. Ray Cooper and I were meant to provide entertainment at Prince Andrew's twenty-first birthday party at Windsor Castle. It had been a really bizarre evening. The outside of the castle was adorned with psychedelic lighting, and before we performed, the ballroom was entertained by a mobile disco. Because the Queen was present and no one wanted to offend the royal sensitivities, the disco was turned down as low as it could go without being shut off completely. Over the music, you could clearly hear your feet moving around on the floor. Princess Anne requested me to dance with her to Elvis Presley's "Hound Dog." I say dance because I ended up basically shuffling from foot to foot, attempting to make as little noise as possible so that I didn't drown out the music. You could just about make out that the DJ had switched from Elvis to 'Rock Around The Clock' if you strained your ears and tried hard. The Queen then appeared, holding her handbag. She approached us and asked if she may join us. So now I was trying to dance as quietly as possible with Princess Anne and the Queen - who was still clutching her purse - while Bill Haley played in what appeared to be the world's quietest disco. Strangely, it reminded me of The Band storming into my dressing room or Brian Wilson repeatedly chanting the chorus of 'Your Song' at me when I first came to America. My life had changed beyond recognition eleven years later, and yet here I was, desperately attempting to act normal while the world around me appeared to have gone absolutely insane.

That was the interesting part about my interactions with the Royal Family. They were always quite lovely and funny to me. I understand that the Queen's public image isn't exactly one of wild frivolity, but I believe this is due to the nature of her job. I became aware of it after receiving the CBE and later the knighthood. She has to hand out the items for two and a half hours, making small conversation with two hundred people one after the other. Anyone in that situation would struggle to come up with a succession of fantastic witticisms. She simply asks if you're busy right now, and when you respond 'yes, Ma'am,' she says 'very beautiful' and carries on. In private, however, she has the potential to be amusing. I observed her approach Viscount Linley and ask him to peek in on his sister, who'd been ill and retired to her room, at another gathering. The Queen lightly slapped him across the face and said, 'Don't' - SLAP - 'argue' - SLAP - 'with' - SLAP -'me' - SLAP - 'I' - SLAP - 'am' - SLAP - 'THE QUEEN!'That seems to be effective. She spotted me staring at her as he went away, gave me a wink, and walked away.

Yet no matter how funny or normal the Royal Family seemed, whether they were complaining about the paint job on my Aston Martin, or asking me if I'd done any coke before I went onstage, or winking at me after slapping their nephew across the face, there would inevitably come a moment where I'd find myself feeling slightly out of place, thinking: 'This is just bizarre. What am I doing here as a musician from a council housing on Pinner Road?'But it wasn't like that with Diana. Despite her class and background, she had an extraordinary social ease, the ability to talk to anyone, make herself appear ordinary, and make people feel completely at ease in her company. Her children have inherited it, particularly Prince Harry, who is precisely like his mother, with little interest in formality or grandeur. Diana was the woman in the famous photograph of her holding an AIDS patient's hand at the London Middlesex Hospital. I don't think she was aiming to make a major statement, though she definitely did: in one instant, she forever changed public opinions toward AIDS. She had just met someone who was in pain and dying: why wouldn't you reach out and touch them? It's a basic human instinct to want to console someone.

When she walked into the ballroom that night in 1981, we instantly clicked. We ended up pretending to do the Charleston while laughing at the disco's incompetence. She was great company, the best dinner party attendee, tremendously indiscreet, and a real gossip: you could ask her anything and she'd tell you everything. Her sole peculiarity was the way she spoke about Prince Charles. She never referred to him by name; it was always my husband,' never Charles, and never a loving nickname. It appeared distant, chilly, and formal, which was odd because Diana was everything but formal: she was constantly amazed at how starchy and prim certain other members of the Royal Family could be.

But if Diana stunned me, it was nothing compared to the impact she could have on straight guys. They seemed to lose their heads in her presence: they were fully charmed. When I was working on The Lion King, the head of Disney, Jeffrey Katzenberg, came to England, and we hosted a dinner party for him and his wife Marilyn at Woodside. When I asked them if there was somebody in Britain they really wanted to meet, they immediately responded "Princess Diana." So we invited her, as well as George Michael, Richard Curtis and his wife Emma Freud, Richard Gere, and Sylvester Stallone, who were all in town at the time. The strangest scene unfolded. Richard Gere and Diana appeared to be really taken with each other right away. She had been separated from Prince Charles by this point, and Richard had recently split up with Cindy Crawford, so they ended up sitting on the floor in front of the fireplace, locked in rapt conversation. While the rest of us talked, I couldn't help but notice a peculiar mood in the room. The sight of Diana and Richard Gere's newly developing bond did not sit well with Sylvester Stallone, judging by the stares he kept shooting them. I believe he went to the party specifically to pick up Diana, only to have his intentions for the evening derailed abruptly.

Dinner was eventually served. We entered the dining room and took our seats at the table. Or, at the very least, most of us did. Richard Gere and Sylvester Stallone were nowhere to be found. We sat and waited. There is still no sign. Finally, I sent David to go find them. He returned with both of them, but he had a really glum expression on his face.

'Elton,' murmured him. 'We have... a problem.'

When David went out to find them, he saw Sylvester Stallone and Richard Gere squaring up to each other in the corridor, presumably preparing to settle their disputes over Diana with a fistfight. He'd managed to defuse the situation by acting as if he hadn't observed what was going on - 'Hey, folks! It's time for dinner!' - but Sylvester was plainly still unhappy. Diana and Richard Gere resumed their position in front of the fire after supper, and Sylvester ultimately stormed off home.

'I never would have came if I'd known Prince fuckin' Charming was going to be here,' he snarled as David and I led him out the door. 'If I'd wanted her, I would've took her!''

We managed to hold our laughter until his automobile was out of sight. Diana and Richard Gere were still staring at one other in the living room. She appeared entirely unaffected. Perhaps she hadn't recognized what was going on. Or maybe it happened all the time and she was accustomed to it. Following her death, people began discussing the Diana Effect, or how she was able to shift popular attitudes toward the Royal Family, AIDS, bulimia, and mental health. But every time I heard the words, I remembered that night. There was undoubtedly another kind of Diana Effect: one that could send Hollywood stars to their knees at a dinner party over her attentions, like a couple of love-struck teenage morons.

She had been a close friend for many years before we abruptly parted ways. Gianni Versace's book, Rock and Royalty, was the catalyst for the cause. It featured photographs by notable photographers such as Richard Avedon, Cecil Beaton, Herb Ritts, Irving Penn, and Robert Mapplethorpe. She agreed to write the foreword and donate the revenues to the AIDS Foundation. She then developed cold feet. Buckingham Palace probably didn't appreciate the thought of a member of the Royal Family being associated with a book that portrayed naked men with towels draped about them. Diana removed her preface at the last minute. She claimed she had no idea what was in the book, which was simply not true: Gianni had shown her the entire thing and she had stated she loved it. I responded by calling her out, telling her how much money she had cost the AIDS Foundation, and reminding her that she had read the book. The letter I received was official and severe: 'Dear Mr John...' and that appeared to be the end of it. I was enraged with her, but I was also concerned. She seemed to be losing connection with a wide range of really close friends who were willing to be honest with her and tell her the truth. Instead, she surrounded herself with individuals who told her what she wanted to hear or who would listen and nod when she revealed some of her more paranoid notions about the Royal Family since her divorce. From personal experience, I knew that wasn't a good situation.

I hadn't spoken to her since the day Gianni was murdered. She was the first one to call me after John Reid informed me that he had died. I'm not sure how she acquired the number; we hadn't had the house in Nice for long. She was on Dodi Fayed's yacht in St-Tropez, close to the coast. She inquired as to how I was doing and if I had spoken with Donatella. 'I'm very sorry,' she said. It was a ridiculous squabble. Let us become pals.'

She arrived at the funeral with us, looking stunning: tanned from her vacation, wearing a pearl necklace. She remained the same warm, caring, tactile individual she had always been. When she stepped in, the paparazzi in the cathedral went crazy: it was as if the world's biggest star had arrived, which I suppose she did. They didn't stop throughout the service, though I should point out that the famous shot of her supposedly consoling me - where she's leaning forward towards me, speaking, while I'm red-eyed and glazed with grief - is one of the few times she wasn't. They caught her just as she was reaching for a mint that David had offered her. The words of solace that sprang from her lips at that very moment were, 'God, I'd love a Polo.'

I thanked her and she responded by offering to be a patron of the AIDS Foundation and asked if I would get engaged in her landmine charity. We planned to have lunch and talk about it the following time we were both in London. But there would be no next time.

I received a phone call from Richard Branson a few days following her death. He told me that when visitors signed the book of condolence at St James's Palace, a number of them were penning down passages from the lyrics of 'Candle In The Wind'. They were apparently playing it a lot on the radio in the UK as well - stations had modified their musical format and were broadcasting somber-sounding music to suit the popular mood. Then he asked if I would be willing to rework the lyrics and perform them at the funeral. That was really unexpected. I believe Richard was called by the Spencer family because they wanted the funeral to be something that people could truly connect to: they didn't want a serious, remote royal occasion full of grandeur and procedure, because that would have been completely out of character for Diana.

So I dialed Bernie's number. I believed that was a very difficult job for him. Not only would whatever he wrote be aired live to literally billions of people - it was evident that the funeral would be a massive, worldwide, televised spectacle - but it would also have to be approved by the Royal Family and the Church of England. But he was fantastic: he pretended as if creating a song for the Queen and the Archbishop of Canterbury to approve was all in a day's work. He faxed the lyrics to me the next morning, and I submitted them to Richard Branson, who waved them through.

Even so, I had no idea what to anticipate when I went to rehearse at Westminster Abbey the day before the burial. The recollection of Gianni's memorial ceremony, and the fact that the church officials had plainly felt it inappropriate for me to perform, lingered in my thoughts. And this was merely a hymn at a private service, not a rock tune at a state function. What if no one else wanted me to be here?

But things couldn't have been more dissimilar. The Archbishop of Canterbury was really gracious and sympathetic. There was a strong sense that everyone had to work together to make this thing work. I insisted on a teleprompter next to the piano, with Bernie's new lyrics written on it. I had previously been opposed to their use. Partly because it seemed contrary to the spontaneous spirit of rock and roll - I'm pretty sure Little Richard wasn't reading the words off an autocue when he recorded 'Long Tall Sally' - and partly because I just thought: come on, do your job properly. Onstage, you really just have three things to do: sing in tune, play the appropriate notes, and remember the words. If you can only be bothered with two of them, you might as well find another career - which is why I have an issue with artists miming on stage. But I figured I might relax the rules a little this time. It was a truly one-of-a-kind experience. It felt like the biggest gig of my life - for four minutes, I was literally going to be the center of the world's attention - but it wasn't an Elton John moment, and it wasn't about me at all. It was quite bizarre.

The strangeness was highlighted the next day when we arrived at Westminster Abbey. David and I went with George Michael before we had a falling out over his drug problems. He had called and asked if we might attend the funeral together. We sat in silence on the way there since George was too upset to speak, there was no chat, nothing. Donatella Versace, David Frost, Tom Cruise and Nicole Kidman, Tom Hanks and Rita Wilson were among those there. It all felt a little weird, like a dream rather than something that was actually happening in real life. We were seated in the church's inner sanctum, precisely where the Royal Family entered. William and Harry appeared absolutely stunned. They were fifteen and twelve years old, and I thought their treatment that day was completely horrible. They were compelled to travel through the streets of London behind their mother's coffin, instructed not to exhibit emotion and to keep their gaze fixed ahead. It was a terrible way to treat two children who had just lost their mother.

But I scarcely registered any of it. I wasn't nervous in the least. I'd be lying if I said it never occurred to me that two billion people were watching, but at least I was performing in front of the section of the church where all the representatives from the charities Diana supported were stationed, so there were friends from the Elton John AIDS Foundation there - Robert Key, Anne Aslett, and James Locke. But it wasn't so much stage anxiety as it was a specific fear: what if I slipped into autopilot and sang the incorrect song? I'd done 'Candle In The Wind' hundreds of times before. It wasn't out of the question that I'd get caught up in the performance, forget about the teleprompter, and start singing the original lyrics. What could possibly go wrong if I did that? Appalling. People may have quoted lines from them in the book of condolence at St James's Palace, but large chunks of the songs were clearly improper for the occasion. You'd have a hard time feigning ignorance about Marilyn Monroe being discovered dead in her underwear, or how your sentiments were more than sexual, during a state funeral, in front of a global audience of two billion people, or whatever it was intended to be.

Then something strange happened. I found myself drifting out at the burial and recalling an incident from my first tour of America. I was scheduled to appear on The Andy Williams Show with The Mamas and The Papas' Mama Cass Elliot and Ray Charles. When I arrived, the producers cheerfully informed me that we would not only be performing on the same program, but also performing together. They seemed to think this was a wonderful surprise for me, and that I would be overjoyed. They were mistaken: Mama Cass was OK, Andy Williams was fine, but Ray Charles? Are you serious? Ray Charles, please! Ray, brother! The Mastermind! An artist I fantasized about being as a kid, hiding in my bedroom with my record collection and miming to his Ray Charles at Newport live album. And now some idiot had decided it would be a great idea for him to go on national TV and sing with me, as if a completely unknown English singer-songwriter was some kind of perfect musical equal for the man who'd virtually invented soul music. If it wasn't the worst notion I'd ever heard, it sounded so similar that it didn't matter. And there was nothing I could do to stop it. It was my first appearance on US television, and I was in no position to start upsetting American television bosses by being unpleasant. As a result, I did it. I stood up and sang 'Heaven Help Us All' with Ray Charles, who was on a white piano and I was on a black piano. It went off without a hitch. 'Hey, love, how you doin'?' said Ray Charles, cordial, friendly, and encouraging.' - as artists with nothing to prove tend to be.

And it actually taught me something valuable. Sometimes you just have to walk up to the plate, even if it's far outside your comfort zone. It's as if you dive deep inside yourself, forgetting about any feelings you may be feeling and thinking, "No, I'm a performer." This is my job. Let's get started.

So I started to work. I don't recall much about the performance itself, but I do recall the applause that followed. It seemed to start outside Westminster Abbey and flow into the church itself, which indicated that Diana's family's goal of persuading me to sing had been met: it connected with the people outside. I went immediately to Townhouse Studios in Shepherd's Bush after the burial, where George Martin was waiting: they were intending to release the new version of 'Candle In The Wind' as a single to generate money for a charity memorial fund established in Diana's name. I sang it twice live at the keyboard before leaving, leaving George Martin to do a string quartet overdub. When I returned to Woodside, David was in the kitchen, watching the news on TV. The funeral cortège had arrived at the M1: people were throwing flowers from the bridges over the highway onto Diana's hearse. That's when I finally gave up. I hadn't felt able to express myself emotionally all day. I had a task to do, and my feelings over Diana's death might have hampered my ability to complete it; the funeral wasn't about me, it was about her. So I couldn't afford to be annoyed up to that time.

The reception to the single was out of this world. People were queuing outside record stores, then rushing in and buying armfuls of CD singles. There were all these ridiculous statistics surrounding it. It was projected to sell six copies every second at one point; it was the fastest-selling single ever released; and it was the best-selling single of all time in Finland. I received sales prizes from the most unusual places: Indonesia and the Middle East. And it just kept going and going. It topped the charts in the United States for fourteen weeks. It spent three years in Canada's top twenty. A part of me couldn't comprehend why anyone would want to listen to that. Under what conditions would you play it? Never did I. I sang it three times: once at the funeral and twice in the studio, then once more to check the mix, and that was the end of it: never again. People probably bought it to donate money to charity, which was fine, but a large portion of the £38 million it raised was eventually wasted. The organization became involved in protecting her image rights against persons who were creating Diana products - plates, dolls, and T-shirts - and the money began to be devoured by legal bills. It lost a battle against an American corporation called Franklin Mint and ended up paying them millions of dollars to settle an out-of-court case of malicious prosecution. Whatever the rights and wrongs of the matter were, I believed it made them look bad, as if they were more interested in utilizing the money donated to battle over trademarks than in clearing landmines, assisting disadvantaged women, or doing any of the other activities they were doing.

Finally, the charity single's persistence made me feel uneasy. Because of its success, there was footage of Diana's funeral on Top of the Pops week after week - it felt as if people were somehow wallowing in her death, as if the sorrow for her had gotten out of hand and they were unwilling to go on. It struck me as unhealthy, morbid, and unnatural. I didn't believe it was what Diana would have wanted. I thought the media had shifted from reflecting the popular sentiment to purposefully inflaming it in order to sell papers.

It was getting crazy, and I didn't want to prolong it any longer. So when Oprah Winfrey invited me to her chat show in the United States to address the burial, I declined. I wouldn't let them include the funeral version of 'Candle In The Wind' on a charity CD issued in her honor. It's never been on any of my Greatest Hits albums, and it's never been re-released. For a few years, I even stopped performing the original version of 'Candle In The Wind' live because I believed people needed a break from hearing it. When I went out on tour that autumn, I avoided it and sang a song called 'Sand And Water' from an album by the singer-songwriter Beth Nielsen Chapman, which was released the day Gianni was murdered. I'd played it over and over in Nice: 'I shall see you in the light of a thousand suns, I will hear you in the roar of the waves, I will know you when I come, as we all will come, through the doors beyond the dead'. I always tried to avoid discussing the subject with journalists: the chart nerd in me enjoyed the fact that I'd made the best-selling single since the charts began, but the circumstances around it were so unusual that I didn't want to dwell on it. I conducted one interview on the twentieth anniversary of Diana's death, regarding her AIDS work, because Prince Harry particularly requested it.

Perhaps there was something personal intertwined with my sentiments towards the single. It had been a strange and dreadful summer. From the day Gianni died, it had felt like the world had spun off its axis and gone mad: his murder, the memorial service, the reunion with Diana, the weeks in the house in France caring after his lover Antonio, Diana's death, her funeral, the bedlam around 'Candle In The Wind'. I didn't want to forget anything; I just wanted things to return to some sort of normalcy. So I returned to work. I took a tour. In an event dubbed 'Out of the Closet,' I sold a load of my old clothing to benefit the AIDS Foundation. I recorded a song for the South Park cartoon series, which felt about as far removed from singing 'Candle In The Wind' at a state funeral as I could get. I started talking about doing a joint tour with Tina Turner, which rapidly developed into a fiasco. She called me at home while we were still planning, presumably with the explicit aim of telling me how terrible I was and how I needed to improve before we could work together. She didn't like my hair, she didn't like the color of my piano, which had to be white for some reason, and she didn't like my clothes.

'You wear too much Versace, and it makes you look overweight; you should wear Armani,' she declared.

I could hear poor old Gianni turning in his grave at the thought: the Versace and Armani houses were bitter enemies. Gianni thought Armani was very drab and uninteresting, whereas Armani thought Versace manufactured really vulgar garments. 'She sounded like my fucking mother,' I cried at David as I hung up the phone. I'd like to think I've grown a thick skin over the years, but listening to one of the greatest performers of all time - an artist you're supposed to be working with - express in detail how much they despise everything about you is a dismal experience.

It wasn't the best start to our professional relationship, but our working relationship deteriorated. I agreed to sing 'Proud Mary' and 'The Bitch Is Back' with her at a large event called VH1 Divas Live. My band had gone to rehearsals a few days before me to get a feel for working with a new singer. When I arrived, I was met not by the joyous sight of musicians uniting over the common language of music, but by the news that if I went on tour with Tina Turner, none of my band members would accompany me, citing Tina Turner as a "fucking nightmare." I inquired as to the nature of the situation.

'You'll see,' Davey Johnstone sighed menacingly.

He was correct. Tina never addressed the artists by name; instead, she pointed at them and exclaimed, 'Hey, you!' when she needed their attention. We started singing 'Proud Mary'. It sounded fantastic. Tina abruptly ended the song.

'It's you,' she exclaimed, pointing at my bassist, Bob Birch. 'You're doing it incorrectly.'

He assured her that he wasn't, and we resumed the song. Tina yelled again for us to stop. Curt, my drummer, was supposed to be at blame this time. This went on for a long time, stopping and starting every thirty seconds, with each member of the band being accused of making a mistake in turn, until Tina uncovered the true cause of the problem. This time, her finger was pointing at me.

'It is you!' You're not doing it correctly!'

I asked her forgiveness.

'You're not playing it right,' she said angrily. 'You have no idea how to play this music.'

The subsequent dispute about whether or not I knew how to play 'Proud Mary' quickly grew heated, and I ended it by telling Tina Turner to stick her fucking song up her arse and storming off. I alternated between angry and wondering what her problem was in the changing room. I've had my fair share of temper tantrums, but there are limits: there's an unspoken rule that musicians don't treat their fellow musicians like garbage. Perhaps it was her insecurity. She'd been treated horribly early in her career, having been ripped off, beaten up, and pushed around for years and years. Perhaps this had an impact on how she interacted with others. I apologized to her in her changing room.

She said that the problem was that I was improvising too much on the piano, adding tiny fills and runs. That's how I've always performed, ever since the early days of the Elton John Band, when we would switch and change songs on stage according to the mood. It's one of the things I enjoy about performing live: the music is always a little fluid, not set in stone; there's always opportunity for maneuver, the players rub off each other, and it keeps things fresh. Nothing beats hearing someone in your band perform something unexpected that sounds wonderful in that moment onstage. It's all about catching their eye, nodding, and laughing. Tina, on the other hand, did not think so. Everything had to be exact every time; everything had to be rehearsed down to the smallest movement. That made it clear that the tour was doomed, but we made amends later: she arrived for dinner in Nice and put a large Tina Turner lipstick kiss in the visitors' book.

Instead, I scheduled another round of live shows with Billy Joel. Since the early 1990s, we'd been traveling together, both of us onstage at the same time, playing each other's songs. It struck me as a brilliant concept. We were both pianists, and our approaches to music were similar, yet Billy is a very American, East Coast writer, similar to Lou Reed or Paul Simon. They're all incredibly different, but even if you didn't know anything about them, you could tell they were from New York. We played together for years, but it ended horribly because Billy had a lot of personal difficulties at the time, the most serious of which was alcoholism. In his dressing room, he would wash down medication for a chest infection with liquor, then fall asleep onstage in the middle of singing "Piano Man." Then he'd rouse himself, take a bow, and go back to the hotel bar, where he'd stay until 5 a.m. I eventually indicated that he required the kind of assistance that I had received, which did not go down well. He accused me of being judgmental, although I was not. I couldn't handle it any longer, watching a kind guy do that to himself. But that was in the distant future. Initially, Billy's tours were fantastic: they were unique, entertaining to perform, crowds liked them, and they were extremely popular.

So I had a lot going on, enough to make me feel that the summer's craziness was over. However, the rest of the world appears to have no desire to stop becoming insane. The following time we went to Milan, I saw that people on the street would step aside from me everywhere I went. When they saw me, women crossed their legs and males grabbed their crotches. They thought I was cursed because of my relationship with Gianni and Diana, as if I had the evil eye or something. I'd have gotten a worse reaction if I'd shown there wearing a shroud and brandishing a scythe.

And then, as if a bunch of Italians acting like I was the angel of death wasn't insane enough, something even more ridiculous occurred. I was in Australia, where I'd just begun touring with Billy in March 1998, when David called. He was at his residence in Woodside. He stated that the girls who did the weekly floral arrangements at the house had called to inform him that they couldn't work for us any more because they hadn't been paid for over a year and a half. He called John Reid's office to find out what was going on and was told that the florists hadn't been paid since there wasn't enough money. I was apparently going bankrupt.

It just didn't make sense to me. The official attitude of John Reid and his office was that I'd spent everything and then some. Don't get me wrong: I know exactly who I am, and no one, with the potential exception of Gianni, would describe me as the living personification of frugality and thrifty housekeeping. I spent a lot of money - I had four residences, workers, cars, I purchased art and china and luxury clothes - and every now and then, I'd get a letter from the accountants advising me to cut back, which I would of course ignore. But I couldn't figure out how I was spending more than I was earning. I never took a break from working. I played live all the time, went on extended tours, played a hundred or a hundred and fifty gigs in the largest venues possible, and the shows were always sold out. My most recent albums had all gone platinum throughout the world, and there was a steady stream of compilations coming out that were selling so well that I questioned who was purchasing them. It seemed impossible that anyone who liked 'Your Song' or 'Bennie And The Jets' didn't already have a copy. The album to The Lion King had sold sixteen million copies, the picture had grossed nearly a billion dollars, and the Broadway show was breaking box office records.

Something didn't feel right, and I had no idea what it was. I wasn't very concerned with money. I've been really fortunate and have made a lot of money, but money was never my motivation. I'd be lying if I said I didn't appreciate the rewards of my success, but the mechanics of how money was created didn't pique my interest: if they had, I'd have applied to accountancy school instead of Bluesology. I just wanted to play and record music. I was competitive; I'd always ask how many CDs or gig tickets I'd sold, and I'd keep a close eye on my chart placements, but I never asked how much money I'd earned, never really wanted to look at the contracts and royalty cheques. I've never been a tax exile because I'm British and desire to live largely in the United Kingdom. I'm not passing judgment on those that do it, but I don't see the point. You may save money, but I doubt it will bring you much consolation when you look back on your life and realize you've spent half of it feeling sorry for yourself in Switzerland, surrounded by other tax exiles who don't want to be there too. And, from a creative standpoint, I want to be where things are happening in music, which is not Monaco. I'm sure the principality has a lot to offer, but when was the last time you heard about a fantastic new band from Monte Carlo?

Besides, I didn't need to keep track of my finances. That was what John Reid did for me, in my opinion. It served as the foundation for a new management agreement we struck in St-Tropez in the 1980s. I gave him 20% of my total revenues - a large sum by most artists' standards - with the expectation that he would handle everything. This approach was probably referred to as 'Rolls-Royce service'. I could enjoy a wonderful life of creativity and pleasure, free of little annoyances like studying tax returns, checking bank statements, or reading the fine print on contracts. It made sense to me since I had complete faith in John. We'd been together for what seemed like an eternity, in some ways. It was more than a commercial arrangement: no matter how close other artists claimed to be to their managers, I doubted any of them had lost their virginity to them. I trusted him, even though there were times when I questioned if his Rolls-Royce service was in need of a MOT. There was the time a tabloid newspaper obtained a lot of my financial information, including one of the letters from the accountants telling me to cut back on my expenditures. I was convinced they had been leaked, but it turned out that a man named Benjamin Pell had discovered them while searching through the garbage cans outside John Reid's office. They'd just tossed confidential information on the street without destroying it, which didn't say much about the firm's security or how well they looked after my interests: it appeared their methods for dealing with personal data could use a makeover.

And then there was John's scheme to sell my master recordings. It meant that I would receive a large lump payment, and whoever purchased them would receive a royalty every time one of my records was sold or a song of mine was broadcast on the radio. It was a huge issue since it included not just everything I'd recorded previously, but also everything I planned to record in the future. I consented when John brought in lawyers and music business executives who assured me what a terrific idea it was. However, the lump sum turned out to be significantly less than I had anticipated and far less than the value of my master recordings. Everyone seemed to be focused on the gross figure rather than the net. After John had got his commission and the attorneys and tax had been paid, the money left over didn't appear to be sufficient to justify signing away every song I'd ever recorded and would ever record. But I quickly forgot about it. It was still enough to buy the Nice house, furnish it with art and furniture, and ensure that everyone around me benefited. When John received his commission, I decided to pay off the mortgages of many of my employees, including my PA Bob Halley, Robert Key, my driver Derek, and Bob Stacey, who had been my roadie and wardrobe manager for decades. And, anyway, I didn't want to get into a major fight with John about it.

But now I knew something wasn't right. David and I decided to seek expert assistance from a lawyer named Frank Presland, who had previously worked with me. He agreed that something didn't appear right and suggested that I get John Reid Enterprises audited independently. When I informed John, he said he thought it was a fantastic idea and would assist in any way he could.

When the auditors arrived, I was in Australia, and I began to dread David's phone calls with his daily report from his meetings with Frank Presland and the accountants. He called one night, clearly shaken: Benjamin Pell, the same guy who'd been rummaging through the garbage outside John Reid's office, had contacted him, telling him that David was being watched and our phone lines were being tapped, and that he should be careful what he said. At the time, such behavior was common in the UK press. How bad might things get?

Finally, the auditors noted a variety of concerns about how various financial items had been handled. I was avoiding John's calls and asked Frank Presland to explain what we were arguing over. To make a long and sad story short, John agreed to settle the possible lawsuit and agreed to give me $5 million, taking into account his financial circumstances at the time.

I couldn't tell you how I actually felt because it changed by the minute. I was devastated. I felt deceived because, whatever the legal rights and wrongs, I expected John to prioritize my interests and alert me if there was anything I should be concerned about. I was furious, both with myself and with John. I felt like a fucking idiot for being so keen to avoid becoming engaged in my own company operations. I was humiliated. Most importantly, I felt like a coward. It was insane: I was still afraid of confronting him about the situation and upsetting him. We'd been together for so long that I couldn't picture my life without him. Our lives had been completely entangled since the minute he appeared in the lobby of the Miyako Hotel. We'd been lovers, friends, partners, a team that had endured everything: fame, drugs, brawls, all the folly, all the extremes that came with my becoming Elton John. You name it, it had happened, and Sharon and Beryl had stuck together through it all. Whenever someone said he was violent or complained about his temper, I remembered Don Henley's comment about The Eagles' manager, Irving Azoff: "he may be Satan, but he's our Satan." It was all over now.

John terminated his management contract and relinquished his rights to my future revenues. The next year, he closed John Reid Enterprises and resigned from management. And then I went on tour again. I needed to pay off some debts.

CHAPTER 15

One of the many things I admire about Bernie is that he has no qualms about telling you that the last album you made together - an album that sold millions of copies, charted in the Top Ten around the world, and spawned a string of hit singles - was a disaster of unimaginable proportions that necessitated an immediate crisis meeting to ensure nothing like it happened again. Bernie and I had been doing a lot of commercials. We'd released two new albums, Made in England in 1995 and The Big Picture in autumn 1997, and they'd both done really well, going platinum in countries ranging from Australia to Switzerland. But, as far as Bernie was concerned, The Big Picture was the issue. He despised everything about it, including the songs, his lyrics, the production, and the fact that we'd recorded it in England and he'd had to travel from the US for the sessions. As he sat on the patio of our Nice home three years later, he commented that the ultimate result was a pile of clinical, boring, middle-of-the-road garbage. In fact, he went on, clearly gaining traction, it was the worst album we'd ever made.

I wasn't a huge fan of The Big Picture, but I felt that was a little much. I didn't think it was as horrible as Leather Jackets, which, to be fair, wasn't much. Leather Jackets, as you may recall, was more of an experiment in attempting to produce music while taking so much cocaine that you've effectively left yourself psychologically insane. But even that meager defense was ineffective. No, Bernie insisted, The Big Picture was far worse.

I didn't agree, but Bernie was plainly irritated: irritated enough to fly from his home in America to the south of France to discuss it. And there was certainly something to what he said. I've been listening to Ryan Adams' Heartbreaker album a lot. He was a true country rock singer-songwriter, and I could picture him onstage at the Troubadour in the 1970s. But it had a hardness and a freshness about it that made The Big Picture feel strangely antiquated and boring. Perhaps I had lost sight of the importance of my solo albums. I'd gotten increasingly fascinated in film and stage music since the triumph of The Lion King. I'd created the soundtrack for the comedy The Muse, as well as an instrumental piece for David's British comedy-drama Women Talking Dirty. I wasn't writing songs, but rather actual instrumental soundtracks, for which I had to sit and watch the film and come up with thirty or sixty seconds of music to complement each scene. I expected it to be dull, but I thoroughly enjoyed it. It's extremely inspiring when you get it right because you can literally see the effect music can have: a small snippet of it can completely affect how a scene feels or how it functions emotionally.

And Tim Rice and I had written the songs for the DreamWorks animation picture The Road to El Dorado, which I had told Jeffrey Katzenberg I would create, and then written Aida, another stage musical. That had been far more difficult than working on The Lion King. The set had issues, the directors and designers were replaced, and I walked out of one of the Broadway previews midway through the first act because they hadn't changed the arrangements of a couple of the songs as I'd requested. If they weren't going to listen to me politely asking, maybe they'd listen to me stomping up the aisle and out of the theater. But the effort - and, yes, the stomping - paid off. It lasted for four years on Broadway, and we earned a Grammy and a Tony Award for Best Score. And I already had another musical idea in the works. We went to watch Billy Elliot at the Cannes Film Festival, and I'm afraid I made a bit of a fool of myself. I didn't know what the movie was about. I just figured it would be a charming little British comedy starring Julie Walters. I was completely surprised at how deeply it would hit me emotionally. The part where his father observes him dancing in the gym and understands that his son is truly skilled, even if he doesn't recognize it; the ending, where his father goes to see him perform and feels proud and affected; it was simply too close to home. It was as if someone had scripted a happy ending to mine and my father's story instead of what had actually transpired in real life. I couldn't take it anymore. I was so upset that David had to carry me out of the theater. If he hadn't, there's a good chance I'd still be sitting there, sobbing.

I mustered the courage to attend the reception that followed. We were conversing with the film's director, Stephen Daldry, and writer, Lee Hall, when David said that it might make a good stage musical. He seemed to have a valid point. Lee felt the same way, albeit he was curious about who would compose the songs. I told him he was: it was his tale, and he was from Easington, the setting for the film. He lamented the fact that he'd never written a lyric in his life, but vowed to try. I couldn't believe what he brought back. Lee has a natural talent. I never had to edit a single word he'd written, and even better, they were unlike any words I'd dealt with before. His words were rough and political: 'You think you're smart, you Cockney shite, you want to be suspicious - while you were on the picket line, I went and raped your missus,' he said. There was a song called 'Only Poofs Do Ballet' that didn't make it into the final play. It was an entirely new challenge. Perhaps the prospect of recording Elton John's twenty-seventh album seemed a tad mundane in comparison.

Or perhaps there was a way to alter that habit. Bernie had started talking wistfully about how we used to make albums in the 1970s: on analogue tape, with few overdubs, and with my piano at the front and center of the sound. It was ironic because I had been thinking about exactly the same issue. Perhaps it was the experience of viewing Cameron Crowe's film Almost Famous, which was a sort of love letter to early 1970s rock, symbolized by a fictional band called Stillwater. In one moment, the band begins singing along to 'Tiny Dancer' on their tour van. In fact, that incident catapulted 'Tiny Dancer' into one of my most popular songs overnight. People forget that when it was released as a single in 1971, it was a flop. It failed to chart in America, and the record label in the United Kingdom refused to distribute it at all. When it appeared on the soundtrack of Almost Famous, I believe many people had no idea what it was or who wrote it. I believe the film unconsciously implanted certain assumptions in my mind about the type of musician I was back then, about how my music was made and received, before I got totally massive.

It wasn't that I wanted to go back in time. I wasn't interested in doing anything retro. Nostalgia, I believe, can be a tremendous trap for an artist. When you reminisce about the good old days, you naturally see everything through rose-colored glasses. In my instance, I believe it is forgivable because I was most likely wearing rose-colored spectacles with flashing lights and ostrich feathers attached at the time. But if you wind up convincing yourself that everything was better in the past, you might as well stop writing music and retire.

What I liked was the concept of recapturing that energy, that directness, which I heard in Ryan Adams' work: stripping things down, focusing on making music rather than thinking about whether it would be a hit; going backwards to go forwards.

So we made the second album, Songs from the West Coast, in this manner. It was released in October 2001 and received the best reviews I'd gotten in years. Bernie penned powerful, straightforward, direct lyrics such as 'I Want Love,' 'Look Ma,' 'No Hands,' and 'American Triangle,' a very harrowing, passionate song about the 1998 homophobic murder of Matthew Shephard in Wyoming. We used a facility in Los Angeles that we hadn't used in years and a new producer, Pat Leonard, who was best known for his work with Madonna but was completely immersed in seventies rock. He was the guy who co-wrote 'Like A Prayer' and 'La Isla Bonita,' yet he was utterly infatuated with Jethro Tull. He'd be happy if Madonna had played the flute while standing on one leg.

It turned out to be a pretty California-sounding record. It's just different writing there vs recording an album in London when it's raining every day. It's as though the warmth penetrates your bones and soothes you, and the sunlight reflects in the music you create. I was pleased with the results, and I've taken the same method on many of my subsequent albums: thinking about what I'd done before, taking a concept and extending it in a new way. The follow-up, Peachtree Road, continued in the same vein, delving into the country and soul elements of Tumbleweed Connection and songs like "Take Me To The Pilot." The Captain and the Kid was a follow-up to Captain Fantastic and the Brown Dirt Cowboy, with Bernie writing about what happened to us after we went to America in 1970, from that stupid double-decker bus they picked us up from the airport into the way our partnership temporarily fell apart. The Diving Board included me performing with just a bassist and drummer, similar to the original Elton John Band, but doing things I'd never done before, such as improvising musical parts between songs. I assume I was thinking of the pop side of Don't Shoot Me I'm Only the Piano Player and Goodbye Yellow Brick Road when I wrote Wonderful Crazy Night. I recorded it in 2015, when the news was nothing but depressing: I wanted something light and cheerful, a sense of escape, plenty of bright colors, and a 12-string guitar.

Those albums were not flops, but they were also not enormous commercial triumphs. When that happens to an album you believe is amazing, it's always frustrating at first, but you have to accept it. They weren't commercial albums with built-in smash singles; The Diving Board, in particular, was quite dark and sad. But those were records I wanted to make, music that you could listen to in twenty years and be proud of. Of course, I would have preferred it if they had reached No. 1, but it wasn't the most essential thing anymore. I've had my moment of selling millions of records, and it was fantastic, but I knew it wouldn't last forever. If you believe it will, you could get yourself into a lot of trouble. That, I believe, was one of the factors that pushed Michael Jackson over the edge: he was confident he could make an album bigger than Thriller and was shattered when it didn't happen.

I was approached to do a residency at Caesar's Palace in Las Vegas just before we started working on The Captain and the Kid. The Colosseum, a massive new theater, had been constructed. Celine Dion was performing there, and they wanted me to perform as well. My first reaction was that I didn't want to do it. In my mind, Las Vegas was still connected to the cabaret circuit from which I'd escaped in 1967. The Rat Pack and Donny and Marie Osmond were there. It was Elvis I'd met in 1976, and performers in tuxedos talking to the audience: 'You know, one of the wonderful things about showbiz...' But then I wondered if it was possible to do something completely different with a Vegas show. David LaChapelle, a photographer and director, had directed an excellent video for 'This Train Don't Stop There Anymore,' one of the hits from Songs from the West Coast. It had Justin Timberlake lip-syncing to the song while dressed as me backstage in the 1970s, complete with a John Reid figure beating up a reporter and knocking off a cop's hat. I fell in love with it and approached him about designing an entire show. I told him he could do whatever he wanted, let his imagination run wild, and be as outrageous as he pleased.

If you're familiar with David's work, you'll recognize this isn't something you say to him lightly. He's amazing, but at that point in his career, he couldn't take a Christmas photo of someone unless they dressed up as Jesus and stood on top of a large stuffed flamingo surrounded by neon lights and strong boys in snakeskin jockstraps. This is the same man who captured Naomi Campbell as a topless wrestler trampling on a man's face in stiletto-heeled boots in front of a mob of masked dwarf men. One of his fashion shoots included a well dressed model standing next to the body of a woman murdered by an air-conditioning unit falling from a window, her skull splattered into a gory mess on the sidewalk. He persuaded Courtney Love to pose as Mary Magdalene, with what appeared to be Kurt Cobain's dead body draped over her knees. He constructed a set full of neon signs and inflatable bananas and hot dogs and lipsticks for my Vegas act, and you didn't have to have a filthy imagination to see that every single one of them looked suspiciously like an erect penis. He developed a series of videos for each song that were arty, crazy, and shamelessly gay. Back in the sixties, there was a reconstruction of my suicide attempt in Furlong Road - it was a dramatization in the sense that it made my suicide attempt look tremendously dramatic rather than miserable in the extreme. Blue teddy bears were ice skating and feeding honey to homoerotic angels. There were videos of people sniffing cocaine from a bare boy's bottom. in one scene, the transsexual model Amanda Lepore was naked on an electric chair, with sparks coming out of her vagina. The show's title was The Red Piano, which seemed benign given what it contained.

I took it all as proof that David LaChapelle was a genius. When I noticed a few individuals going out in disgust and my mother telling me she despised it, I knew we'd nailed it. She arrived the first night, expressing her displeasure with what was occurring onstage by theatrically donning a pair of dark glasses after about five minutes, then returned stage with a thunderous scream, telling everyone that it was so bad that it would kill my career overnight. Sam Taylor-Wood was also present; David and I knew her from the art world. I admired Sam's photography; I had purchased her version of Leonardo da Vinci's The Last Supper and hired her to direct a video for 'I Want Love,' another hit from Songs from the West Coast. She couldn't believe my mum's reaction - 'I felt like pulling my shoe off and striking her over the head with it,' she added - but to be fair, she didn't know my mum all that well. The rain of criticism that had begun in the mid-1970s had continued unabated ever since: the woman didn't like anything. I'd become accustomed to blocking it out or laughing it off, but it tended to startle others when they came into contact with it.

Some people disliked The Red Piano because they did not receive what they expected, which was the whole idea. But what they got showed that they hadn't been paying attention to the rest of my career. The entire enterprise had been built around wild and over-the-top live performances. The Vegas residency worked because it suited my personality and the way I'd previously presented myself. It wasn't just a bunch of frightening graphics slapped on for emphasis; it was a modernized version of the 1970s shows where I'd been introduced onstage by famous porn actresses and brought Divine out in full drag. Despite the occasional irate letter to management and Mum's terrible warnings, they were hugely popular shows, and I believe they were groundbreaking as well. Perhaps they altered the image of Las Vegas, making it appear less showy and more edgy; it became a location where Lady Gaga, Britney Spears, and Bruno Mars could perform without anyone raising an eyebrow.

In the United Kingdom, the law governing gay marriage was evolving. A handful of minor technical issues aside, it became legal for same-sex couples to enter into civil partnerships at the end of 2005: marriages in all but name. David and I discussed it and agreed we wanted to be the first in line. We'd been together for almost a decade, and it was a crucial piece of legislation for gay couples. I'd watched so many individuals lose their partner as a result of AIDS, only to realize they had no legal rights as a pair. Their late boyfriend's family would rush in, cut them out of the equation completely - either out of greed or because they didn't like the fact that their son or sibling was gay - and they would lose everything. Despite the fact that we had discussed it calmly and rationally, I managed to catch David off guard. I proposed to him while we were having a dinner party for the Scissor Sisters at Woodside. I got down on one knee the right way. Even though I knew he'd say yes, it was an incredibly sweet moment. We'd re-blessed the rings we'd bought for each other in Paris - the weekend I imagined I'd be able to blend in while wearing the complete Versace spring/summer menswear collection at once.

The new law went into effect in early December, with a fifteen-day waiting period. The 21st of December was the first day we could legally become civil partners. There was enough to do. The wedding would take place at the Guildhall in Windsor, where Prince Charles married Camilla Parker Bowles. That was going to be a small, personal gathering with only me and David, Mum and Derf, David's parents, Arthur, our dog, Ingrid and Sandy, and our friends Jay Jopling and Sam Taylor-Wood.

The initial intention was to hold a large event in the evening at Pinewood Studios, but the planner managed to come up with a budget that even I felt was preposterous, which was an incredible feat in and of itself. I remember gazing at it and thinking, 'I could go insane in Sotheby's Old Masters department for that kind of money.' We couldn't find someplace else to host our reception - it was right before Christmas, and everything was already booked - so we decided to have the party at Woodside. We built three interconnected marquees in the grounds: one for a reception, one for a dining room, and one for a massive dance floor. There would be live entertainment, including performances by James Blunt and Joss Stone. There were 600 people, and David insisted on making the seating arrangements himself. He was quite conscientious. One of his pet peeves is the type of party where everyone is placed together at random and you find yourself sitting next to someone you've never met before. Besides, we needed to be cautious because the guest list was as diverse as it could be: there were people invited from virtually every aspect of our lives. I was rather pleased with the fact that members of the Royal Family had been invited, as had a selection of celebrity performers from the gay porn studio BelAmi, but it seemed prudent to ensure they weren't seated together. So David meticulously organized everything around what he called tribes: there was a table for the visiting sports stars, a table for people from the fashion industry, and a table for the former Beatles and their associates. Then I ruined his careful work, leaving my unique imprint on them.

A prevalent belief among psychiatrists holds that a person cursed with an addictive personality can become addicted to almost anything. It was a theory I spent most of the early 2000s seeking to test with the help of a paper shredder we'd purchased for the Woodside office. I'm not sure when my obsession with it started. It was partly motivated by a desire for security: after all, our bank statements had been published all over the front pages of the press because some fool in John Reid's office had tossed them out intact. But it was largely because there's something indescribably wonderful about using a paper shredder: the sound it produces, the sight of the paper slowly disappearing into it, the tendrils of shredded paper coming from the other end. It was fantastic. I could sit in a room full of beautiful works of art and find none of them as interesting as the destruction of an old travel schedule.

But even if I don't remember when my obsession began, I know when it ended. It was about two minutes after I saw the state of the room where David was working on the seating plan - there were sheets of paper everywhere - and decided that this was a great opportunity both to help him out by tidying up a bit and to feed my burgeoning passion for turning old documents into confetti. I'm not sure how many pages of David's perfectly prepared seating plan I managed to shred before he wandered back into the room and began ranting. David was never a man for volcanic eruptions of fury, but it looked that throughout the course of our twelve years together, he'd been discreetly taking notes from a master of the art and waiting for the appropriate moment to put what he'd learned into action. He began enthusiastically describing images of uncontrollable social disaster in which the BelAmi actors ended up discussing their work on Boys Like It Big 2 with his mother or my auntie Win. He was shouting so loudly that you could hear him from anywhere in the house. You could definitely hear him upstairs in our bedroom. I know this because I chose to hide there, carefully shutting the door behind me as a precaution. I didn't think he was going to smash the paper shredder over my head, but the sounds coming from downstairs suggested it wasn't completely out of the question.

But everything else in the run-up to the event went down without a hitch. Patrick Cox, a friend of ours, threw us a wonderful joint stag party at Too 2 Much, a homosexual bar in Soho. A full cabaret performance was hilarious. Paul O'Grady hosted the event and sang a duet with Janet Street-Porter. Sir Ian McKellen donned the role of Widow Twankey. Bryan Adams sang, and Sam Taylor-Wood performed a cover of "Love To Love You Baby." In between performances by the famed New York drag act Kiki and Herb and Eric McCormack, who portrayed Will in Will and Grace and was an old school friend of David's back in Ontario, there were video messages from Elizabeth Taylor and Bill Clinton. Jake Shears of the Scissor Sisters became so thrilled that he stripped naked and demonstrated the pole-dancing talents he'd developed working at New York strip joints before the band's breakthrough. It was a wild night.

We awoke to a wonderful winter day, sunny and brisk, on the morning of the ceremony. In the midst of the chaos, the house had a beautiful Christmas Morning atmosphere. David's family had come from Canada, and my old school friend Keith Francis had traveled all the way from Australia with his wife. Outside, people were finishing up the marquees and inspecting the fairy lights in the trees. We'd seen on TV the night before about the first civil partnerships in Northern Ireland - there was a shorter registration period there - and how the couples had faced protests outside their ceremonies, evangelical Christians yelling at them about sodomite propaganda,and people throwing flour bombs and eggs. I was honestly concerned: if this was happening to ordinary people, how would a renowned homosexual couple be received? David told me that everything would be fine: the police were completely aware of the threat and had set up a protest area where they wouldn't be able to disrupt the day. But, according to the latest reports from Windsor, there were thousands lined the streets and a party atmosphere. No one wanted to harm us; instead, people had come bearing banners, cakes, and gifts for us. There were CNN and BBC news vans parked outside, with reporters doing segments for the camera.

I turned off the TV and instructed David not to watch anything. I just wanted us to be present in the moment, without distractions. Of course, I'd been married before, but this was different. I was truly being myself, being allowed to express my love for another man in ways that seemed incomprehensible when I first realized I was gay or when I first came out in Rolling Stone - partly because no one ever talked about gay marriage or civil partnerships in 1976, and partly because I seemed no more capable of ending up in a long-term relationship than I did of flying to Mars. But here we were. It felt intense: not only personal, but also historic, as if we were a part of a world that was changing for the better. I was as happy as I had ever been in my life.

And that's when my mother appeared, dressed as a raving sociopath.

The fact that she refused to get out of the automobile was the first indication that something was awry. She and Derf had arrived at Woodside on time, but she flatly refused to enter the home. Despite numerous invitations to join us, they remained stone-faced. David's family had to come out and greet him through the car window. What the fuck was wrong with her? I didn't get a chance to inquire. Everyone was intended to travel together in a convoy of automobiles to the Guildhall as part of the security measures for the ceremony. But Mum abruptly drove away, saying she wouldn't be joining the convoy and wouldn't be coming to the private lunch we were having at Woodside after the civil partnership.

That's fantastic. The most crucial day of my life had arrived, and one of Mum's moods, which I'd lived in fear of since I was a child, appeared to be upon us. I'd inherited some of her sulking ability. The difference was that I soon snapped out of it: I'd realized what I was doing - dammit, I'm not just behaving like an idiot, I'm behaving like my mother - and about apologizing to everyone involved. Mum never snapped out of it, never showed sorry, never appeared to believe she was in the wrong or acting inappropriately. The best you could expect was a nasty disagreement - in which she had to have the last word, as she always did - followed by an awkward smoothing over, a tenuous ceasefire that lasted until she went off again. Sulking had progressed to epic proportions throughout the years. She was the Cecil B. DeMille of bad moods, the Tolstoy of huffing. I'm only slightly exaggerating. We're talking about a woman who went ten years without speaking to her own sister because of a disagreement about whether Auntie Win used skimmed milk in her tea or not. A woman whose sulking was so intense that, at its peak, it drove her to pack her entire existence and flee the country. It happened in the 1980s; she had a falling out with me and one of Derf's sons from his first marriage at the same time and fled to Menorca as a result. She'd rather relocate to another nation than back down or apologize. There's hardly much point in attempting to argue with someone like that.

I saw her car pull out the driveway and wished she was in Menorca right now. Or even on the moon. Anywhere but my civil partnership ceremony, which I had a bad feeling she was going to do her hardest to ruin. I hadn't intended for her to be there in the first place. I had a nagging dread that she would do something similar, just as I did when I married Renate. That was one of the reasons I insisted on getting married in Australia so quickly - I didn't want Mum there. But I had changed my mind a few weeks ago, figuring that not even Mum would be insane enough to try such a thing. It appears that I was mistaken.

She didn't want to - couldn't - ruin the day. It was too magical, with crowds cheering outside the Guildhall and, later, cars arriving at Woodside and what seemed like everyone I knew and loved climbing out to join the party, like your life flashing before your eyes in the most beautiful of circumstances: Graham Taylor and Muff and Zena Winwood, Ringo Starr and George Martin, Tony King and Billie Jean King. But, to be fair to Mum, she did her greatest best. When David and I exchanged our vows, she began talking over us, very loudly, about how she didn't like the setting and couldn't imagine getting married in a place like this. She signed her name, snapped, 'It's done, then,' slammed the pen down, and walked off. It was strange; my feelings alternated from pure ecstasy and intense terror over what she was going to do next. Worse, I was unable to stop it. I knew from experience that trying to talk to her would be like lighting the blue touchpaper on a massive row that would wreck everything and, even worse, could happen in front of the entire world's media or 600 guests. I wasn't a fan of the coverage of Britain's most publicized civil partnership, which included a segment in which Elton John and his mother delighted the nation by yelling at one other on the steps of the Windsor Guildhall.

During the speeches at the evening celebration, she tutted, moaned, and rolled her eyes. She grumbled about the seating arrangements, claiming that she wasn't close enough to me and David - 'you might as well have stuck me in Siberia' - but it was difficult to see how she could have been any closer without sitting in our laps. I avoided her as the evening progressed, which was simple because there were so many friends to talk to, all of whom wanted to wish us well. But out of the corner of my eye, I noticed a continual stream of folks approaching her, then rapidly leaving with tremendously long expressions. No matter how benign their attempts at conversation were, she was unpleasant to everyone. Jay Jopling made the fatal error of telling her, 'Isn't this a great day?'It appeared to be considered a ruthless provocation. 'I'm happy you fucking well think so,' Mum snapped back. Tony King went to say hello because he'd known Mum and Derf for years and was told he was looking elderly. Sharon Osbourne approached me as I stood there watching.

'I know she's your mother,' she grumbled, 'but I want to murder her.'

I didn't discover what had triggered all of this until much later. She told the reporters she was furious because she was informed she couldn't be in any of the photos because she wasn't wearing a hat, which was nonsense. David's mother had requested a hat for the ceremony, and he had offered to take her and my mother shopping, but my mother had declined. Given that she was in all of the family photos, this was obviously not a problem. David's parents had known what was wrong with her all along, but they didn't tell us before the wedding because they didn't want to upset us. They had called her as soon as they arrived in the UK because they had always gotten along well with Mum and Derf. They'd even gone on vacation together. My mother had persuaded them that they needed to act together to prevent the civil partnership from proceeding. She didn't like the idea of two males 'becoming married,' as she phrased it. She believed that LGBT couples should be treated the same as straight couples. The concept had terrified everyone she had spoken to. It was going to be detrimental to my career. David's mother told her she was crazy, that their children were doing fantastic things and that she should encourage them. My mum hung up the phone on her.

She said the same thing to me a few years later, in the middle of a row. It made no sense. Mum had always been a hard worker, but she was never homophobic. When I told her I was homosexual, she was encouraging, and she was unflappable when the press cornered her after I came out in Rolling Stone, telling them she thought I was brave and didn't care if I was gay or straight. Why would she, thirty years later, conclude she had a problem with my sexuality? Maybe she had all along and had managed to keep it hidden until now. As again, I believe the true issue was that she despised everyone who was closer to me than she was. She'd been chilly to most of my lovers, and cold to Renate, but this was something else. She understood the men were never going to be long-term relationships because I was too unstable from the coke. Even though I married Renate, Mum was convinced it wouldn't last because she knew I was gay. But now I was sober and happily married to a man I adored. I'd met my life companion, and the civil partnership confirmed it. She couldn't bear the thought of the umbilical connection finally being severed: it had become so all-consuming that she couldn't see beyond it, didn't care about anything else, not even the fact that I was finally happy.

That was unfortunate for her. I was finally pleased, and I wasn't about to change that for anyone, no matter how many mood swings they went through. Maybe she'd change her mind once she realized that.

I have a lot to be thankful for. Not just in my personal life: with the Vegas concerts, Billy Elliot, and the new CDs, I was having so much fun making music that my excitement spread. David became interested in the musicians and albums that had inspired me at the outset of my career, artists and albums that he was too young to have experienced firsthand. He'd create iPod playlists of stuff I'd recommended to him. When we went on vacation to South Africa with our friends Ingrid and Sandy, he brought them with him to play in our hotel room.

If you want to see how a deep, lifelong friendship can be formed from the most unlikely of beginnings, look no further than Ingrid and me. I'd met her when she was working on a profile on me for Interview magazine, which she edited. Or, more accurately, I'd gone out of my way to avoid meeting her while she was preparing a story about me: I was grumpy and canceled our interview. She called back and said she was coming anyway. I advised her not to bother. She said she was coming nonetheless. I told her she needed to fuck off. She hung up the phone and appeared at my hotel room door in what seemed like seconds. I had fallen in love with her in a matter of minutes. Ingrid was brave. Ingrid has her own point of view. And Ingrid's ideas were worth hearing because she was clearly as bright as heck. When she was twenty-seven, she was appointed editor of Artforum magazine and seemed to know everything there was to know about - and everyone there was to know in - the worlds of art and fashion. She didn't take crap from anyone, even, it had now become clear, me. She was quite amusing. By the end of the afternoon, she not only had her interview, but she also had my commitment to write a column for her magazine, and I got the same feeling I had when I first met Gianni Versace: if he felt like my long-lost brother, Ingrid seemed like my missing sister. We talked all the time; I enjoyed talking to her, partly because she was a fantastic gossip, partly because every time you spoke to her you learnt something new, but largely because she always told you the truth, even if it wasn't what you wanted to hear.

Ingrid was born in South Africa but moved away when she was a child. Because her mother faced arrest for her engagement in the anti-apartheid movement, the family relocated to Edinburgh, then to New York. But Ingrid adored South Africa, which is how she and Sandy ended up joining us on our vacation. We were getting ready for supper one evening while listening to one of David's early 1970s iPod mixes. 'Back To The Island' by Leon Russell came on as he was in the shower. It really caught me by surprise. It's a beautiful song, but it's also extremely sad: about loss, regret, and the passage of time. I sat on the bed and began to cry. Leon walking into the Troubadour dressing room, the tours I performed opening for him, Eric Clapton, and Poco: it all seemed so long ago. I used to listen to this song all the time when I lived on Tower Grove Drive. In my mind's eye, I could still see it. The interior's dark wood; the suede on the walls of the master bedroom; the way the sunshine fell on the swimming pool in the morning. The clouds of heady Californian grass and the glasses filled with bourbon, and the blue eyes of a guy I lured up to the games room, who said he was straight but whose smile suggested he was persuadable, and the blue eyes of a guy I lured up to the games room, who said he was straight but whose smile suggested he was persuadable. Dusty Springfield returns home from a night of gay club hopping and falls out of the car onto the drive. After someone in our party invaded the kitchen and decided, in their altered state, to concoct a new kind of Bloody Mary, with a lump of raw liver on the side of the glass, Tony King and I ended up with the shrieking horrors. We were alarmed just by the look of it.

But my memories of Los Angeles in the 1970s were haunted. All of the old Hollywood legends I'd made an effort to meet had died in old age. Ray Charles had done the same. Thirty-four years after he'd invited me to appear on American television for the first time, I'd been the last person to record a song with him for a duets album. We sang 'Sorry Seems To Be The Hardest Word' while seated since he couldn't stand. I requested a copy of the tape from the engineers, not for the music, but to have a recording of us speaking between takes. I guess I needed verification that it truly happened, that a child who aspired to be Ray Charles ended up chatting to him like a friend. There were other ghosts, too, folks who didn't die of old age: AIDS victims, people who'd drunk or drugged themselves to death. People who had died in car accidents, people who had been murdered, people who had died of the things that kill you in your fifties and sixties if you're unlucky. Dee Murray, my former bassist. The Troubadour was run by Doug Weston. Graham, Bill. Dudgeon, Gus. Harry Nilsson, George Harrison, and John Lennon. Dusty Springfield and Keith Moon. Endless boys I'd fallen in love with, or believed I had, on the dance floor at After Dark.

David's face sank when he returned from the bathroom and discovered me in tears.

'Oh my God,' he groaned, 'what's the matter?'

He was so used to dealing with my emotions that his first idea was that I didn't like some little feature of the holiday and was going to start ranting about how we had to leave right away. I explained that it was nothing like that: I was simply thinking about the past. Leon was still singing on the iPod, 'Well all the fun has died, it's raining in my heart, I know down in my soul I'm truly going to miss you'. That dude had a beautiful voice. What had become of him? I hadn't heard his name mentioned in years. I picked up the phone and contacted my friend Johnny Barbis in Los Angeles, asking him if he could locate Leon. He responded with a Nashville song. I dialed it, and a voice responded. It sounded a little gravelly, but it was certainly him - that same Oklahoma drawl. I inquired about his health. 'I'm fine,' he said, lying in bed and watching Days of Our Lives on TV. 'It's just about making ends meet,' was one way to phrase it. Leon had made some poor business decisions, had numerous ex-wives, and the times had changed. He was now touring anywhere he could get work. One of the world's best musicians and composers was performing at sports bars and pubs, beer festivals and motorcycle conventions in communities I'd never heard of in Missouri and Connecticut. I explained that I was in the middle of nowhere in Africa, listening to his music and reflecting on the past. I thanked him for everything he'd done for me and expressed my appreciation for his music. He sounded deeply moved.

'Well, that's quite thoughtful of you,' he said. 'I really appreciate it.'

I set the phone down and looked at it when we finished talking. Something was wrong. I couldn't explain it, but I knew I hadn't phoned him for that reason. I picked up the phone and dialed his number once more. When he picked up the phone, he laughed.

'My God, I haven't heard from you in forty-five years, and now twice in 10 minutes?'

I asked him if he wanted to record an album with me. There was a long pause.

'Are you sure?' he explained. 'Do you think I can pull it off?' He groaned. 'I'm quite elderly.'

I told him I was getting on in years, and if I could, he could if he wanted to.

He laughed once more. 'I'd do it in a heartbeat.'

It wasn't a charitable act. It was pure enjoyment for me: if you'd told me in 1970 that I'd one day record with Leon Russell, I'd have laughed. And it wasn't always simple. Leon had expressed some health difficulties over the phone, but I didn't know how ill he was until he arrived at the LA studio. He resembled the ailing patriarch from a Tennessee Williams play, with his long white beard, heavy glasses, and cane. He found it difficult to walk. He'd sit in a La-Z-Boy recliner in the studio for a few hours a day, singing and playing. That was all he could manage, but what he accomplished in those two hours was amazing. There were times when I wondered if his contributions to the album would be released after his death. His nose started running one day because fluid was draining from his head. He was brought to the hospital for surgery and was treated there for heart failure and pneumonia.

But we finished the album. We called it The Union, and it charted in the top five in the United States. We went on tour together in the autumn of 2010, playing 15,000-seat arenas, which Leon claimed he hadn't been inside in decades. He had to come onstage in a wheelchair some nights, but it made no difference to how he sounded. Every time, he nailed it.

Leon was finally given his due as a result of that album. He received a new record deal and was inducted into the Rock & Roll Hall of Fame. I was so happy for him that I forgot about my pledge never to return and offered to give his induction speech. He made money, bought a new bus, and toured the world in larger and finer venues than he'd played in for years.

He continued to tour until his death in 2016. I'm sorry if you didn't see him: you missed out. Leon Russell was unrivaled.

CHAPTER 16

It happened for the first time in South Africa in 2009, at a drop-in center for children living with HIV and its complications. It was located in the heart of Soweto, and it was a location where orphaned children and youngsters who had been forced to stand up and become the head of their household could go to obtain what they needed, whether it was a hot meal, counseling, or simply assistance with their homework. We were there because the Elton John AIDS Foundation had funded it, and they had put on a presentation for us, with the women who operated the center and the children who benefited from it explaining how it worked. A tiny boy wearing the type of brilliantly patterned shirt made famous by Nelson Mandela handed me a small spoon, a symbol of South Africa's sugar industry. But he wouldn't return to sit with the other youngsters. I'm not sure why - he had no idea who I was - but he just appeared to like me. He was named Noosa, and he stayed by my side for the duration of my tour. I held his hand, made faces at him, and made him laugh. He was just lovely. I pondered what his life would be like in the outer world: God, the horror stories you heard in South Africa about how AIDS had wrecked lives that weren't exactly a picnic to begin with. When he left here, where was he going? Back to what, exactly? But when I looked at him, I knew I was feeling something other than pity or fondness. There was a glimmer of something else there, something more powerful than 'awww,' something I couldn't quite place. I went up to David.

'This child is really fantastic,' I said. 'He was orphaned. Perhaps he requires assistance. What are your thoughts?'

David was extremely perplexed. He'd mentioned starting a family before - the thought of a gay couple adopting children was no longer as unusual as it previously had been. But every time he mentioned the notion, I provided him with a laundry list of objections that wore him down.

I adored children. I have a slew of godsons and goddaughters - some famous, like Sean Lennon and Brooklyn and Romeo Beckham, and some not so well-known, like the kid of my AA sponsor - and I adore them all. Having your own children, on the other hand, was a completely other story. I was far too old. I'm too stuck in my ways. Too absent - he's always on tour. Too obsessed with china, photos, and modern art, none of which respond well to being knocked over, drawn on with crayon, smeared with Marmite, or any of the other things that tiny children are famous for doing. Too preoccupied to make the time in my life that was clearly required to be a mom. I wasn't being grumpy; I was simply being truthful. But, in reality, every objection stemmed from my own childhood. Bringing up children was a huge challenge, and I understood from personal experience how terrible it was if you messed it up. You certainly want to believe that you will not make the same mistakes as your parents, but what if you do? I couldn't bear the prospect of making my own children as unhappy as I was.

All those protests, and now I'm recommending that we adopt an orphan from Soweto. It's no surprise David was perplexed; I was as well. What in the world was going on? I had no notion, but something had clearly happened that was utterly out of my hands. It was almost as if a true paternal instinct had finally kicked in in my sixties, just as mine libido had arrived unexpectedly, years after everyone else's, when I was twenty-one.

It didn't matter what it was. We conducted some inquiries and discovered that the small guy was in a relatively nice situation. He lived with his grandmother, sister, and another relative, and they were well cared for, a close-knit family - so close-knit that when Noosa attached himself to me, his sister burst into tears, fearing we would take him away from her. That was the end of it. We would not be able to help him by removing him from his culture and identity and bringing him to the UK: it was better to invest in his future in his own nation. When I returned to South Africa to perform or work with the AIDS Foundation, I saw him a couple more times, and he was still utterly adorable and clearly very happy.

It was a strange occurrence, but I put it out of my mind since I knew we had done the right thing. I reverted to my previous position on children. I don't believe either of us brought it up again. The following year, we traveled to Ukraine.

The orphanage is located in Donetsk, a large industrial city in the country's center. It was a location where children aged one to eleven could be watched to see if they contracted HIV - not every child born to an HIV-positive mother tests positive. If they did, they received antiretroviral therapy, care, and support. We were walking around, handing out food, nappies, and schoolbooks - not costly gifts, but necessities for the caregivers and the children. I performed 'Circle Of Life' for them on a piano that I had donated. Soon after, a young boy went over to me, and I took him up and cuddled him. They informed me his name was Lev. He was fourteen months old, but he appeared younger because he was so little. His story was harrowing. His father had been convicted of murder after strangling a teenage girl. His mother was HIV-positive, a persistent drinker with TB, and unable to care for her children. They didn't know if he had HIV yet, but he had an older half-brother named Artem who had tested positive for it. Lev had blond hair, brown eyes, and a grin that appeared out of place given his surroundings and the hand fate had handed him. Every time he smiled at me, I absolutely melted.

I didn't put him down for the remainder of our time there. Whatever happened in Soweto happened again, only this time it was more intense: there was an instant bond, some type of really deep connection. I was already in a raw emotional condition. Guy Babylon, who'd played keyboards in my band for eleven years, had died unexpectedly a few days ago. He was just fifty-two years old and appeared to be in good health, but he suffered a heart attack while swimming. It was a reminder that time is limited, and you never know what's around the corner. Perhaps this provided me with some true clarity about what was essential to me in life. Why try to hide your own feelings about something as essential as fatherhood?

The rest of the party left, but I remained in the room, playing with Lev. I didn't feel like leaving. David eventually returned to see where I was. I started crying as soon as he walked into the room.

'This little guy is exceptional; his name is Lev, and he is an orphan. I didn't find him, he found me. I believe this is a calling. I believe the cosmos is communicating with us, and we should adopt him.'

David appeared even more astonished than in Soweto. Clearly, he hadn't expected his straightforward 'what are you doing?' question.' to be met with a deluge of information regarding higher callings and messages from the universe. But he could tell I was serious. He encouraged me to calm down and keep things low-key for the time being since we needed to learn more about Lev's circumstances, his family, and whether he could leave the orphanage before they knew if he was HIV positive.

For the rest of the day, I carried Lev. When we were hurried outside for a press conference in a makeshift marquee, I was still holding him. While I answered the reporters' queries, I placed him on David's lap. The last one was about how I'd previously stated that I didn't want children: had seeing youngsters in need of homes in the orphanage altered my mind? This was an excellent opportunity for me to demonstrate that I fully understood what David had stated about the importance of keeping any thoughts I had concerning Lev's future private. Instead, I blurted out that my mind had changed, that the little boy sitting next to David in the first row had grabbed our hearts, and that if it were possible, I would want to adopt him and his brother.

You may recall that I mentioned a few chapters back why I'm glad I became popular before record companies and managers pushed artists to acquire media training and monitor what they say: that I'm proud of always giving direct answers and expressing my mind. Perhaps I should qualify that statement by saying that there have been a couple of times in my career when media training has suddenly seemed like a very good idea, when I've wished that, for once in my life, I just answered a question by saying something unbelievably boring, bland, and evasive, rather than telling the truth. This was undoubtedly one of them. I realized I shouldn't have said it as soon as it came out of my mouth, not least because I saw David lower his head, close his eyes, and say something that sounded suspiciously like 'oh shit'.

'That comment,' he grumbled as we drove back to the airport, 'is going to get everywhere, in minutes.'

He was correct. When we arrived in Britain, his BlackBerry was full of texts and voice messages from friends congratulating us on our fantastic news, indicating that it had already made the headlines. Certain elements of the British press would have reacted much more adversely if I had said I had a pathological hatred for children and intended to burn down the Donetsk orphanage that night. The Daily Mail and the Sun sent journalists to Ukraine right away. One got hold of a government minister, who claimed adoption was out of the question since we were a lesbian couple, and I was too elderly. Another paid a visit to Lev's mother, bought her vodka, and took her to the orphanage for a photo opportunity, which automatically delayed any adoption process by a year: in order for a child to become a ward of the state, they had to be in an orphanage for twelve months without receiving any visit from any family member. The journalist either didn't know or didn't care because they hadn't considered it. There was something horrifying, if unavoidable, about how the story became wholly about me and David, rather than the children involved. It was difficult not to imagine that if I hadn't spoken up during the press conference, none of this would have happened. Maybe it wouldn't have made a difference. But we'd never know.

We tried again and again, looking at the logistics of adoption, but it became clear that it would not work. We could have appealed to the European Court of Justice, but it didn't seem worth it because Ukraine was not a member of the EU. We had called a psychologist to inquire about the emotional process of integrating children from orphanages into families, and something he stated truly caught us off guard. He warned us that any child who had been in an orphanage for more than eighteen months would be psychologically damaged indefinitely. They would not have received adequate nurturing, such as being picked up, held, and loved, and this would have had long-term consequences for them. So we abandoned trying to adopt Lev and Artem and instead focused on getting them out of there before their eighteen-month period expired, working with a charity in Ukraine. Their mother died, and their father was returned to prison, but they had a young grandma, and it was agreed that they should live with her.

We secretly supplied cash assistance to them through the charity. Because of the way the media had pounced on them, we were urged to keep everything quiet - so anonymous that not even Lev and Artem's grandma would know we were assisting - because if they found out I was their benefactor, there was a risk they would never leave the kids alone. We did not provide excessive Elton John-style assistance, which would have only served to further alienate them. But we made sure they had enough of the items the charity said they needed: quality furniture, food, schoolbooks, and legal assistance. We worked with the same organization that had supported the orphanage to transfer them to Kiev when the Russians occupied that portion of Ukraine. We'll keep an eye on them at all times.

I saw Lev and Artem last year when I returned to Ukraine with the AIDS Foundation. They entered the room wearing matching hoodies, and we hugged, cried, and spoke and talked. Such a long period had passed. Lev had grown up. He was a ten-year-old who was funny, cheeky, and charming. But, in one regard, nothing had changed: I still felt the same way about him that I had the day I first met him. I still wish we had been able to adopt him. But I knew his grandmother did an excellent job.

We'd tried and failed several times to become adoptive parents. It was upsetting, yet the paternal sensation did not dissipate this time. It was as if someone had flipped a switch: I now want children as much as David. However, it was not an easy process. Adoption was still extremely difficult for a gay couple, and the other alternative, surrogacy, was equally difficult. Although transactional surrogacy is legally illegal in the UK, you can have a child in another country and then bring them back to live in the UK. We consulted with our doctor in California, who recommended California Fertility Partners. The process is extremely complicated: there are egg donation agencies and surrogacy agencies, as well as complicated legal requirements, especially if you live abroad. The more we looked into it, the more difficult it appeared. My mind began to race with hormone therapy and blastocysts, embryo transfers and parental orders, and egg donors.

We were encouraged to choose an unmarried surrogate because there have been examples in the past of married surrogates' husbands claiming legal custody of the child despite having no biological tie. We chose to share the sperm sample so that we wouldn't know which of us was the biological parent. Everything had to take place behind a shroud of extreme secrecy, we were told. We were to remain anonymous to the surrogate by posing as Edward and James, an English gay couple vaguely characterized as 'working in the entertainment world,' while everyone else involved had to sign severe legal non-disclosure agreements. I thought that made great sense, having lately received a powerful lesson in the virtues of keeping my mouth shut. When the identity of

Matthew Broderick and Sarah Jessica Parker's surrogate was revealed, the unfortunate woman was pushed into hiding: no one wanted an expectant mother being harassed by the press.

Surrogacy requires a significant leap of faith. Your fate is totally in the hands of others once you've chosen your egg donor and left your sperm sample at the fertility clinic. We were quite fortunate. We discovered Guy Ringler, a gay man who specialized in fertility for LGBT parents. And we found the most extraordinary surrogate. She resided north of San Francisco and had previously worked as a surrogate. She had no interest in popularity or money; all she cared about was assisting loving couples in having children. She figured out who Edward and James were about three months into her pregnancy and didn't even blink. David arrived outside of her hometown in case he was recognized. Everything suddenly became very real when he returned, talking about how great she was. I didn't experience any trepidation or doubt about our decision; no panic, no 'what have we done?' - nothing but enthusiasm and expectation.

The rest of my pregnancy was a blur. The child was expected on December 21, 2010. We became fast friends with the surrogate, her boyfriend, and her family. I grew to despise the term 'transnational surrogacy' as I got to know them more. It seemed clinical and mercenary, but these folks were anything but clinical or mercenary: they were warm and compassionate, and truly happy to be assisting us in realizing a dream. We hired the same nanny who had looked after our friend Elizabeth Hurley's children. We knew her since Liz had stayed at Woodside after giving birth to avoid the attention of the media. We started putting together a nursery at our LA apartment, but everything had to be done behind closed doors: everything we bought was sent to our office in LA, unpacked, and wrapped so it appeared like a Christmas present for David or myself when it came at our house.

As the due date approached, the surrogate and her family relocated to a hotel in Los Angeles. We had requested Ingrid and Sandy to be godparents, and they traveled in for the birth. We had intended to surprise our friends in LA with the news that we had formed a family during a Christmas lunch, but we had to postpone the meal since the baby was late. The surrogate eventually became tired of the sleepless nights, back discomfort, and swollen ankles and took drastic action. There was a restaurant on Coldwater Canyon in Los Angeles that featured a watercress soup that was said to induce labor. The reputation was clearly well-deserved: on the afternoon of Christmas Eve, we received a phone call instructing us to rush to Cedars-Sinai.

I arrived in disguise, dressed down and wearing a cap, still anxious about the veil of concealment. As it turned out, I could have arrived at the hospital wearing Tommy's four-foot-high Doc Martens and my old glasses that lit up in the shape of the word ELTON and no one would have noticed because no one was there. The area was completely vacant. The maternity ward resembled the motel from The Shining. We discovered that no one wants to have a baby over the holidays, so they either induce or have cesareans to avoid staying in the hospital. Except for us, no one. We had purposefully planned for the birth to occur while I was not working or on tour. So there was no one else around but us and one other woman in the room next door, an Australian with twins. And our kid, who arrived at 2:30 a.m. on Christmas morning.

I severed the umbilical cord - I'm typically really uncomfortable, but the emotion of what had transpired took over totally. We removed our shirts to allow the baby to have skin-to-skin contact. Zachary Jackson Levon was his given name. Everyone thinks his surname is derived from the song Bernie and I wrote for Madman Across the Water, but they're wrong: he's named after Lev. He had no choice. Lev was like an angel, a messenger who taught me something I didn't truly comprehend about myself. We were on a maternity ward, holding our son, knowing that our lives had just altered forever because of Lev.

We asked Lady Gaga to be Zachary's godmother, in addition to Ingrid and Sandy. I'd begun working with a lot of younger musicians, ranging from the Scissor Sisters to Kanye West. It was always humbling to be allowed to collaborate with people who weren't even born when my career took off, but of all the young musicians I worked with, Gaga stood out. I fell in love with her the instant I laid eyes on her: her music, her outlandish attire, her sense of theater and spectacle. We were quite different people - she was a young woman from New York, barely out of her twenties - but as soon as we met, it was clear we were cut from the same cloth: I dubbed her Elton John's Bastard Daughter. I was so in love with her that I got myself into even more difficulty with the press. I'd always gotten along well with Madonna. I used to mock her for lip-syncing onstage, but the real problem began when she ran Gaga down on an American talk show. I understood that Gaga's single 'Born This Way' sounded similar to 'Express Yourself,' but I couldn't understand why she was so ungracious and nasty about it, rather than taking it as a compliment that she influenced a new generation of artists, especially since she claims to be a champion for women. It's simply unfair, in my opinion, for an experienced artist to dismiss a younger artist at the outset of their career. I was enraged, and I told a TV journalist in Australia, Molly Meldrum, whom I'd known since the 1970s, some very heinous things about her. You can tell from the footage that it wasn't part of the interview, that I was just ranting to an old friend between takes - you can hear people moving cameras around to set up the next shot while we're talking - but they broadcast it anyway, effectively ending that particular old friendship. Nonetheless, I should not have said anything. I apologized later when I ran into her in a French restaurant, and she was really kind about it. Gaga proved to be an excellent godmother, appearing backstage and insisting on giving Zachary a bath while dressed in full Gaga regalia, which was quite a sight.

Everything about fatherhood is fantastic. I don't have any great insights regarding fatherhood that you haven't previously heard a hundred times. All of the clichés about it anchoring you, changing your perspective on the world, experiencing a love unlike any other love you've felt in your life, and how awe-inspiring it is to see a person form before your eyes are true. But maybe I felt all of those emotions more strongly because I never imagined I'd be a father until much later in life. If you tried to tell Elton John in the 1970s or 1980s that changing a nappy was more fulfilling on a deep and profound level than writing a song or playing a gig, you would probably have had to flee the room at high speed, with thrown crockery flying past your ears. And yet, it was true: the responsibility was enormous, yet there is nothing I don't enjoy about being a father. I even thought the toddler tantrums were amusing. My tiny sausage, do you think you're being difficult? Have I ever told you about the night I drank eight vodka martinis in front of a film crew, stripped naked, and shattered my manager's nose?

We knew we wanted another child almost immediately. It was mostly because we adored being parents, but there was more to it. Whatever we attempt to make our child's childhood regular, the fact is that it would never be completely normal because of what one of his parents did for a career and everything that comes with it. Because, before starting school, Zachary usually accompanied me on tour; he'd gone around the world twice by the age of four. Lady Gaga had bathed him and he'd jigged up and down on Eminem's knee. He'd stood in the wings of Las Vegas performances and been photographed by paparazzi, which he tolerated more than enjoyed: a chip off the old block, there. These are not typical toddler experiences. There is definitely a degree of privilege that comes with being Elton John's kid, but you would be delusory if you didn't also believe there is a degree of hardship. I had despised being an only child, and it felt natural that he should have a sibling with whom he could share his life experiences. We used the same surrogate, agencies, and egg donor, and everything came into place wonderfully again: Elijah was delivered on January 11, 2013.

My mum was the only one who didn't seem overjoyed for us. My marriage to her had always been difficult, but it never fully recovered following our civil partnership ceremony in 2005. As usual, I smoothed things up as best I could, but something about her had altered, or at least been exaggerated. The rain of criticism became a steady downpour. She seemed to go out of her way to express her displeasure with what I was doing. If I released a new record, it would be a waste of time: why didn't I strive to be more like Robbie Williams? Could I no longer make songs like that? If I bought a new painting, it would be hideous, and she could have done better herself. If I performed at a charity event, it would be the most boring thing she'd ever sat through in her life, with the evening only spared from total disaster by someone else's performance, which had stolen the show. If the AIDS Foundation had a dazzling fundraising dinner attended by celebrities, it was proof that I was just interested in fame and kissing celebrities' arses.

She tossed in the occasional thunderclap of genuine rage for variation. I never knew when they'd show up or what would set them off. Spending time with her was like inviting an unexploded bomb to lunch or on vacation with you: I was constantly on guard, wondering what would set her off. It used to be that I'd purchased a kennel for the dogs we maintained at our Nice home. It was formerly Billy Elliot, reportedly the only thing I'd done in the previous 10 years that she thought was excellent. The musical had taken off in ways that no one had predicted, not only in the UK, but in countries where people had never heard of the Miners' Strike or the impact of Thatcherism on the British manufacturing industry: the story at its center proved to be global. Mum saw it dozens of times in London until one afternoon, when the box office misplaced her tickets for the matinée and waited five minutes to find them, which she assumed I had done on purpose to disgrace her. Fortunately, I followed Billy Elliot with The Vampire Lestat, a musical Bernie and I co-wrote, which bombed - everything went wrong, from the timing, to the staging, to the dialogue - and normal service was resumed: it provided my mother with the unmissable opportunity to inform me that she had known it would be a terrible flop from the beginning.

I tried to shrug it off or dismiss it, but it wasn't that easy. Mum always knew which buttons to hit when she wanted a row because she had installed the buttons in the first place. She could still make me feel like a terrified ten-year-old in Pinner, as if everything was my fault: I was constantly afraid of getting smacked, metaphorically speaking. The end outcome was precisely what you'd expect: I began to purposefully avoid her. On my sixtieth birthday, I had a magnificent celebration in New York at St John the Divine, the same church where I later saw Aretha Franklin perform for the final time. Mum had been one of the honorees at my fiftieth, the famous fancy dress party where she and Derf came dressed as the Queen and the Duke of Edinburgh, and I donned a Louis XVI costume with a train supported by two men dressed as Cupid and a wig so large that I had to get there in the back of a furniture van. When the furniture van got stalled in traffic for an hour and a half, I had plenty of time to ponder the soundness of this approach. I decided not to invite her this time. I knew she'd show there and put a damper on the whole thing; she wouldn't enjoy herself, and neither would I. I pretended it was too far for her to travel because she hadn't been feeling well, but the truth was that I didn't want her there.

We hadn't spoken in years by the time Zachary was born. Mum had progressed from continually criticizing to going out of her way to be hurtful. After our professional connection ended, she rejoiced in informing me she was still friends with John Reid: 'I don't know what you're upset about,' she shouted when I pointed out that this sounded a little disloyal. 'It's simply money,' was surely one way to describe what had occurred. However, the final row appeared after my PA, Bob Halley, left. We'd been together since the 1970s, but our relationship had grown difficult. By proxy, Bob lived a very expensive lifestyle, and he was irritated when management tried to cut back on expenditure to make my tours more cost-effective: it's strange how fame affects others around you more than it affects you. The point of contention was a disagreement about which vehicle service we should hire. A more competitive company had been brought in by the management. Bob had fired them and replaced them with a more expensive one. The management office overruled him and reinstalled their preferred mode of transportation. Bob was enraged. We had a heated debate about it at the St. Regis hotel in New York. He said that his authority had been called into question. I explained that we were only attempting to save money. When he said he was leaving, I lost my cool and told him that was alright with me. After I had cooled down, I returned to speak with him. This time, he told me that he despised everyone in the Rocket office, including my whole management team. I wasn't sure what to say in response: your entire team or your PA? It's not the most difficult decision in the world. Bob stormed out, announcing that he was quitting his job and saying that my career would be over in six months without him. Whatever Bob's abilities were, clairvoyance was not one of them. The only difference in my profession after he left was that the invoices for touring expenses shrank substantially.

My mother was furious when she learned Bob had left; they had usually gotten along well. She refused to listen to my version of events, telling me that Bob had been more of a son to her than I had ever been.

'You care more about that fucking thing you married than you do about your own mother,' she snarled.

After that phone call, we didn't communicate for another seven years. There comes a moment when you know you're just hitting your head against a brick wall, and no matter how many times you do it, you'll never break through, only wind up with a continuous headache. I nevertheless made certain she was financially secure. I purchased her a new property when she said she wanted to move to Worthing. I paid for everything and made certain she received the best possible treatment when she needed a hip replacement. She auctioned off every item I'd ever given her, from jewelry to platinum discs imprinted with her name, but she didn't need money. She told the papers she was downsizing, but it was just another way of telling me to fuck off, similar to hiring an Elton John tribute act for her 90th birthday celebration. I ended up purchasing some of the jewelry myself, items that held sentimental meaning for me even if they no longer did for Mum.

It was heartbreaking, but I didn't want her in my life any more. When the law regarding gay unions changed again and David and I married in December 2014, I did not invite her to the wedding. It was a much smaller and more personal affair than the civil partnership. We went to the registry office in Maidenhead on our own, and then the registrar returned to Woodside to execute the ceremony. We tied the same gold bands we used in the civil partnership - the ones we bought in Paris years ago - to a couple of toy rabbits with ribbon, and Zachary and Elijah carried them in.

I'd say Mum missed out on her grandsons' childhoods - my auntie Win and cousins rushed around, as normal families do when there are babies and toddlers to be fussed over, played with, and treated - but she didn't care. When Zachary was born, a tabloid journalist knocked on her door and inquired how she felt about not seeing her first grandchild, hoping to get a scoop on the callously abandoned grandmother. He didn't understand. She said she wasn't disturbed and that she didn't like children and had never liked them. When I read it, I laughed: no points for winning sympathy, Mum, but ten out of ten for honesty.

When I learned she was gravely ill, I contacted her again. I emailed her with some images of the kids attached. She hardly noticed them, saying merely, 'You've got your hands full,' in her response. I invited her to join me for lunch. Nothing had altered substantially. The first thing she said when she went into Woodside was, 'I'd forgotten how small this place is.' But I was resolved not to respond, not to take the bait. My kids were home, playing upstairs, and I asked my mother if she wanted to see them; she said no. I told her I didn't want to talk about John Reid or Bob Halley; I simply wanted to tell her I loved her after everything we'd been through.

'I love you as well,' she added. 'But I don't like you in the least.'

Oh well, at least things remained pleasant. We would occasionally converse on the phone. I never asked her what she thought of anything I did, and whenever I brought up the kids, she always changed the conversation. I was able to re-establish contact between her and Auntie Win after they had a falling out when Derf died in 2010 and Mum refused to let Win's son Paul to attend the burial, claiming that 'Fred never liked him' - so that was something. But she had no luck bridging the gap with Uncle Reg. I have no idea what that disagreement was over, but they were still not talking when she died in December 2017.

When Mum died, I was devastated. I'd gone down to Worthing to see her the week before; I knew she was terminally ill, but she didn't seem to be on the verge of death that day. It was an unusual meeting: when I knocked on her door, Bob Halley answered. We greeted each other and shook hands, which looked to be the highlight of the afternoon for Mum.

Mum was never one of life's tactile, nurturing, come-here-and-hug-me mothers, and she had a mean streak to her that went beyond just being prone to bad moods, or a victim of the Dwight Family Temper, into something else entirely, something that scared me. She seemed to actively love picking conflicts, and not just with me: there wasn't a single member of the family with whom she had a falling out throughout the years. And yet, there had been occasions when she was encouraging, and others when, in the start of my career, she was a lot of fun. People who knew her in the early 1970s told me after she died, "Oh, your mother was such a laugh."

We held a private family funeral for her in the Woodside chapel: "I wanted to remember the good things, with just relatives around me." I cried while I spoke about her at the service. I truly missed the person I was describing, but I'd been missing her for decades before Mum died; she just seemed to go as fast and unexpectedly as she appeared. In the end, her casket was transported in a hearse. We all stood there, what remained of the Dwights and Harrises, silently watching it drive down the long road at Woodside. My uncle Reg shattered it by addressing his sister for the last time.

'You can't respond to anyone now, Sheila, can you?' He muttered something.

CHAPTER 17

I've been a professional musician my entire adult life, and I've never gotten tired of performing live. Even when I believed I had - when I was on the cabaret circuit with Long John Baldry, or when I was in my mid-seventies and absolutely fatigued - I clearly hadn't. You could tell by the way I would declare my retirement and then return to the stage weeks later. That feeling I get before I go on each night, the mix of adrenalin and nervousness, has never changed throughout my life, and thank God it hasn't, because that feeling is fucking fantastic. It's quite addictive. You may become tired of the traveling, the promotion, and everything else that comes with playing live, but that sensation will always keep you going back for more. That, plus the awareness that even at the worst event - horrible sound, uninteresting audience, bad venue - something fantastic will always happen onstage: a spark, a flash of inspiration, a song you've played a thousand times that unexpectedly triggers a long-forgotten memory.

So the music will always surprise you, but after fifty years, it begins to feel as if nothing else at a show can. It's easy to believe that you've done everything there is to do onstage except slump over and die. I've performed while sober, while drunk, and, to my shame, while high as a kite. I've played shows that made me feel as delighted as a human being can feel, as well as shows that made me feel hopeless. I've played pianos, jumped on pianos, fallen off pianos, and pushed a piano into the audience, hitting a member of the audience with it and spending the rest of the night apologizing to them. I've performed with my boyhood heroes and some of music's greatest artists; I've performed with folks who were so dismal they had no business being onstage; and I've performed with a gang of male strippers disguised as Cub Scouts. I've performed as a woman, a cat, Minnie Mouse, Donald Duck, a Ruritanian general, a musketeer, a pantomime dame, and, on rare occasions, a normal human person. I've had shows stopped by bomb threats, student rallies against the Vietnam War, and gigs disrupted because I flounced offstage in a fury and then came scuttling back shortly afterwards, apologetic for losing my cool. I've had hot dogs hurled at me in Paris, been knocked out by a hash pipe while dressed as a huge chicken in North Carolina (my band believed I'd been shot), and ran onstage in a gorilla costume to startle Iggy Pop. That was not one of my brightest ideas. It was 1973, and the night before I had seen The Stooges. It was the most spectacular thing I'd ever seen - 180 degrees away from my music, but incredible in its energy, sheer cacophony, with Iggy climbing all over the place like Spider-Man. So I went to see them again the next night; they were doing a week of gigs at an Atlanta club called Richards. I thought it would be amusing if I dressed up as a gorilla and ran onstage during their set, simply to add to the general mayhem and anarchy. Instead, I learned an important life lesson: if you're going to run onstage in a gorilla suit and surprise someone, always check first to see if the person you're surprising has taken so much acid before the show that they can't tell the difference between a man in a gorilla costume and an actual gorilla. I learned this when my arrival was met with Iggy Pop shrieking and retreating away from me in panic, rather than gales of laughter. This was shortly followed by the realization that I was no longer on stage and was instead speeding into the air. Another member of The Stooges had stopped playing, scooped me up, and tossed me into the mob, sensing the need for immediate action.

You can see why I sometimes think I've covered every possible live situation, that there's nothing left to do during a show that I haven't previously done. But, of course, when you start thinking that, reality has a way of proving you incorrect. Which leads us to the night in Las Vegas in 2017 when I found myself springing from the piano as the final chord of 'Rocket Man' faded away and strolling across the stage of the Colosseum, relishing in the crowd's enthusiasm, punching the air, and pointing at fans who were going especially wild. Nothing out of the ordinary, except that while I walked across the platform, reveling in the ovation and punching the air, I was also, unbeknownst to the audience, urinating copiously into an adult nappy concealed beneath my suit. Pissing in front of an audience while wearing a massive nappy was definitely unknown terrain. There aren't many advantages to having prostate cancer, but it did allow me to have an altogether new and unprecedented experience onstage.

My life is seldom tranquil, but the previous few years had been especially chaotic. Some of them were really complimentary. I adjusted to parenting far more smoothly than I had anticipated. I loved going to the movies with the boys on Saturdays, going to Legoland, and meeting Father Christmas at Windsor Great Park. I had a great time taking them to see Watford. They are football enthusiasts. I could talk about it for hours, answering their queries about its history: 'Who was George Best, Dad?' 'How did Pelé become such a brilliant player?' They came to Vicarage Road for the opening of a stand named after me, which I'm quite proud of; there's also a stand dedicated after Graham Taylor. They've been mascots at sports since then, and they frequently attend them.

And I liked how having children anchored me in the village closest to Woodside. I'd been there since the mid-1970s, but I'd never really gotten to know anyone. However, when the boys started nursery and school, they made friends, and the parents of their friends became our friends. They didn't give a damn about who I was. A harassed mother at the school gates is less interested in asking you how you wrote 'Bennie And The Jets,' or what Princess Diana was really like, and more interested in talking about uniforms and packed lunches, and the difficulty of putting together a costume for the nativity play with only 48 hours' notice - which was fine by me. We ended up with an entirely new social group that we would not have had if David and I had simply been a famous, jet-setting gay couple.

In 2011, I debuted a new Vegas act, The Million Dollar Piano. It was less contentious than its predecessor, but it was equally magnificent and successful. I brought in Tony King as creative director - he'd been working for The Rolling

Stones for years, touring the world with them - and he did an outstanding job. He's been with my company since then, and his formal title is Eminence Grise, which wonderfully describes Tony. The next year, I released Good Morning to the Night, a unique record that debuted at number one. Or, more precisely, I did not make Good Morning to the Night; instead, I sent the master tapes of my 1970s albums to Pnau, an Australian electronic duo I admired, and instructed them to do anything they wanted with them. They reworked various components from earlier songs into completely new tracks, making me sound like Pink Floyd or Daft Punk. I thought the results were amazing, but I didn't understand the process they employed; there was a number one record with my name on it, and I had no idea how it was made. We performed together at an Ibiza festival, which was wonderful. I'm always nervous before a gig - I believe the day you stop feeling nervous is the day you start phoning it in - but this time I was scared. The audience was so young that they could have been my grandchildren, and the first section of the play was just myself and a piano. They adored it. There's something extremely satisfying about seeing an audience that isn't like the ones who usually come to see you love what you do.

Pnau were not the only folks I worked with. I collaborated with a wide range of artists, including Queens of the Stone Age, A Tribe Called Quest, Jack White, and the Red Hot Chili Peppers. I enjoy getting into the studio with artists who you wouldn't expect me to play with. It reminds me of working as a session musician in the late 1960s: the challenge of adapting your approach and thinking on your feet musically is still quite interesting to me.

I was in the studio with Clean Bandit when I was summoned to the phone: Vladimir Putin allegedly wanted to speak with me. There had been a lot of buzz over a number of shows I'd done in Russia where I came out onstage regarding LGBTQ rights. I'd dedicated a show in Moscow to the memory of Vladislav Tornovoi, a young man tortured and murdered in Volgograd for being gay, and in St Petersburg I'd discussed how ridiculous it was that a statue of Steve Jobs in the city had been demolished when his successor as Apple CEO, Tim Cook, came out. It turned out to be a prank call made by two men who had done the same thing to a variety of important individuals, including Mikhail Gorbachev. They taped everything and aired it on Russian TV, but I wasn't humiliated because I hadn't said anything stupid to them; I'd just expressed gratitude and expressed a want to meet face to face to discuss human rights and AIDS treatment availability. Besides, the real Vladimir Putin called me at home a few weeks later to apologize and request a meeting. The meeting never took place; I've returned to Russia since, but my invitation to the Kremlin appears to have gotten lost in the mail. But I have hope.

Cutting people off accomplishes nothing. It's similar to when I performed at the wedding of right-wing talk show host Rush Limbaugh in 2010. I was astonished to be asked - the first thing I said onstage was, 'I assume you're wondering what the fuck I'm doing here' - and I was dragged through the mud in the media: he said some extremely idiotic things about AIDS, how can you possibly perform for him? But I'd rather try to construct a bridge to someone on the other side of the fence than erect a wall. In any event, I gave my performance fee - and believe me, as a wedding singer, I don't come cheap - to the Elton John AIDS Foundation. So I managed to turn the wedding of a right-wing talk show DJ into an AIDS charity event.

But a lot of terrible things happened throughout those years as well. Bob Birch, who had played bass in my band for almost two decades, took his own life. He'd been ill since a car accident in the mid-1990s - a truck had hit him on the street before a gig in Montreal, and he never fully recovered from his injuries - but I didn't realize how much pain he was in or the psychological toll it was taking on him. He appeared to be extraordinarily resilient; they told him he'd never walk again, but he was back on tour within six months. His musicianship was flawless, and he never complained, even when he had to perform while sitting. But then, during our 2012 tour's summer break, his injuries worsened to the point where they had to be excruciating. At six o'clock in the morning in Nice, I received a phone call from Davey informing me that Bob had shot himself outside his home in Los Angeles. I wished he'd reached out and said something. I'm not sure what I could have done, but the thought that he had suffered in silence haunted me after his death.

Then Ingrid Sischy passed away. She'd had breast cancer before, in the late 1990s: she'd contacted me in Nice, in tears, asking if I could assist her get an appointment with a famous oncologist named Larry Norton, the same oncologist who had treated Linda McCartney. The cancer went into remission, but Ingrid was scared that it would return. She was so obsessed with it, hunting for clues that it had reappeared in the most unusual places, that it became a running gag between us.

'Elton, my hands are shaking; do you think I have hand cancer?'

'Oh, sure, Ingrid, you've got hand cancer now. You most likely have cancer of the teeth and hair.'

It was amusing at the time since I couldn't fathom her dying. I'd never met somebody with such much energy; she was always doing something, juggling a million projects at once. And she was so prevalent in my life that I would call her every weekday, Monday through Friday, for gossip and to seek her opinions, which she seemed to have in abundance. When someone has that much life force inside them, when they take up so much space, it seems unfathomable that life could be taken away.

Until it was not. The disease returned in 2015, and she died unexpectedly - so unexpectedly that I had to rush from Britain to America to visit her before she died. I just finished it. I got to say goodbye, which had not happened with many of my deceased pals. In a way, I was relieved it was so sudden: Ingrid was terrified of cancer and dying, and at least she didn't have to face death for weeks or months. But it wasn't much of a consolation. I'd already lost Gianni, and now I'd lost another best buddy, another half-sibling. I never stop thinking about her; I have images of her all over my house, so she's constantly with me. I miss her advice, her brilliance, her enthusiasm, and her laughter. I'm missing her.

There was also David. I can't claim I didn't notice he was drinking more, perhaps too much. He began bringing a glass of wine to bed with him most evenings and sipping it while reading and chatting. Or he'd stay up far longer than I did, and the next morning there'd be an empty bottle by the kitchen sink. Occasionally, two. He didn't come to bed at all on a couple of occasions while we were on vacation at the house in Nice. I'd find him in the morning, sparking out in front of his computer or on the living room sofa. But I honestly didn't believe he had any problems. Regardless of what happened the night before, he'd be up at seven a.m. and on his way to work. There were occasions when we were out and he'd get drunk - I remember having to hold his arm and steer him quite firmly to the vehicle after a joint birthday party I had with Sam Taylor-Wood, so he didn't weave around in front of the cameras - but he never made a fool of himself. Given that I was capable of everything from verbal abuse to violence to public nudity after a few vodka martinis, you can understand how I missed David's major problem.

I had no idea he was bolstering himself with alcohol. I always assumed David had stepped into Elton John World with incredible ease and confidence, but it turned out that many of the things I was fully used to living with, that I just accepted as a fact of life, made him anxious. He didn't appreciate being photographed all the time, being scrutinized by the press, or giving public speeches at AIDS Foundation events. He was always a scared flier, but in my life, you don't spend a week without stepping foot on a plane. After a few beers, he found it easier to deal with everything. Plus, we were frequently separated - I was away playing gigs all the time, while he was at home. I don't want to make him sound like a rock and roll touring widow - he had a lot going on in his life - but he became lonely and bored after a while, and one way to feel less lonely and bored is to crack open a bottle of excellent wine or knock back a few vodkas. And then there were the kids to contend with. As any new parent will tell you, no matter how much you adore it, there are times when the weight of responsibility overwhelms you. David would not be the first parent in history to rush to the fridge after night, desperate for a glass of something cool, alcoholic, and calming. We obviously had support, but it doesn't really matter if you had the best nannies in the universe: every new parent who cares about their children has moments when they feel overwhelmed by the concept of bringing new humans into the world and making their lives the best they can be.

When you medicate your fears with alcohol, it usually works, at least while you're drinking: the next morning, you're more nervous than ever. That's exactly what happened to David. Everything came to a head in Los Angeles in 2014, just two days before I was set to begin a US tour. That night, I was heading for Atlanta; Tony King was flying in, and I was looking forward to catching up before the tour started. David was in a bad mood and asked me to spend the night with him. No, I said. We had a long line. I went regardless. The next morning, David called, and we had a row that made the previous day's row look like a light-hearted disagreement over what to have for lunch: the kind of argument that leaves you teary and reeling, where things are said that make you wonder if the next time you communicate will be through lawyers. Indeed, the next time I heard from David, he had checked himself into a Malibu treatment clinic. He informed me he had lain in bed after getting off the phone. He could hear Elijah and Zachary playing down the hall but was too melancholy and anxious to get up and go see them. That was it: he called the doctor and told her he'd had enough and wanted help.

I was relieved that he was receiving treatment. I felt horrible for not seeing things had gotten so awful: once I did, all I wanted was for David to get better. But I was also strangely nervous. There is no stronger advocate for sobriety in the world than me, but I also understand that it is a massive undertaking that can profoundly transform people. What if the man I loved returned home as someone else? What if our relationship deteriorated, as it had with Hugh when we got sober, and became unworkable? It was enough to keep me awake at night, but when David returned, he didn't appear to have changed much, despite having more energy and focus, and he was determined to work on his rehabilitation in a way that touched me. I resumed attending AA meetings. I hadn't gone since the early 1990s, and I only went to keep David company and show support, but once inside, I discovered I really enjoyed it. You always hear something encouraging, and you always leave with your spirits elevated. We began having a meeting at our house every Sunday, inviting people in recovery, such as Tony King. I think it's similar to going to church in that you're just thankful for your sobriety. I usually leave on a high note.

David appeared to be bouncing as well. I parted ways with Frank Presland, who'd gone from being my lawyer to my manager, not long after he got sober. Since John Reid, I'd had a slew of managers, but none of them had truly worked out. I considered many choices before wondering if David couldn't do it. He was a successful advertising executive before we met. He handled large campaigns and worked with budgets - the talents required for that didn't seem so dissimilar to the skills required for rock management. There were definitely concerns about entering into a commercial connection with your partner, but I liked the notion of us working together: we had kids, so it would be like a family business. David was hesitant to accept the part, but he eventually consented.

He attacked the assignment with zeal: never underestimate the zeal of the newly sober. He streamlined the business and saved money. He began to make changes to accommodate the changing nature of the music industry, such as incorporating streaming and social media. I was completely ignorant of the subject. I've never had a cell phone. As you might think, given my collector's attitude, I'm not interested in streaming music: I prefer to possess albums in large quantities, ideally on vinyl. And, having considered my temper as well as my outstanding track record of expressing what you could call robust and honest thoughts, I understood that coming near anything like Twitter was sure to result in complete chaos, at best.

But David figured it out. He assembled an excellent squad. He seemed genuinely interested in aspects of the music industry that I was completely uninterested in. He became increasingly insistent on making a biography of my life. Years previously, I'd seen David LaChapelle's films for The Red Piano concerts in Vegas and thought that if a film was going to be made about me, it should look like them. They were gritty, but fantastical, surreal, and over-the-top, and my career has always been fantastical, surreal, and over-the-top, so they fit well. We hired Lee Hall, the screenwriter behind Billy Elliot, to write the screenplay, which I adored, but it took years and years to get it off the ground. Directors and main characters came and went. Originally, David LaChapelle was going to direct it, but he preferred to focus on his fine art career. Tom Hardy was supposed to play me, but he couldn't sing, and I really wanted whoever played me to sing the songs rather than lip-synch to them. There was a lot of bickering with studios over funds and the film's substance. People kept urging us to tone down the gay sex and drugs so it could be rated PG-13, but I'm a homosexual man and a recovering addict: there doesn't seem to be much purpose in making a sanitized film about me that takes out the sex and the coke. There were times when I doubted it would happen, but David persisted, and eventually it happened.

And he had some revolutionary new ideas. When he handed me a piece of paper one morning in LA, I realized how radical he was. He had jotted down a slew of dates pertaining to Zachary and Elijah's schooling - when each term would begin, how long the holidays would be, the years they would progress from infants to juniors and then secondary school, and when they would take tests.

'How long do you want to be around for?'He inquired. 'You may organize your tours around it.'

I examined the piece of paper. It effectively charted their lives. By the time they reached the end dates, they would no longer be children, but teenagers or young men. And I'd be in my late nineties.

'Everything,' I finally said. 'I want to be there for it all.'

David cocked his brow. 'In such a case, you should consider changing your life,' he advised. You should consider retiring from touring.'

It was a significant decision. I've always considered myself a working musician, just as I did when Bluesology was driving up and down the highway in the van that Arnold Tendler had paid for on our behalf. That is not feigned modesty. Obviously, I'm not the same as I was in the sixties - it's been a long time since I arrived at a show in the back of a transport van - but the basic idea, if you will, has never changed. Back then, if you got a gig, you went and played it: that's how you made a livelihood and identified yourself as a musician. I took pride in the fact that my timetable now resembled my routine from the early 1970s. Obviously, bigger venues, more expensive accommodations and travel arrangements, and less time spent locking myself in the backstage lavatory to evade the attentions of female groupies. Even the most fervent of them had long since realized that Elton John was unlikely to be influenced by their charms. But I did the same number of concerts every year: 120 or 130. I wanted to perform more shows the following year, no matter how many I did the previous year. I kept a list of nations I still wanted to play in -

places I hadn't gone to yet, such as Egypt, where I'd been barred from performing because I was homosexual. I used to say that I would be content to die onstage.

But David's list of school dates had caught me off guard. My children would only grow up once. I didn't want to be in Madison Square Garden, the Staples Center in Los Angeles, or the Taco Bell Arena in Boise while it was happening, as much as I adored the fans who came to see me there. I didn't want to be with anyone but Zachary and Elijah. I'd finally found something that matched the stage's allure. We started planning a farewell tour. It had to be bigger and more spectacular than anything I'd done before, a massive party to thank everyone who'd bought albums and tickets over the years.

When I was diagnosed with cancer, the arrangements for the farewell tour were already in the works. During a routine check-up, they noticed it. My doctor noted a modest increase in the level of prostate-specific antigens in my blood and referred me to an oncologist for a biopsy. It was found to be affirmative. It was strange: I wasn't as surprised to hear the term 'cancer' as I had been in the 1980s, when they suspected I had it in my throat. I believe it was because he had prostate cancer. It's no laughing matter, but it's quite common, they discovered it early, and furthermore, I'm blessed with the kind of constitution that allows me to recover quickly from illnesses. I'd had a few significant health scares in the past, but they didn't stop me. I became ill on my way to David and Victoria Beckham's wedding in the 1990s. I felt faint while playing tennis that morning and passed out in the car on the way to the airport. I missed the wedding and went to the hospital, where doctors monitored my heart and diagnosed me with an inner-ear infection. The next day, I was playing tennis again when David yelled from the house that I needed to stop immediately. My feelings about being interrupted while playing tennis are well documented - you may recall the incident in Tantrums and Tiaras in which I declared that I was leaving France immediately and never returning because a fan waved at me and shouted 'yoo-hoo!' while I was attempting to serve. I had just started telling David to fuck off when he shouted that the hospital had called; they had made a mistake - I had a cardiac abnormality and needed to fly to London right now to receive a pacemaker. I was only in the hospital for one night, and instead of feeling incapacitated, I thought the pacemaker was amazing. It appeared to provide me with more energy than previously.

I'd recently managed to play nine gigs, fly twenty-four times, and perform with Coldplay at an AIDS Foundation fundraiser ball despite having a burst appendix: the doctors informed me I had a colon infection and I was fatigued, but I simply kept going. When your appendix bursts, it usually causes peritonitis, which kills you within a few days. I had my appendix removed, spent a couple of days in the hospital on morphine, hallucinating - I won't lie, I enjoyed that part - then a few weeks in Nice recuperating before getting back on the road. It's just the way I am. All of the medications I consumed would have killed me decades ago if I hadn't had the constitution I do.

My oncologist informed me that I had two options. The first was prostate surgery. The other was a regimen of radiation and chemotherapy that required me to return to the hospital dozens of times. I went straight to the operation. Many guys will refuse since it is a huge operation, you can't have sex for at least a year afterwards, and you can't control your bladder for a while, but my children basically made the decision for me. I didn't want cancer to hover over me - or us - for years to come; I just wanted it gone.

I had the operation done quickly and quietly in Los Angeles. We worked hard to keep knowledge of my illness from reaching the press: the last thing I needed was a slew of hysterical stories in the media and photographers outside my door. The operation went off without a hitch. They revealed that the cancer had spread to two lobes of my prostate, something that targeted treatment would not have detected.

I'd made the correct decision. Within ten days, I was back onstage at Caesar's Palace.

It wasn't until I landed in Las Vegas that I realized there was something wrong. I awoke in the morning feeling a little uneasy. The pain became increasingly severe over the day. It was unimaginable by the time I got backstage at the show. I burst into tears. The band considered canceling the event, but I refused. Before you start praising my guts and unrivaled professionalism, let me clarify that I did not agree to play out of any show-must-go-on stoicism or sense of duty. Surprisingly, getting on stage seemed preferable to sitting at home with nothing to do in the same amount of discomfort. So we continued. It kind of worked. At the very least, the gig gave me something to think about other than how sick I was, especially when I realized that the radical prostatectomy's aftereffects on my bladder were becoming apparent.

That was really funny if only the audience knew, but if pissing yourself in front of 4,000 people is the highlight of your day, you're obviously in a foul mood. It was discovered that I had an uncommon and unanticipated consequence after the surgery: fluid was leaking from my lymph nodes. The pain disappeared once I had it drained at the hospital. The fluid reaccumulated, and the discomfort returned. Another fantastic evening of anguish and incontinence on the Caesar's Palace stage. The cycle continued for two and a half months before being cured by accident: a regular colonoscopy permanently relocated the fluid, just days before my seventieth birthday.

My party was held at Hollywood's Red Studios. David surprised Zachary and Elijah by bringing them over from London. Lady Gaga, Ryan Adams, and Rosanne Cash all performed. Prince Harry sent me a video in which he wished me well while donning Elton John spectacles. Stevie Wonder played for me, having either forgotten or forgiven me for refusing to come out of my bedroom the last time he tried to sing 'Happy Birthday' to me, forty-four years before, on board the Starship. And Bernie was there, together with his wife and two young girls - it was a kind of dual celebration, because it had been fifty years since we'd met, in 1967. We stood for photos together, myself in a maroon suit with satin lapels, a ruffled blouse, and velvet slippers, and Bernie in jeans, his hair chopped, and his arms covered in tattoos. We were just as much a study in contrasts today as we had been when Bernie first arrived in London from Owmby-by-Spital. Bernie had wound up back in the country, on a ranch in Santa Barbara: he'd returned to his roots while also becoming one of the Old West characters he loved to write about, like something out of Tumbleweed Connection. He literally won cow roping events. I collected porcelain, and the Tate Modern was putting on an exhibition of my vast collection of twentieth-century photography, one of which was the original Man Ray photograph Bernie and I had bought a poster of when we were trying to decorate our shared bedroom in Frome Court. We were on different planets. I'm not sure how it all worked between us anymore, but I never understood how it worked in the first place. It just happened. It simply does.

It had been a magical evening. I can normally live without events where everyone tells me how beautiful I am - I've never been good at accepting compliments - but I was in a great mood. I was rid of cancer and pain. The procedure had gone well. The issues had been resolved. I was set to embark on another tour, this time to South America, to perform with James Taylor. Everything had returned to normal.

Until I almost died.

I started feeling nauseous on the flight back from Santiago. We had to change aircraft in Lisbon, and I was sick by the time I boarded. Then I became quite cold. I couldn't stop trembling. I wrapped myself in blankets to be warm, but something was definitely wrong. When I got back to Woodside, I contacted the doctor. My fever had dropped slightly, and he urged me to rest. I awoke the next morning feeling worse than I had ever felt in my life. I was brought to London's King Edward VII Hospital. They ran a scan on me and discovered that something was seriously wrong. My situation was deemed so bad that the hospital lacked the necessary equipment. I was transferred to the London Clinic.

I arrived around lunchtime. My final memory is of hyperventilating while they were looking for a vein to inject me. It's always been difficult for me because I have very muscular arms, which is exacerbated by my aversion to needles. They eventually came in a Russian nurse who looked like she had just changed into her uniform after a morning of training with the Olympic shot put squad, and by 2:30 I was on the operating table: there was more lymphatic fluid seeping, this time in my diaphragm, and it needed to be drained. I was in critical care for two days following that. When I arrived, they informed me that I had developed a serious infection in South America and that I was being treated with enormous doses of antibiotics administered intravenously. Everything appeared to be fine until the fever returned. They collected an infected sample and cultured it in a Petri dish. It was considerably worse than they had expected; they had to modify the medications and increase the dosage. I had MRI scans, as well as who knows how many additional treatments. I just laid there feeling miserable, being pushed around, having tubes inserted and removed, not really understanding what was going on. The physicians informed David that I was only twenty-four hours away from death. If the South American tour had continued, it would have been the end of it: brown bread.

I was extremely fortunate to have a terrific team surrounding me and the best possible medical care - though, to be honest, I didn't think of myself as particularly fortunate at the time. I couldn't fall asleep. All I can remember is lying in bed all night, awake, wondering whether I was going to die. I didn't know the details, or how near I was to death - David had sensibly kept that information to himself - but the fact that I was sick was enough to make me think about death. This was not how or when I had planned to travel. I wanted to die at home, surrounded by my family, preferably after having lived to a ripe old age first. I wished to see the lads once more. I required additional time.

I was allowed to depart after eleven days. I couldn't walk because of shooting sensations down my legs, and the sheer quantity and strength of the medicines I had to take absolutely exhausted me, but at least I was home. I spent seven weeks recovering and relearning how to walk. I only ever left the house to see a doctor. It was the kind of forced leisure that would normally have driven me insane - I couldn't remember the last time I'd spent this much time at home - but, despite how sick I was, I realized I rather enjoyed it. It was spring, and the gardens at Woodside looked lovely. There were considerably worse places to be stuck in the globe. I fell into a sort of domestic pattern, pottering around the grounds and enjoying the garden throughout the day, waiting for the boys to come home from school and tell me what was going on.

I'd prayed in the hospital alone at night: please don't let me die, please let me see my kids again, please give me a little more time. In a strange sense, the time I spent healing felt like an answer to my prayers: if you want more time, you have to learn to live like this, you have to slow down. It was as if I had been shown an alternative existence, one that I concluded I preferred over being on the road. Any reservations I had about retiring from touring have now vanished. I knew I'd made the proper choice. Music was fantastic, but it didn't sound as good as Zachary talking about what occurred at Cubs or football practice. I couldn't keep pretending I was twenty-two any longer. Pretending I was twenty-two would do what drugs, drink, and cancer had failed to do: it would kill me. And I wasn't prepared to die just yet.

EPILOGUE

The farewell tour began in Allentown, Pennsylvania on September 8, 2018. David had planned the perfect opulent event for me. He had commissioned a series of spectacular films to accompany the songs: animations that brought Captain Fantastic's cover to life, archival footage of me from every point of my career, and edgy flicks made by modern artists. Tony King was on hand to inspect them and make sure they were all perfect: half a century after he initially walked into my life, looking spectacular, I still trusted his artistic sense wholeheartedly. The feedback was fantastic - the last time I'd gotten feedback like that, I had a full head of hair and the reviewer had to spend half the piece explaining who I was. The sweetest thing about them was their genuine regret that I'd decided to quit touring, that an era was coming to an end.

I saw a rough cut of the biopic Rocketman for the first time about halfway through the first dates. David was visibly concerned about my reaction. When I heard Taron Egerton sing 'Don't Let The Sun Go Down On Me,' I knew he was the right man for the part; he got through it without threatening to murder anyone or screaming about Engelbert Humperdinck, which was an improvement over the first time I sang it. I'd invited Taron to Woodside and we'd spoken over a takeaway curry, and I'd allowed him to read some of the old diaries I'd kept in the early 1970s to give him a flavor of what my life was like back then. Those diaries are unintentionally hilarious. Everything was written down in a matter-of-fact manner, which further adds to the absurdity. 'Got up. I cleaned the house. I was watching football on TV. "Candle In The Wind" was written by him. I visited London. Purchased a Rolls-Royce. Ringo Starr stopped by for supper.' I believe I was attempting to normalize what was happening to me, despite the fact that it was clearly not normal.

But I'd avoided the set and avoided looking at the rushes because the last thing you want is the person you're playing staring at you while you're pretending to be him. But watching the film was like the first time I saw Billy Elliot all over again: I started bawling during the scene set in my gran's house on Pinner Hill Road, where my parents and dad and gran are singing 'I Want Love'. Bernie wrote that song about himself, a middle-aged man with a few unsuccessful marriages behind him, wondering if he'll ever fall in love again. However, it could have been written about the residents of that residence. The most important thing to me was that it felt right. It's the same as my book: I wanted something my children could see or read in forty years to learn about my life and how it felt to me.

When the farewell tour was announced, a number of journalists wrote articles implying that I would never truly retire. They backed up their claim with deep knowledge of my background and remarkable psychological insights into my personality: tried to retire previously, addictive personality, born entertainer, music fanatic. They could have backed it up even more by repeating what I said at the press conference, which was that I had no intention of retiring from music or even live concerts. All I stated was that I wasn't going to schlep around the world any longer: one last big tour - 300 shows over three years, spanning North and South America, Europe, the Middle East, Asia, and Australasia, with the kids having a tutor and accompanying us - and that was the end of it.

It's not the end. I was excited because ending traveling would give me more time to accomplish other things. I'd like to write more musicals and cinema scores. I wish to volunteer with the AIDS Foundation, particularly in Africa. I want to advocate for the LGBTQ population in Uganda, Kenya, and Nigeria, and try to influence legislators to alter the way people are treated. I'd like to work with a variety of artists. I'd like to host a large exhibition that spans my entire career, and perhaps even consider building a permanent museum where people can view some of my art and photography collections. I want to spend more time crafting records, and to do so in the same manner I did at the beginning of my solo career: get Bernie to spend time writing a lot of lyrics and developing a stockpile of content. Since Madman Across the Water, forty-eight years ago, I haven't gone into the studio with a large collection of songs to choose from; instead, I've just turned up and written on the spot, like a painter with a blank canvas. I want to go back to writing without recording anything, like we did with Captain Fantastic, memorizing what comes to mind as I go. I'd like to perform live, but in much smaller venues where I can focus on other content. If there's a drawback to writing songs like 'I'm Still Standing,' 'Rocket Man,' or 'Your Song,' it's that they become so massive; they take on a life of their own and overpower everything else you do. I adore those songs, but I've created other songs that I believe are as excellent as them but dwell in their shadow, and I'd like to give those other songs a chance to shine.

But, above all, I want to spend time being... normal, or as normal as I can ever expect to be. Less time on the road means more time doing the school run, more Saturday afternoons taking the kids to Pizza Express or around Daniel's, Windsor's department store - activities the boys like that I would never have considered doing before. I spent my entire life trying to get away from Reg Dwight because he wasn't a happy budgie. But running away from Reg Dwight taught me that when I got too far away from him, too far away from the normal person I used to be, everything went horribly wrong; I was more miserable than ever. I, like everyone else, require some link to reality.

I live and have lived an exceptional life, and I honestly wouldn't alter anything about it, even the portions I regret, since I'm so pleased with how things have ended out. I certainly wish I'd just kept walking when I saw John Reid slicing coke in the studio, rather than putting my nose in - in every sense - but then again, maybe I had to go through all of that to get to where I am now. It's not where I anticipated to be - married to a man, father of two children, both of which seemed inconceivable to me not long ago. But that's not the only thing my bizarre life has taught me. Nothing has ever gone as planned for me since I was hustled out of a failed audition and handed an envelope containing Bernie's lyrics as I approached the door. My life is filled with what ifs, strange small events that affected everything. What if, after failing my audition, I threw Bernie's mail in the trash on my way to the station? What if I had refused to go to America when Dick James advised me to? What if Watford had beaten West Bromwich Albion that Saturday afternoon in the early 1990s, and I hadn't felt the need to phone a friend and urge him to bring several homosexual men to dinner? What if I hadn't noticed Lev in the Ukrainian orphanage? What would I be doing now? What kind of person would I be now?

You can drive yourself insane by wondering. But it all occurred, and now I'm here. What's the point of wondering what if? The only question that matters is, "What's next?"

Printed in Great Britain
by Amazon

30870831R00187